COLLAPSED
STATES

SAIS African Studies Library

General Editor
I. William Zartman

COLLAPSED STATES

The Disintegration and
Restoration of
Legitimate Authority

edited by
I. William Zartman

LYNNE
RIENNER
PUBLISHERS

BOULDER
LONDON

Published in the United States of America in 1995 by
Lynne Rienner Publishers, Inc.
1800 30th Street, Boulder, Colorado 80301
www.rienner.com

and in the United Kingdom by
Lynne Rienner Publishers, Inc.
3 Henrietta Street, Covent Garden, London WC2E 8LU

Library of Congress Cataloging-in-Publication Data
Collapsed states : the disintegration and restoration of legitimate
    authority / edited by I. William Zartman.
    (SAIS African studies library)
    Includes bibliographical references and index.
    ISBN 1-55587-518-1 (alk. paper)
    ISBN 1-55587-560-2 (pb, alk. paper)
    1. Africa—Politics and government—1960– . 2. Legitimacy of
governments—Africa—Case studies. 3. Political stability—Africa—
Case studies. 4. Authority—Case studies. I. Zartman,
I. William. II. Series: SAIS African studies library.
JQ1879.A15C647 1994
320.96'09'045—dc20   94-25734
                                                          CIP

British Cataloguing in Publication Data
A Cataloguing in Publication record for this book
is available from the British Library.

Printed and bound in the United States of America

The paper used in this publication meets the requirements
of the American National Standard for Permanence of
Paper for Printed Library Materials Z39.48-1992.

5   4

Contents

Acknowledgments

Collapsed States is the thirteenth in the series of the SAIS African Studies Program's publications that result from the program's annual country day conference. We are grateful for the participation of the contributors in the conference and for the comments from our annual audience.

This book represents a new direction in our activities, shifting from the earlier focus on the political economy of individual African states to a broader focus that enables the world to learn from Africa and enables Africa to learn from the rest of the world.

We are grateful for the assistance of Theresa Simmons, who was the fine organizer of the conference and the editorial work on this book. Our thanks also go to John White, who compiled the index, Katarina Vogeli, who provided bibliographical support, and Lynne Rienner and her staff, who were particularly helpful in this effort.

—*I. William Zartman*

1

Introduction: Posing the Problem of State Collapse

I. William Zartman

In the world after the Cold War, not only has the bipolar, interstate system of world order dissolved, but in many places the state itself has collapsed. State collapse is a deeper phenomenon than mere rebellion, coup, or riot. It refers to a situation where the structure, authority (legitimate power), law, and political order have fallen apart and must be reconstituted in some form, old or new. On the other hand, it is not necessarily anarchy. Nor is it simply a byproduct of the rise of ethnic nationalism: it is the collapse of old orders, notably the state, that brings about the retreat to ethnic nationalism as the residual, viable identity. Indeed, one hypothesis to be pursued is that when the state collapses, order and power (but not always legitimacy) fall down to local groups or are up for grabs. These ups and downs of power then vie with central attempts to reconstitute authority. For a period, the state itself, as a legitimate, functioning order, is gone.

The phenomenon is historic and worldwide (Yoffee and Cowgill 1988; Tainter 1988), but nowhere are there more examples than in contemporary Africa. The African state is a new state, successor to a colonial, nonsovereign creation, and this newness at sovereignty, coupled with colonialist claims of African unreadiness for independence, led to early skepticism about its viability. Against all predictions, so surprisingly that it had to be explained (Jackson and Rosberg 1986), the African state persisted. It overrode lustier proclamations of continental and regional unity, formed a dominant bloc in the United Nations (UN) and other world fora, and imposed itself on its citizens' lives. But here and there, it collapsed.

That collapse, as seen in the modern state phenomenon in Africa and elsewhere, is different from the historical phenomenon associated with giant civilizations of the past, and in its difference throws some light on its own nature. Current state collapse—in the Third World, but also in the former Soviet Union and in Eastern Europe—is not a matter of civilizational decay. Society carries on, in ways to be discussed below, and while ideology, regime, and order change, it is hard to claim that a civilization has been destroyed. Nor is the process merely an organic characteristic of growth and decay, a life cycle in the rise and fall of nations or "a continuous aspect in the life of human societies and not an anomalous response to some sort of irregular or periodic stress" (Eisenstadt 1988: 236; Eisenstadt 1969; Eisenstadt 1967). State collapse, as a current phenomenon, is much more specific, narrow, and identifiable, a political cause and effect with social and economic implications, and one that represents a significant anomaly. Indeed, discussion of the problem is based on an assumption, characteristic of the current era, that territory and population are expected to be divided into political jurisdictions that determine, however unevenly, the identity, order, and authority within their confines.

Rather than pose the nature of that phenomenon and then proceed to examine its occurrence deductively against a logical construct, this study of state collapse reverses the procedure and develops an initial analysis inductively from a brief empirical review. It then returns to individual case studies to apply and expand the original analysis, leading to policy-relevant conclusions about the restoration of legitimate authority. This path has been chosen in order to make the most of Africa's experience. Our purpose here is not merely to learn about Africa—an exercise of current interest to a small audience—but to learn from Africa—a project of much wider importance. Even in its misfortunes and malfunctions, Africa has much to teach the world.

■ State Collapse in Africa

It might be said that contemporary African history began in state collapse, in the famous events associated with the collapse of the colonial state in the Congo (now Zaire). But it is more remarkable that the Congo was an isolated exception to the otherwise successful transfer of authority from colonial to independent rule throughout the continent (Callaghy 1984). In the Congo in 1960–1961, the state that collapsed was the colonial state, marked by the refusal of state institutions (army, executives, local governments, and populations) to recognize each other's authority (Leslie 1993). While these characteristics reappear in independent state collapse in the following decades, the Congo case is of greater relevance for its lessons about state reconstitution. An international intervention to restore law and order, a strongman installed with foreign connivance—these were the means of restoring the state and the elements in its gradual collapse again two or three decades later.

State collapse in independent Africa is not a postcolonial phenomenon, but a condition of nationalist, second- or later-generation regimes ruling over established (i.e., functioning) states. The phenomenon has occurred in two waves. One came toward the end of the second decade of independence, when regimes that had replaced the original nationalist generation were overthrown, carrying the whole state structure with them into a vacuum. In Chad in 1980–1982, state collapse resulted from a factional civil war among the guerrilla victors over the previous regime, a war that caused the destruction of all of the branches of central government: executive, legislative, judiciary, and bureaucracy. In Uganda in 1979–1981, it came about after Idi Amin Dada had concentrated all power in his own delegitimizing hands and then fallen to a coalition of oppositions, leaving a power vacuum. In Ghana, under the Third Republic of Hilla Limann (1979–1981), between the two interventions of Flt. Lt. Jerry Rawlings, where collapse was less total than in the previous cases, the center nonetheless lost its control over the countryside and its ability to perform government functions even in the capital, as opposition became more organized than the state and coercion and corruption replaced government. In all of these cases, an established but poorly functioning regime had been replaced by a military regime that concentrated power but was unable to exercise it effectively or legitimately, making the state contract and implode. But the characteristics and tenure of the various governments differed widely.

The second round came another decade later and continues to extend into the 1990s and into new cases. A recent study (Nellier 1993) characterized half the African states as being in serious[1] or maximum[2] danger of collapse, if not already gone. Their condition is not too different from the earlier cases: the authoritarian successors of the nationalist generation were overthrown by a new successor regime that can destroy but not replace, and government functioning and legitimacy have receded. In Somalia after 1990, Siyad Barre so concentrated power in the hands of his clan that the whole country rose against him, using their own clans as their organizing base and delegitimizing both the idea and the practice of central state government. In Liberia after 1990, Samuel Doe's concentration of power in his hands for the benefit of his ethnic group alienated the rest of the country into support of Charles Taylor's rebellion, but international intervention and other groups arose to grasp for power as it fell from Doe to Taylor.

Beyond these two cases of clear collapse are others of similar characteristics. In Ethiopia, also after 1990, the thirty-year Eritrean rebellion (first against the emperor and after 1974 against the Marxist military regime that overthrew him) finally overcame the military with the aid of other ethnic rebellions, but was unable to combine ethnic self-determination with effective central government. In this case, the state retracted in effectiveness and legitimacy; but state collapse was not as complete as in Somalia and Liberia.

In Angola and Mozambique, on the other hand, the postcolonial state has been contested by a regional rebellion since independence in 1974. In Angola, a truce was finally negotiated in 1991 between the People's Movement for the Liberation of Angola (MPLA) government and the

National Union for the Total Independence of Angola (UNITA), but the resulting election was rejected by UNITA and civil war continued. In Mozambique, a truce was negotiated in 1992 between the Front for the Liberation of Mozambique (FreLiMo) government and the Mozambican National Resistance Movement (ReNaMo), promising elections in 1993, postponed to 1994. In neither case did central government disappear, but its exercise and legitimacy were severely restricted throughout the countryside and its effectiveness limited, even in its own territory. The pattern here is different from the cases mentioned earlier.

The current wave is not over; other cases are certainly looming on the horizon. In Sudan, in a situation similar to Angola and Mozambique but also in part similar to Ethiopia, the southern rebellion that raged between 1955 and 1972 reemerged after 1982. As the rebellion became broader, moving from southern regionalism to national revolution, the government became more restricted in its identity and response, moving from national assertion to Islamicist repression, alienating many regions of the country. As in Southern Africa, the writ of the government does not run nationwide; collapse at the center is possible. In Rwanda and Burundi, agreements to democratize the political system in late 1993 ran up against traditional (and coincident) ethnic and class animosities and, in 1994, turned both countries into bloodbaths, sweeping away the order and authority of both states. In Zaire, in a pattern similar to that of the 1980s wave. Mobutu Sese Seko, the answer of the 1960s, has found himself isolated and alienated—and, moreover, broke. A parallel government born of the democratic movement whines for power, impotent. Interestingly, the greatest barrier to anarchy is the restraining memory of the bloody disorders of three decades ago; but the state, as a national authority, collapsed.

Two other cases that may well avoid total state collapse have enlightening similarities. In South Africa, against all precedent and predictions, negotiations between the majority, led by the African National Congress (ANC), and the apartheid government of the National Party (NP) arrived at elections in 1994 and an agreement for powersharing over a five-year transition period, averting the bloodbath that the leadership of both sides feared. But a deeper drama underlay the efforts to escape the dilemma of a government, trying to maintain law and order as it negotiated its own replacement in the face of its own illegitimacy, and an opposition, hoping to maintain law and order over its followers while de-legitimizing the government. On the wings, extremist fringes from both sides sought to take advantage of the reduced authority of the government and the restricted ability of the transition to meet inflated expectations, and challenge government's legitimate monopoly on violence. State collapse was the threat that kept the negotiations on track. In Algeria, a reputedly strong state suddenly showed its clay feet in the massive popular riots and intragovernment dissension of 1988. Struggling to keep ahead of its own collapse, it has not been able to make and carry out decisions since then and has resorted to a state of emergency to hold off the popular authoritarianism of an Islamicist opposition's electoral victory. The state remains in place but paralyzed.

Behind these instances lie broader questions. In looking at the causes and characteristics of state *collapse,* what separates this phenomenon from conflicts and changes that occur without the state's being destroyed? What preemptive measures are appropriate to meet the causes? How can state collapse be recognized on the horizon and prevented? What are effective remedies for the perceived causes and characteristics? And how can collapsed states be put back together?

■ The Concept of State Collapse

Why do states collapse? Because they can no longer perform the functions required for them to pass as states. A state is the authoritative political institution that is sovereign over a recognized territory (Dawisha and Zartman 1988: 7). This definition focuses on three functions: the state as the sovereign authority—the accepted source of identity and the arena of politics; the state as an institution—and therefore a tangible organization of decisionmaking and an intangible symbol of identity; and the state as the security guarantor for a populated territory. Because these functions are so intertwined, it becomes difficult to perform them separately: a weakening of one function drags down others with it. It also becomes difficult to establish an absolute threshold of collapse.

Collapse means that the basic functions of the state are no longer performed, as analyzed in various theories of the state. As the decisionmaking center of government, the state is paralyzed and inoperative: laws are not made, order is not preserved, and societal cohesion is not enhanced (Badie and Birnbaum 1983). As a symbol of identity, it has lost its power of conferring a name on its people and a meaning to their social action (Dyson 1980; Migdal 1987). As a territory, it is no longer assured security and provisionment by a central sovereign organization (Poggi 1978). As the authoritative political institution, it has lost its legitimacy, which is therefore up for grabs, and so has lost its right to command and conduct public affairs (Weber 1958; Ferrero 1942). As a system of socioeconomic organization, its functional balance of inputs and outputs is destroyed; it no longer receives supports from nor exercises controls over its people, and it no longer is even the target of demands, because its people know that it is incapable of providing supplies. No longer functioning, with neither traditional nor charismatic nor institutional sources of legitimacy, it has lost the right to rule.

Does this pervasive incapacity occur because the state itself collapses as the authoritative political institution? Or because society beneath it has become incapable of providing the supports and demands it needs? *Civil society* is used here to designate the social, economic, and political groupings that structure the demographic tissue; it is distinct and independent of the state but potentially under its control, performing demand and support functions in order to influence, legitimize, and/or replace the state (cf. Gramsci 1967; Hegel 1952; Kean 1988). Although the current debate over state-society relations has produced useful insights into the two overlapping parts of the polity, it is an exercise in scholasticism to try to isolate and incriminate one part or the other for the occurrence of collapse. Indeed, state collapse is conceptually significant because it shows the necessary imbrication of the two components, the degeneration of one necessarily entailing the debilitation of the other.

State collapse, on one hand, is the breakdown of good governance, law, and order. The state, as a decisionmaking, executing, and enforcing institution can no longer take and implement decisions. Societal collapse, on the other hand, is the extended breakdown of social coherence: society, as the generator of institutions of cohesion and maintenance, can no longer create, aggregate, and articulate the supports and demands that are the foundations of the state (Hyden 1992). These are two aspects of breakdown and between them the links and overlaps of state and society fall away. The normal politics of demands and responses atrophies; the political processes for popular legitimization are discarded or prostituted; politics and economics are localized; and the center becomes peripheral to the workings of society.

A more specific version of the causal question is: Did the state fall apart because it was the wrong institution? Taking Africa as the example, was it because the state was not appropriately African? Various ways of answering the question turn up negative. On one hand, no common theme or characteristic runs through the cases of collapse that would indicate that collapse was the result either of the same "Western-style" malfunction in the state or of particularly badly adapted Western institutions. While parliaments, parties, and bureaucracies in Africa seem to have difficulties in living up to Montesquieu's, Madison's, or Weber's standards, these shortcomings do not seem to be the key to collapse; nor do these institutions function any better in noncollapsing states in Africa. Nonetheless, it can be said that the poor performances of their functions—representation, interest articulation, output efficiency—are broad causes of state collapse, whether performed by the "proper" institution (in Western terms) or by a surrogate more suited to African conditions. It can also be affirmed, perhaps axiomatically, that there is no typical "African state" especially adapted to African circumstances, or specifically derived from a precolonial protoinstitution;

rather is there a set of functions that need to be performed for the coherence and the effectiveness of the polity—*anywhere.*

Similarly, another intuitive version of the causal question might be: Did the state collapse because it had turned into an evil or tyrannical institution, in which the necessary balance between coercive and rewarding functions was disrupted in favor of coercion? As the longstanding debate over the state as a social contract has brought out, individuals in society, in creating a state, trade in their freedom in exchange for security and constraints. When the state overplays its control functions, it loses the willing allegiance and legitimizing support of its population. This is the hard state, often confused with the strong state (Myrdal 1971). The events of the early 1990s—the collapse of ideologized tyranny in the Soviet Union and of constitutionalized racism in South Africa—support the hypothesis that authoritarianism is the cause of state collapse and that tyranny, in the end, will destroy its own hard state. The cloud on this silver lined conclusion is that society, too, pays the price of tyranny: it is the tyrant's destruction of the institutions of civil society that make the hard state's destruction a matter of collapse rather than one of simple replacement.

Comforting though the positive aspects of this conclusion might be, they are not the whole story. While the cases of Idi Amin in Uganda, Mengistu Haile Miriam in Ethiopia, Samuel Doe in Liberia, Siyad Barre in Somalia, and Mobutu Sese Seko in Zaire bear out the hypothesis that the origins of collapse may be found in tyranny, many other cases are not that clear-cut. In Chad, and perhaps partially in the cases of Ghana, Mozambique, Algeria, and South Africa, the regime was indeed so bad that people rose up against it, yet—as in the more extreme group of cases—the opposition was unable fully to fill the vacuum. These regimes were bad in their unwillingness—institutionalized in South Africa—to meet the needs of their people, in the managerial incapacity of the center to care for the periphery. They were instances of neglect, corruption, and incompetence: the tyrannical aspects of the regime were adopted to repress the resulting dissatisfaction. The state pulled into itself and imploded; became a black hole of power.

These two categories—the extreme and the not so clear-cut—are not so distinct from each other. What holds them together is not the basic maleficence of the state as a cause of collapse but, paradoxically, the effectiveness of the state before collapse, through repression and neglect, in destroying the regulative and regenerative capacities of society. Hard or soft, evil or merely incapable, the collapsing state contracts, isolates itself, retreats. As it implodes, it saps the vital functions of society. State collapse involves the breakdown not only of the governmental superstructure but also that of the societal infrastructure.

The important question then becomes: How do states collapse? The pattern is remarkably similar across the cases. The most striking character-istic of state collapse is that it is not a short-term phenomenon; not a crisis with a few early warnings; nor simply a matter of a coup or a riot. State collapse is a long-term degenerative disease. However, it is also one whose outcome is not inevitable: cure and remission are possible. The process may be likened to the movie version of a car falling slowly, in stages, down a cliff—or to the progress of an object tumbling down a staircase, landing and teetering on each step it hits, then either regaining its balance and com-ing to rest or losing its balance again and bouncing down to the next step, where the exercise is repeated. Many states recover their balance and return to more or less normal functions, but the states that reach the bottom of the stairs are the cases of collapse. Collapse, then, is an extreme case of gover-nance problems; or excessive burdens on governing capacity, a matter of degree but not a difference in nature from the normal difficulties of meet-ing demands and exercising authority (Yoffee and Cowgill 1988: 259–266).

In more detail, this means that a regime—which is often ruled by the independence generation of civilians—after being in power for a long time wears out its ability to satisfy the demands of various groups in society. Resources dry up, either for exogenous reasons or through internal waste and corruption (selective misallocation). Social and ethnic groups feel neglected and alienated, causing an atmosphere of dissatisfaction and oppo-sition, which in turn draws increased repression and use of the police and military to keep order. With nobody to watch the watchmen, the military moves in to take over and some military regimes are able to reverse a downward spiral. In the cases under consideration, the new government is no better at generating resources, stabilizing allocations, and productively channeling the opposition groups than was its predecessor and so it relies even more on control and coercion. This inability may take a short or a long time to become apparent. When it does, and the regime falls, it brings down with it the power that it has concentrated in its hands. The regime falls into a vacuum that it has created by repressing the demand-bearing groups of civil society.

What distinguishes this scenario from other instances of government change is the inability of civil society to rebound: to fill positions, restore faith, support government, and rally round the successor. The maimed pieces into which the contracting regime has cut society do not come back together under a common identity, working together, sharing resources. The whole cannot be reassembled and instead the components of society oppose the center and fend for themselves on the local level. Organization, participation, security, and allocation fall into the hands of those who will fight for it—warlords and gang leaders, often using the ethnic principle as a source of identity and control in the absence of anything else.

There are variations on the scenario, usually occurring at the beginning or the end of the military reaction. The military takeover may come not from the army but from an armed rebellion against the government. A clear victory usually provides central control and reinvigorating leadership, at least for a while. But often the rebellion becomes bogged down on the way to the capital, falling prey to the same type of divisions as those that have splintered the society. Full takeover is averted and a weak government hangs on, its authority gone and its de facto power limited to the capital. As in the case of full collapse, government retracts and the countryside is left on its own, organizing its own life, for or against the rebellion or the remnant state. In general, relations between the state and the local institutions were already tenuous or exploitative in the period immediately preceding state collapse.

State collapse is marked by the loss of control over political and economic space. The two effects work in opposite directions. Neighboring states encroach on the collapsing state's sovereignty by involving themselves in its politics directly and by hosting dissident movements who play politics from neighboring sanctuaries. As a result, the political space—the territory where politics is played—of the collapsing state is broader than its boundaries (Zartman 1989). On the other hand, its economic space retracts, in two ways. The informal economy tends to take over, overshadowing the formal economy in its transactions and escaping the control of the state. At the same time, parts of the national territory become lost to neighboring economies. Such areas often use the neighbor's currency and tie in to the neighboring region's trade. Neighboring currencies were in use in Chad in 1980, in Ethiopia in the late 1980s, and in Zaire in the 1990s. Reconstructing the state means, among others, constricting national politics to the national territory and restoring national economic flows throughout the territory.

What is notable in these scenarios is the absence of clear turning points, warning signals, thresholds, or pressure spots. The momentary respites (the stairtreads) are often evident, but the elements of the next round of fall (the risers) are unclear. To blur the image, the slippery slope, the descending spiral, and the downward trend are the marks of state collapse, rather than deadlines and triggers. The road is not marked with ripe moments and clear, appropriate responses. Incumbents have a tendency to view slippery slopes as merely grades on the normally bumpy terrain of politics, making it difficult to focus their attention on the gravity of the problem until it is too late and difficult to prescribe preventive measures.

Nonetheless, the slippery slope has some notable characteristics near the bottom and these do serve as ultimate warnings. Once they are identified, the question then becomes: Can anything be done about the situation or is it simply too late? Five of these ultimate signposts are identifiable, even though it is not clear whether they are in the right order or not (or whether there is an order at all).

• Power devolves to the peripheries when (because) the center fights among itself. Those in central power are too busy defending themselves against attacks from their colleagues to hold onto the reins of power over the countryside. Local authority is up for grabs and local power-grabbers— future warlords—grab it.

• Power withers at the center by default because central government loses its power base. It no longer pays attention to the needs of its social bases and they withdraw their support. The center instead relies on its innermost trusted circle: this may be an ethnic or regional group, or a functional group such as an army officers' clique. Attention to the needs and demands of the smaller group diverts allocations from the broader social sources of support.

• Government malfunctions by avoiding necessary but difficult choices. As a result, such measures mount in urgency and difficulty, facing the state with a governing crisis. Decisional avoidance can take place either because of institutional incoherence, in which the mechanisms of government are inadequate to their challenges, or because of political flabbiness, in which the politicians themselves are incapable of biting the bullet. The effect is the same.

• The incumbents practice only defensive politics, fending off challenges and reducing threats, concentrating on procedural rather than substantive measures. Such measures include both repression and concession, both taken to get the opposition off their back. What is absent is a political agenda for participation and programs. Elections are postponed; platforms are absent.

• Probably the ultimate danger sign is when the center loses control over its own state agents, who begin to operate on their own account. Officials exact payments for their own pockets, and law and order is consistently broken by the agents of law and order, the police and army units becoming gangs and brigands.

The antidote to these ultimate signs of collapse is simply to reverse them. But it is obvious that their very nature makes reversal extremely difficult. It might almost be said that, at this point, the process needs to run its course before a new structure of law and order or legitimate authority can be constructed.

These then are the characteristics and causes of state collapse as taught by African experience. The following chapters examine three groups of cases against the background of this understanding, drawn from the two waves of collapse at the end of the 1970s and the end of the 1980s and from the impending instances of the 1990s. The case studies have a dual focus: the causes of collapse, as discussed above; and the means, or potential means, of reconstruction. State reconstitution is the subject of the book's last section.

■ **Notes**

1. Algeria, South Africa, Sudan, Cameroon, Madagascar, Malawi, Kenya, Djibouti, Nigeria, Niger, Togo, Mali.

2. Angola, Mozambique, Rwanda, Burundi, Zaire, Ethiopia, Chad, Sierra Leone.

PART 1

STATES COLLAPSED AND RECONSTRUCTED

2

Reconstructing the State of Chad

William J. Foltz

A ctive revolt against the Chadian state began in 1965. Initially, it took the form of a peasant *jacquerie,* a violent protest against an overbearing, venal, and incompetent administration. At first a local affair, it quickly found echoes across the northern two-thirds of the country. As revolt produced reprisal, reprisal in turn produced rebellion—then civil war, coups d'état, foreign military intervention, regional secession, and the division and recombination of alliances and futile governments. No part of the country escaped armed violence; no Chadian family escaped the violence unscathed. State authority collapsed definitively in 1980 when civil war touched virtually every corner of the country, reaching a ferocious peak in the battles fought back and forth across the capital, Ndjamena. Government functionaries—and the entire diplomatic corps—fled the capital. What remained of the administration lost contact with its agents in the countryside: the last government salaries were paid in August 1979. In those few localities where schools and clinics kept their doors open, they did so on local initiative and without supplies. Banks and post offices were looted. Even Cotontchad, the privileged state-within-a-state that controlled cotton production and marketing in the deep south, suspended most operations for want of cash and transport. Libyan troops occupied a third of the national territory and began introducing their own currency. As 1980 drew to a close, *Le Monde* (December 30, 1980) told its readers: "In Chad, the 'modern' state inherited from the colonial period no longer exists." Ordinary Chadians expressed the same thought more pithily: *"Tchad khalass. . . .* Chad is finished."

Since then Chad has undergone more than its share of wars, coups, and conquests, yet remarkably a recognizable state has emerged out of the violence. In retrospect, the reconstruction could be said to have begun in June 1982, when the fighters of Hissein Habré's Forces Armées du Nord (FAN) seized the burned-out, bullet-pocked remains of the capital from the loose alliance of rival armed groups known as the second GUNT—the second Transitional Government of National Unity—headed by Goukouni Weddeye. What looked like one more reversal of fortunes in endless factional warfare actually was a turning point. Habré pursued a double strate-gy: military reconquest of Chadian territory (particularly against Libyan occupation) and incorporation of domestic opponents into the central gov-ernment through a policy of coercive "national reconciliation." By the time Habré celebrated his fifth anniversary in power, he had succeeded in driv-ing the Libyans out of all but the area around their principal military base in the disputed Aouzou Strip and in establishing central government authority across most of Chad. Once again, something recognizable as a Chadian state functioned, albeit at a very basic level.

Increasingly, personalized rule and quarrels over the spoils of victory pushed some of Habré's lieutenants into armed rebellion and Habré was ousted in November 1990. The state that Habré left has changed little under his successors. This chapter investigates how the Chadian state was recon-structed and the challenges it continues to face.

The reconstruction of a state involves putting back into place at least five basic elements:

1. A central political authority, be that a tyrant, an oligarchic clique, or a democratic parliament
2. Control over national boundaries, to prevent penetration by external forces and hemorrhaging of national resources
3. Control over national territory, to establish a tolerable level of order and to prevent armed challenge to state authority
4. Capacity to extract resources from the domestic and international environment sufficient for the state to function and reproduce itself
5. Control over the actions of state agents sufficient to coordinate and execute policy and to limit freebooting so it does not threaten the preceding elements

How the central political authority is constituted, and how and to what degree it establishes these other basic elements, will determine the state's strength and its relationship with civil society. It has not been easy to estab-lish any of these elements in Chad.

■ Background on Chad

Specific characteristics of Chadian society and political life contributed to the breakdown of state structures and defined the reconstruction task. First is the absence of large-scale solidaristic structures. Chad's 5 million people make up one of the most ethnically diverse social mosaics in Africa. Depending on the criteria used, scholars count between 72 and 110 differ-ent language groups in Chad (Chapelle 1980: 39–57). The largest of these, the Sara, is in turn divided into 12 (or in some classifications more) socio-logically distinct subgroups (Lanne 1979; Magnant 1986). Furthermore, virtually all of these group identities are highly segmentary: it would be unusual for a whole linguistic or ethnic group to mobilize behind a single leader or cause. As Magnant (1986: 261) notes, both for the Sara and more northern populations: "Traditions report more bloody fights between frac-tions of the same ethnic group allied to fractions of neighboring ethnic groups than conflicts in which ethnic groups confronted one another as blocs." While, as elsewhere in Africa, colonization had the effect of accen-tuating, and indeed creating, ethnic group solidarity, the extraordinary pres-sures of the post-1965 conflicts in Chad more often broke solidarities down to lineage or family level, instead of promoting and sustaining cohesion of larger social groups.

Social segmentation accentuated the tendency toward factionalism in political and military organization. The agreement of August 21, 1979, set-ting up the first GUNT, was signed by eleven "principal" factions. Two and a half years later, when the FAN began its long march back to Ndjamena, it was one of seventeen politicomilitary factions contending for power, not counting several more whose principal assets consisted of an engraved let-terhead and a post office box in a neighboring country (Soulas de Russel 1981: 2). Religion, ethnicity (at various levels of inclusiveness), personal loyalty, level and place of education, opportunism, and region have all pro-vided reasons for cleavages underlying factions and alliances of factions. Only social class, ideology, and political program (except as a set of con-ventional symbolic markers to distinguish a particular coalition at a particu-lar moment) seem definitively absent from the list of conventional cleav-ages. Much attention has focused on the north-south regional dimension of the Chadian conflict, leading some quite erroneously to see Chad's civil wars as contests between Islam and Christianity or animism; or, even more absurdly, as white (or Arab) African versus black African conflicts. With trivial exceptions, all Chadians, including the Saharan populations, are black; and one or another of the highly segmented Arab groups has been found at some time in most of the factional alliances. The most consequen-tial personal rivalries have opposed Habré first to Goukouni Weddeye and then to Idriss Deby—all three of them northerners of different branches of the Tubu peoples, an extremely segmented and individualistic society (Chapelle 1982).

Chad has no natural borders that would clearly delimit its peoples or their livelihoods from those of its six immediate neighbors. A landlocked country, its goods and peoples have long transited through neighboring states, and its central location has historically been traversed by many West Africans on their way to and from Mecca. Such lack of natural boundaries has contributed to the ambiguities of the dispute with Libya over the

Aouzou Strip along the northern border, and to the much less virulent dispute with Nigeria over the constantly shifting islands of Lake Chad. It has also meant that many Chadians could flee and find refuge with related communities across the border, and that they also might recruit factional support in neighboring lands. This is particularly true in the northern two-thirds of the country, where, on the east, Zaghawa and Wadaians overlap very substantially into Sudan's Dar Fur Province; on the north, Tubu overlap into Libya and Niger; on the west, Kanembou, Fulani, and Kotoko overlap into Niger, Nigeria, and Cameroon—while Arabs regularly cross all these borders, following historic grazing and trading routes.

Weak national boundaries, abetted by Chad's general poverty and the active solicitation of foreign help by all of Chad's factions and governments, have involved most of Chad's neighbors and several farther-flung nations in some aspect of the Chadian struggle. Of its neighbors, Libya, Nigeria, and Sudan, each with a different favorite, have each at some time tried to assure that what they took to be their faction came to power. Among noncontiguous African states, Morocco, Zaire, Egypt, Algeria, Congo, and Gabon have tried to play significant roles as part of their search for allies and influence; and even such improbable states as Benin and Burkina Faso have gotten involved on behalf of an external patron. Further afield, Saudi Arabia and Iraq have supplied arms and diplomatic support. The United States and, above all, France have assured, by their direct involvement, that Chad's factional contests would be played out on a vastly larger international field.

Warfare is nothing new to the Chad region, as is suggested by the title of Stephen Reyna's major study of nineteenth-century Bagirmi and its neighbors, *Wars Without End* (Reyna 1990). At the best of times, the colonial and postcolonial Chadian states have functioned as a "loosely-coupled system," capable of surviving and supporting a level of local disruption and dissidence that would be intolerable in more tightly integrated states. Particularly in the north, among Tubu and related peoples like the Bideyat and Zaghawa, fighting prowess is a normal and practiced male attribute, with feuds an integral part of social life (Baroin 1985: 387–389).

Nonetheless, by 1982 a full generation of civil war waged with artillery and automatic weapons had raised the level of social disruption to a point unknown since French conquest at the beginning of the twentieth century. War-weariness was a fact of life and to much of the population any sign of governmental stability and effectiveness was attractive. While most people were distrustful of what any group would do with power, they were likely to be at least as distrustful of opposition promises as they were of those of a government and they were hardly inclined to lead a public challenge to armed authority. Few Chadians felt they could trust anyone outside of their immediate group, and most defined that group in very restrictive terms.

■ Enter Habré

Hissein Habré and the Forces Armées du Nord (FAN) brought with them specific attributes that distinguished them from other leaders and groups. These attributes affected the strategies they would adopt in power. The FAN, as its name implies, had its base in the north, from which Habré himself comes (he was born in the large Saharan oasis, Faya, the capital of the vast and sparsely populated Borkou-Ennedi-Tibesti [BET] prefecture). The FAN's irreducible core was composed of members of Habré's own Anakaza, a subgroup of the Daza branch of the Tubu peoples. Other important groups represented were the Zaghawa, from the northeast Biltine Prefecture, who made up the largest single group in the army; the Hadjerai, a congeries of mountain folk (the name is roughly equivalent to *hillbilly*) from the center-east Guera Prefecture; some Kim and Moundang from the southwest Mayo-Kebbi; and scatterings of individuals and *groupuscules* from most corners of the country except the Sara and closely related peoples of the cotton-producing deep south.

Habré was a seasoned and ruthless fighter, at the time best known outside Chad as the faction leader who had kidnapped and held the French archaeologist Françoise Claustre hostage for two and a half years and who had executed the French intelligence officer who tried to arrange her freedom. Habré was also an educated man with a French law degree—something highly unusual for a Tubu—who could appeal to other educated Chadians, most of whom were from the capital and from the south. Among the many factional leaders, he stood out by his uncompromising nationalism and dedication to a unified Chad, and by his refusal of any compromise with Libyan attempts to play a significant role in Chadian politics or to control Chadian territory (which in Habré's view most emphatically included the Aouzou Strip).

Habré's and the FAN's antipathy to Libya had been one of the issues on which the FAN had split from the other factions in the first GUNT, and it was a massive infusion of Libyan troops and heavy armor that had driven the FAN from Ndjamena in December 1980. Opposition to Libya structured Habré's pattern of external allies. Following their defeat, the FAN regrouped in Kulbus, across the border in Sudan's Dar Fur Province. Sudan's President Nimeiry was only too happy to aid a dedicated opponent of Libya's Qadhafi, as was his Egyptian ally and patron, Anwar Sadat, whom Habré visited at Aswan in January 1981. For the new Reagan administration and its activist CIA director, William Casey, Habré's anti-Libyan credentials and Sadat's support were decisive. Participation in the clandestine reequipping of the FAN became the Reagan administration's first covert action (Woodward 1987: 94–97). By the end of February, the FAN had reestablished a toehold within eastern Chad in the Biltine, home of the

FAN's operational commander, Idriss Deby, and had begun the "long march" back to Ndjamena (Devoluy 1981).

Habré's FAN seized power by exploiting a window of opportunity. The self-styled transitional GUNT had never risen above a loose alliance of warlords and symbolic ethnic placemen. Corruption was rampant at the higher levels, as the warlords shared out the spoils; and it spread downward when, in January 1982, the GUNT decreed a 50 percent cut in civil service salaries: disabused civil servants sought to compensate for their reduced circumstances by emulating their leaders. When the FAN attacked, the natural strategy of each GUNT faction was to hold back so that its partners' forces would pay the price of engaging the attacker, in the expectation that it would sweep to untrammeled power over the bodies of those who had done the fighting (Buijtenhuis 1987: 185–187, 222–225).

Qadhafi, meanwhile, had overplayed his hand. First, in January 1981 he persuaded Goukouni to sign an agreement setting forth steps to be taken toward the full union of Chad and Libya. The uproar this caused in the rest of Africa, including a denunciation of Libyan interference by the Organization of African Unity (OAU) committee on Chad, put Qadhafi on the diplomatic defensive (Thompson and Adloff 1981: 138–143). This was of more than casual moment to the Libyan leader, since he aspired to election as chairman of the OAU in 1982. Bowing to African pressures, Qadhafi agreed to withdraw Libyan troops from Chad in favor of an OAU-sponsored inter-African force of peacekeepers. To the general surprise, he stuck to his agreement. Thus, by the beginning of 1982, the FAN confronted only the squabbling military factions of the GUNT and an OAU force of Nigerians, Senegalese, and Zairois, whose uncertain mandate gave them neither orders nor inclination to fire on Habré's seasoned fighters (Pittman 1984: 297–326). Under strict orders not to put the OAU forces in a position where they might have to fight, the FAN units simply walked around the peacekeeping forces and on June 7, 1982, entered Ndjamena against only token resistance from Goukouni's personal army, the FAP (Forces Armées Populaires). Several former members of the GUNT who did not command factional armies on which they could fall back quickly rallied to Habré.

■ Extending State Control

Having taken control of the capital, Habré faced the task of spreading central power outside the city limits. The actual task had two principal regional foci, the south, where the campaign lasted from 1982 to early 1986, and the north, where the campaign, in two phases, continued to mid-1987.

The south, at the time Habré came to power in Ndjamena, was in poorly organized secession, under the authority of a *comité permanent* made up of senior southern civil servants. The head of the comité was Wadal Kamougué, nominally a member of the GUNT and commander of the FAT, which had once been the national army. Kamougué had been the southern warlord in the GUNT, but his rule over the south had been singularly inept and the *comité permanent* had been torn by quarrels over money (Lanne 1984: 35). Also present, by virtue of their participation in the GUNT, were isolated garrisons of troops of the (predominantly Arab) Conseil Démocratique Révolutionnaire (CDR). Like the FAT, the CDR had stayed on the sidelines as Habré's forces retook Ndjamena. Habré immediately opened discussions, held in Gabon, with Kamougué and Acheikh Ibn Oumar of the CDR, and it looked at first as if some peaceful arrangement about the south might be possible. Whatever Habré's true intentions may have been, FAN units began moving south while the talks were going on. The FAT split, with several commanders from the Mayo-Kebbi going over to the FAN and leading the attack against the largely discredited Kamougué. With these reinforcements, Habré's forces cleared the CDR out of their strongholds and, in the August 1982 rainy season, launched a surprise offensive into the Sara heartland.

With the economy and administrative structures disrupted, ex-soldiers and young men out of desperation or adventure took to the bush to form a variety of commando groups, known as *codos*. Habré sent his leading Sara recruit, Dono Djidingar, on a mission to the South to negotiate the codos' surrender, but also sent along a trusted FAN commander, Issaka Hassan, to keep watch over Djidingar and to handle the military side of operations. Over the next year the negotiations, supported by continued military pressure, seemed to make progress. At a crucial point, however, the codo commanders backed out of an agreement, claiming that Habré offered insufficient economic compensation and no guarantee of the safety of their members once they were in the hands of Habré's army. Part of the problem seems to have been the choice of Djidingar as negotiator. The fact that he was a prominent southerner led some southerners to fear that Djidingar would advantage his own clan group at the expense of other southern peoples, while others feared that, as a southerner in a regime dominated by northerners, Djidingar would have no authority to deliver on his promises. The violence resumed, more fiercely than ever (Buijtenhuis 1987: 293–300).

In October 1984, Habré sent out a single spokesman, one of his most trusted lieutenants, Mahamat Itno, to start negotiations all over. Itno, a Zaghawa, had the authority to rein in the northern army leaders and oblige them to control the depredations of their men. He also showed great personal courage and persistence in contacting the codos and—still very much with the aid of military pressure—convincing them that they had a future by cutting a deal with the Habré regime (*Info-Tchad,* August 6, 1986). This was a classic military "hearts and minds" campaign, one that worked. Violence was essential to its success; weariness and time also helped; but none of this would have been enough had the Habré regime not had positive incentives to offer, including a believable military and political framework into which the codos and the rest of the southerners could be integrated. Key to this was the integration of the FAT into the FAN, to form FANT—the Forces Armées Nationales Tchadiennes. The symbolic unity was given some solid underpinning with the appointment of several ex-FAT commanders to senior positions—though always with an ex-FAN combattant exercising final control.

Also, despite objections from many FAN stalwarts, Habré had turned his army-commanded government into a republic, with ministerial posts distributed to southerners and others who rallied to the cause. In June 1984, Habré and his colleagues created a political party, the Union Nationale pour l'Indépendance et la Révolution (UNIR). This provided additional patronage positions and, in particular, a palatable mechanism for civil servants and other "intellectuals" (most of them southerners) to be associated with the regime. By the early days of 1986, deals had been cut with the codo commanders, and by the following year those of their followers who preferred to stick with the military life were integrated into the FANT and given plenty of opportunity to fight on the northern fronts.

Habré sent FAN units north immediately after the conquest of Ndjamena in June 1982, but they were unable to hold back the Libyan forces. By August 1983, Libyan troops and civil authorities administered most of the northern BET Province, while their Chadian allies, the FAP and CDR, bivouacked in separate encampments and patrolled the countryside. Ndjamena's writ stopped at the fifteenth parallel. Even to hold there, Habré's government depended on a French expeditionary force, Opération Manta, which guaranteed a line at that parallel against Libyan invasion. In September 1984, the Mitterrand government arranged a deal with Colonel Qadhafi that both countries would withdraw their troops. The French did, the Libyans did not (Spartacus 1985). With the French out of the way, FAP and CDR forces struck across the demarcation line in February 1986, but were decisively beaten and chased back north by the FANT. Renewed activity by Libyan air power brought the French back, in what they baptized Operation Epervier, whose principal mission was to protect against Libyan military aviation south of, this time, the sixteenth parallel.

With Libyan air power neutralized, neither the GUNT nor any of its factional armies was going anywhere. Goukouni spent most of his time in Tripoli, as did the CDR leader, Acheikh Ibn Oumar. In this unpromising stalemate, the GUNT's propensity toward factionalism flourished: minor leader after minor leader cut a deal to return to Ndjamena. From Paris, Kamougué announced in July 1986 that he would "suspend cooperation" with the GUNT (an announcement greeted by derision) and a few months later an agreement presided over by Gabon's President Omar Bongo brought him back to Ndjamena where Habré made him minister of agriculture. More seriously for the GUNT, open conflict broke out in August 1986 between FAP and CDR units in northern Chad, a rivalry exacerbated by the Libyan policy of playing off one group against another. In the fighting, the Libyan forces seemed to have favored the CDR, interpreted by most Chadians as Qadhafi's picking the Arabs over the Tubu.

The effect of the Libyan action was to put the FAP in a position where they were unable to function as a separate military faction. In need of supplies and money, they behaved like any other Chadian faction and searched for the best deal. Habré and his men provided it. Through secret contacts across the desert, Tubu ways of doing business clinched the deal, and common Chadian nationalism provided a convenient language in which to make the deal public. The bulk of the FAP forces joined up with the FANT, setting the stage for Habré's reconquest of the north.

By now France and the United States had provided the FANT with significant equipment for fighting on the ground, and enough antiaircraft capability (mostly U.S.-made Redeyes—though they also had Soviet-made SAM-7s) for them to make low-level attack hazardous for Libyan pilots. However, much against French advice, the FANT started moving north in December 1986. They linked up with the FAP, drove the CDR from the field, and in surprise after surprise ousted the Libyan garrisons from all their heavily fortified positions south of the Aouzou Strip (Devoluy 1987; Foltz 1988). The flow of factional leaders to Ndjamena increased, and in November 1988, CDR leader Acheikh Ibn Oumar and a group of other holdouts cut their deal with Habré, with Iraq providing the diplomatic auspices. Habré promptly made Acheikh his minister of foreign affairs, with particular responsibility for heading off Libyan initiatives with Arab governments. Goukouni remained the only significant factional leader who had not been integrated into Habré's new order (or forced into retirement), and Goukouni was a leader without troops and without much in the way of international support. In these terms, national reunification and control over the national territory under Hissein Habré's leadership was all but complete.

■ How Did Habré Do It?

Habré's success in reestablishing a Chadian state can be traced to many factors. Among these factors, *military prowess* must take pride of place. Habré's ability as a field general and then commander in chief, the boldness and bravery of succeeding commanders, the tactical inventiveness of the FANT, and the courage and ferocity of the ordinary soldiers were all extraordinary. No single-factor analysis—certainly not sociological reductionism to "charismatic leadership" or "warlike traditions"—will get one very far in explaining military effectiveness. Though both of these played some part, any adequate explanation must take into account the experience acquired in twenty years of fighting, courageous battlefield leadership (normally in the front of the attack), daring tactics featuring rapid movement and sudden concentration of firepower, and taking advantage of available military technology creatively adapted to the task at hand. Above all, in Chad-like circumstances, effective military performance is an extension of statecraft, and shares in all the complexity characterizing other branches of that difficult art. Without military tenacity and eventual superiority, Habré's other advantages would not have mattered. When those military skills decayed, he was overthrown.

But, however essential, the deployment of superior military force was not sufficient to achieve Habré's ends. With only a little stretching, the idea of the "hurting stalemate" may be applied to the situation in southern Chad after 1982. Habré's soldiers dispensed the most obvious immediate hurt to the local populations and to those codos they could catch. But if Habré was to rebuild an effective Chadian state, it would not suffice to dominate the south, nor to deny it to enemy factions. He needed to make southern Chad useful once again to the rest of the country, to rebuild its economy—the source of three-quarters of Chad's foreign exchange—and reintegrate its educated manpower (and its fighting forces) into the national system. For this, a series of convincing political deals had to be struck.

The next element to be considered also contributed to military prowess, but it is of more general application: the FAN's experience in *delegating tactical authority to trusted colleagues*. Well before it came to power, the FAN distinguished itself from other factions by its sense of cohesiveness and even, in Chadian terms, by its discipline. Some of this reflects personal loyalty to Hissein Habré, but that loyalty has been reciprocated. Responding effectively to guerrilla-war conditions, the FAN learned to decentralize tactical responsibility and decision authority to the local operative level, within the framework of generally understood strategic goals. The immediate beneficiaries of such responsibilities and delegated powers were the core of trusted comrades, mostly men who made the long march into and out of Sudan in 1980–1982. These comrades often carried no formal rank or relevant portfolio, yet were trusted to act on their own initiative to get something done. Allegedly, the sum total of procedural instructions Habré gave to Itno for negotiating the surrender of the codos was "*débrouille-toi*" (get it done any way you can). He had authority to control military actions, wide latitude in cutting deals with the rebel commanders, and credibility that he could deliver on the deals he cut. The person on whom responsibility for a task devolved might or might not be the senior individual in the formal chain of command. This was most obvious in the military, where the true commanders had no rank and were deferred to by officers with gold bars on their epaulettes. This style of decisionmaking relied on a high level of common understanding and trust among leaders. While that trust was there, fighters could be sure that their actions would be covered and any inconvenient bodies quietly buried; when it was lost, for reasons of incompetent performance or political unreliability, the fall from grace was precipitous and painful.

Key instruments of control, notably the secret police (DDS) and the elite presidential guard regiment (SP), were entrusted to individuals whose past loyalty to the president was reinforced by ethnic ties. The activities of these units, together with the prerogatives of the inner core, not only limited the effective power of former opponents who had rallied to the regime; it also curbed their ability to disrupt the new order through old-style factional politics. They also made it easier for Habré's old comrades to accept that newcomers could be given prestigious jobs; experience had taught them that real power had nothing to do with public position.

A third factor, *Habré's nationalism,* was a major symbolic advantage and initially he manipulated it with skill. Surrender ceremonies, whether with opposing faction troops or with individual political leaders, were carried. out under the Chadian flag with a flourish of fraternal rhetoric, which almost disguised the fact that the flag stood for Habré's continued rule. This "commitment to the national idea" made it possible for those outside the original FAN coalition to rally to Habré's side with some dignity preserved: such an action need not be seen as a surrender, but rather as a selfless act of "offering one's service to *la Nation Tchadienne.*" Though hardly lacking in ego, Habré had, when necessary, the self-discipline to subordinate concerns of *amour-propre* to reasons of state, extending his hand to formerly dedicated enemies who accepted the new order. His opposition to even a tactical alliance with Libya, the powerful Arab state—and self-proclaimed champion of Islam—to Chad's north, provided at least a modicum of reassurance to southern Christians and animists. Nationalistic appeals drew a strong response from civil servants: after initial hesitation, southerners as well as others readily, even eagerly, took up their old bureaucratic positions. Habré's personal pragmatism and the absence of meaningful ideological discourse in any branch of Chadian politics helped to make nationalism the sole ideology of reconciliation. In this, Habré much resembled the political leaders of the 1960s, in the early days of African independence. Now, "Libyan imperialism" replaced European colonialism as the all-purpose external enemy.

A fourth factor in Habré's success was *negotiating skill.* In this arena, the skills of Habré and his principal lieutenants were honed to a keen edge.

By 1984, experience had taught Habré to stay out of the internationally sponsored roundtables of Chadian factions (such as those that originally created the GUNT). In these, the combination of several internal factions and several foreign powers—however well-intentioned the latter may have been—worked to give each faction hope that it could find an external patron and, in Habré's opinion, tended to treat his side as just another faction, albeit one occupying the capital city (Dadi 1987: 147–149). Rather, Habré maneuvered to deal one-on-one with his opponents, isolating them as much as possible, and then offering a bargain. It is no wonder that the Chadian government had twenty-seven ministers and a dozen junior ministers; and that senior positions in the civil service and parastatal enterprises were doled out with regard to qualities other than technical competence, narrowly conceived. At the same time, the person welcomed back into the national fold was expected to continue to deliver the goods, in the sense that he continued to hold the loyalty of a significant group and publicly transferred that loyalty to the regime. Those whose followers stepped out of line, and those who joined Habré early but whose constituencies were more effectively delivered by latercomers, found their portfolios and perquisites reassigned. The establishment of a formal state and a political party opened up institutional frameworks in which even minor factional leaders could find a job and their followers could find a home.

Habré used third-party mediators to advantage in his negotiations. Gabon's Bongo and Congo's Sassou-Nguésso have vied for the honor of presiding over the surrender of the greatest number of Chadian dissidents. Less friendly places like Algeria, Burkina Faso, and Benin were also manipulated into service, the latter two as Libyan clients who could facilitate the "reconciliation" of GUNT members. Iraq became Habré's Arab partner of choice, both as a supplier of military equipment and as the presider over negotiations with Chadian Arab factions.

Habré has needed, and received—a fifth factor—much *help from his friends.* American and French military supplies and occasional military intelligence were essential, and the dissuasive presence of a French military contingent has made it impossible for Libyan air power to be deployed against targets in central and southern Chad. Economic support from the same two powers was equally essential, both for buying back opponents and, even more so, for keeping the Chadian economy and the Chadian state afloat. The additional ability of these allies to mobilize other donors has also been essential to a country for which foreign aid represents the largest single category of GNP. Habré also carefully cultivated key African friends, useful for their direct contributions and also for putting pressure on their patrons among the great powers. Zaire's Mobutu was by far the most important, acting, no doubt, out of his usual complex motives, which in this case would include rendering service to the United States, blocking the expansion of Arab influence in sub-Saharan Africa, and acquiring a publicly appreciative client. The Côte d'Ivoire's Houphouet-Boigny and other conservative Francophone leaders played an important role in keeping up French interest and contributions, principally by reminding the French that their reputation for reliability would suffer greatly were they to allow Qadhafi once again to invade Chad. Habré's skill in presenting himself as the embodiment of comprehensive Chadian nationalism and the defender of territorial integrity provided useful normative cover for those states—Western, Arab, and African—that for their own purposes wished to support his regime.

Finally, *mistakes by his enemies* were of incalculable importance for Habré. Persistent underestimation of him as a leader, and of the FAN, then the FANT, as fighting forces, both helped, in part by increasing the surprise and panic factor when Habré and his men prevailed. Opposition leaders like Goukouni and Kamougué never seriously consolidated their political positions or otherwise rose above the segmentary factional politics that epitomized so much of Chad's problems.

The prize set of mistakes was committed by the Libyans, however. The litany is long, and all can be traced to Qadhafi. Had he not withdrawn his troops from Chad out of his vain desire to become chairman of the OAU in 1982, and aroused African opinion against him by his bombastic announcement that Chad and Libya were to be united as one nation, Habré could not so easily have fought his way back into Ndjamena. Persistently, Libya overplayed the Chadian factional game, refusing to place its trust in any one Chadian leader, but seeking to preserve ultimate control by encouraging rivalry among all its client Chadian factions (Lemarchand 1988: 115–117). The fight between the CDR and the FAP in 1986 was the disastrous culmination of a consistent policy that ended up adding most of Goukouni's Tubu forces to the FANT and depriving the Libyan forces of those allies who best knew the difficult terrain of Chad's far north. Indeed, Qadhafi's penchant to divide and rule, in the form of multiple and overlapping chains of command in the Libyan garrisons inside Chad, contributed to the Libyan forces' inability to withstand the surprise assaults of the FANT (Foltz 1988: 63–69). Qadhafi's distrust of his own military agents and their inability to innovate in battle situations contrasted strikingly with Habré's military daring and FAN-style delegation of authority and initiative to trusted men on the spot.

■ The Challenge of Success

By mid-1987 the basic elements of the state were in place. *Central political authority* was exercised through a dual realm of power. At the very center

of power was a core united by the long march and their personal connec-
tions with Habré. Outside this inner circle was a secondary realm of formal
state institutions, including the ministries, the cabinet, and the official
political party, the UNIR. This realm gave a channel for formal association
of social groups with the center, without delegating to them final power
over major decisions.

National boundaries, though far from impervious, were pushed back to
a point where the major centers of Chadian life were not directly threatened. While the ownership of the Aouzou Strip remained contested,
Libya's massive military defeat in the BET region removed the immediate
threat. Indeed, the general disorder in Sudan's Dar Fur Province made
Chad's eastern border a more immediate source of concern.

Internally, *governmental control* had been reestablished in all the populated areas of the country, at about the degree that had prevailed during
most of the colonial period. While the state's ability to deliver services to
the population remained low, its apparatus actually functioned, and most
months its agents were paid (Foltz and Foltz 1991). While local troubles
and banditry were not uncommon, they in no way threatened overall state
sovereignty. The state made serious progress in *extracting resources* from
its domestic and international environments. With basic order reestablished, cotton production in the south exceeded prewar levels, and positive
findings from renewed oil exploration held out the hope that by the end of
the century the Chadian government might be able to pay its own routine
operating expenses. Stability brought increased economic resources from
the international donor community, with "foreign aid" representing the
largest single source of international "earnings" (Foltz 1987).

The system for *control of state agents* grew out of the dual realm of
central authority. The FAN core and its agents watched the others and had
no hesitation about sanctioning behavior that threatened the regime or the
prerogatives of the inner core. Habré came to rely increasingly on his secret
police, the DDS, and the Presidential Security or Guard (SP) recruited from
among his kinsmen. The SP kept the regular army from making trouble,
while the DDS penetrated the civil administration and particularly the
UNIR, the official political party, which was used as prime recruiting
ground for informers. There can be little doubt that the prime purpose of
the control mechanisms was to assure regime security, rather than effective
performance.

■ Habré's Failure

Habré was driven from power in November 1990. The failure of his regime
tells us much about the limitations of military force as the principal tool of
state construction.

Habré's regime failed at its political center: the FAN core cracked along ethnic and family lines. The first signs were not particularly alarming. Banal incidents between Hadjerai and Gorane soldiers in Sahr—where they had previously cooperated enthusiastically in repressing the southerners—brought savage repression by the SP. Several hundred Hadjerai then decamped with their weapons to their native Guera, raising marginally the endemic rate of banditry and disruption. The DDS and SP clamped down on Hadjerai elites in Ndjamena in mid-1987, with a few escaping over the border to safety.

More serious were quarrels over the division of spoils. Corruption in Habré's Chad was a routine matter, but few considered it among the state's major problems. As observers quipped, corruption couldn't be that much of a problem, there was nothing much to steal. This ceased to be true, however, in mid-1987, when Chad began to sell off much of the Libyan heavy armament captured in battle. The market value was variously estimated at between $500 million and $1.5 billion. While no Chadians realized anything like such sums, the numbers may be put in perspective when one realizes that Chadian GNP was less than $1 billion. By late 1987, there was something worth fighting over in Chad, and the sums involved, like the international cast of arms merchants, gunrunners, and government agents who traipsed through in search of a deal, were well beyond anything the Chadian state could manage.

Arms are not just a neutral export commodity: they have a potential domestic use as well. The Anakaza group around Habré moved to make sure that other parts of the FAN alliance did not get their hands on them; this meant, in particular, the Bideyat and Zaghawa, who made up about 40 percent of the FANT and whose ranks had provided the FANT's *comchefs*—first Idriss Deby and then Hassane Djamouss. Also of concern was Mahamat Itno, who as interior minister oversaw the state police and prefectoral systems. The Zaghawa and Bideyat made sure they were not cut out of the profits: they took captured arms themselves and either secreted them in their home areas of Ennedi and Biltine or sold them into the active commercial circuits in nearby Sudan. Whether Deby, Itno, and Djamouss were in fact planning a coup against Habré on April Fool's Day 1989 or fled, as the SP moved to eliminate them, is a moot point. By then the alliance at the center of state authority had collapsed and Habré's real troubles began.

Deby escaped across the border into Sudan, to be joined by many of the FANT's seasoned Zaghawa and Bideyat troops and by the Hadjerai and others who had fled earlier. It did not take long for Libyan money and supplies to meet up with them, and this time Qadhafi appears to have avoided micromanaging the rebels' enterprise.

Habré's response was to unleash the SP and the DDS and to intervene personally and directly in their repressive operations. Rather than reach for broader support, the regime closed in on itself. The excesses of the agents of control increased the quiet opposition to the regime. This was particularly true among the civil servants, who were both harassed and aware that resources that ought to have gone to them were being stolen by the agents of control. Habré did not help his cause abroad by his disdainful reaction to François Mitterrand's La Baule speech urging democratization in Africa. French aid slowed down, and the French military detachment in Chad moved toward a position of neutrality between Habré and Deby's rebels that came to advantage the latter.

Habré himself made basic military mistakes. His SP terrorized the Zaghawa population in the Biltine and across the border in Sudan, which swelled the ranks of Deby's forces. Mistrusting his own commanders, Habré tried to run the operations against Deby himself, radioing in tactical decisions from Ndjamena and traveling to the front to himself assume command. In the ensuing action he narrowly escaped death. In the night of November 30–December 1, 1990, Habré looted the treasury while his kinsmen looted the cities, then they stole away across the border. Ordinary people watched them go, then looted the abandoned government residences and offices and waited for the new masters of the state to arrive.

■ **Habré's Legacy**

Hissein Habré left a functioning, if basic, state structure to his successor. He also left a clear legacy, indicating that neither one-man rule nor a tight and unrepresentative oligarchy can long expect to govern in today's Africa. Habré seized and lost power through military force. There can be little doubt that effective military force is an essential element in reconstructing most African states, but that force must be disciplined and controlled. Many of Habré's problems stemmed directly from the excesses—and excessive privileges—of the military and civil control structures. In particular, reliance on ethnically exclusive agents of control, like the Presidential Security, is a sign that a regime is on shaky ground.

Idriss Deby's successor regime has not had an easy time of it, especially in bringing its Zaghawa troops under control. Indeed, their high-handed looting in Ndjamena and brutal repression of southern dissidents have created a major problem for the regime. In seeking to gain control over a functioning state, the regime has taken two major steps, albeit hesitantly. The first was the convocation of a sovereign national conference that laid plans for a transition to a multiparty parliamentary system by March 1994. Although in the interim Deby retained presidential authority, including command of the army, day-to-day administration and decisionmaking were made the responsibility of a transitional government, headed by a southerner (and sometime Goukounist), Fidèle Moungar. A Conseil Supérieur de Transition, made up of fifty-seven members, was supposed to monitor the implementation of government decisions. The second step taken was to make a major reduction in the size of the army, with particular attention being given to achieving national balance in its makeup and putting it under central, disciplined control.

Both of these initiatives were costly and required external support. They also required a more orderly regional environment, one supportive of state authority, than Chad had previously known. If these requirements are met over the rest of the decade, the Chadian state that Habré reconstituted may continue long after his departure from power.

3

State Collapse and Reconstruction in Uganda

Gilbert M. Khadiagala

To understand how to put collapsed states back together, we need to probe the causes of collapse, its symptoms, and the attempts to reverse it. Most discussions of the predatory, parasitic, and weak African state provide only partial answers to why some states collapse while others survive. In recent years, the antistatism characteristic of the dominant state-society theorists has further clouded thinking about state reconstruction in Africa.

This chapter discusses state collapse and reconstruction in Uganda since the 1970s. It proceeds from two propositions. First, collapse is fundamentally an institutional problem, manifesting itself in the inability of political arrangements to provide meaning to social action. In Zartman's apt introductory remark, states collapse when they "can no longer perform the functions required for them to pass as states." Second, since the state, in its institutional mode of extending authority and deriving legitimacy is indispensable to socioeconomic organization, collapse implies the disappearance of a purposeful entity; put differently, institutional collapse occurs when the state withers away by default. I will, therefore, treat reconstruction as the return of the state to the center of social and political organization.

■ State-making and Collapse: Conceptual Issues

State collapse needs to be located conceptually in ideas that inform state-making. Dominant traditions of the state concentrate upon its territorial, central, and institutional nature, reflected in the definition of the state drawn from the first chapter. The primary process of state-making involves the extension of authority. What Poggi (1978; 1982: 337–360) has characterized as the "phenomenon of rule" finds expression in territorial space, the essential physical basis of the state's institutional mission.

Since Weber, however, scholars have also conceded the inadequacy of mere territorial expansion, hence the importance of legitimacy, the normative basis for the exercise of authority. The state as "the receptacle of legitimacy" (Dawisha and Zartman 1988: 7–8) constitutes the appropriate basis of rule-making and the modalities of power and purpose. Legitimation thus dovetails with "state limiting doctrines" such as constitutionalism and civil liberties (Young 1982: 75). To this end, expansion of state power is accompanied by the establishment of legal controls as it reproduces support and compliance (Marennin 1987: 63; Onuf 1991: 425–446; Parekh 1990: 247–262). As Dyson (1980: 214) notes, "the state tradition of authority has been concerned to provide man with direction in his behavior, and to avoid 'aimless' conduct, through the idea of order in values."

To facilitate the extension of authority and legitimacy, state-makers build institutions, the objective manifestations of the state (Badie and Birnbaum 1983; Poggi 1978). Institutions become the instruments of organizational consensus through which the state derives legitimacy; more pertinent, they are the mediations that transform the private lives of individuals into shared and collective identities (Dyson 1980; Migdal 1988; O'Donnell 1988: 175). *Stateness,* then, refers to the functional ability of institutions to organize constraints and effect compliance to orient human action toward certain expectations and rules of procedure. Dyson (1980: 217) writes:

> The idea of the state lends to a complex set of institutions the appearance of a certain coherence, by providing them with certain common substantive purposes, and authoritativeness, by emphasizing the importance of constraints (in the form of procedures and rules) in order to insure binding decisions of common concern.

Whether in its "relative autonomy" of operations independent of social constraints or as a blatant instrument of specific forces, stateness endows institutions with their authoritative and legitimating purposes. Marennin (1987: 73) is, therefore, accurate in stressing that "legitimations are fundamental to the drive for autonomy, for without proper justifications states cannot gain the right to be distinct, the right to manage for society, and would be forced to depend on force to maintain their rule."

Stateness has a dual face, manifested in the ambiguity of the state as a structure of dominance and as an agent for mobilizing collective interests (O'Donnell 1988: 175). On the one hand, stateness embodies despotic power, the range of actions that state elites undertake without routine, institutionalized negotiations with groups in society; on the other hand, it represents infrastructural power, the ability of the state actually to penetrate and coordinate, from the center, the activities of society (Mann 1984: 185–212).

If stateness is basically the acquisition of capacities for the legitimation and exercise of power, then collapse is an extreme on a range of many outcomes in the arduous process of state-making. More than mere institutional weaknesses, collapse connotes profound reversals in these capacities.

Given that radiation of power across geographic space is a critical dimension of state-making, the loss of territorial scope for such exercise could be seen as one of the vital characteristics of state collapse (Kaufman 1988: 219–235). In sum, collapse occurs when centralized institutions of penetration are unable to "tame" the contiguous periphery. This culminates most often in fragmentation and the emergence of countervailing power centers. Collapse at this level becomes the disintegration of overarching governmental structures, structures that establish and maintain order, coordination, and security (Young 1984: 80–81; Yoffee and Cowgill 1988: 1–19).

Similarly collapse occurs when the state ceases to supply consensus for the exercise of its power and to secure resources from society. The latter aspect depends on the procedural rules by which institutions derive goods and services from organized groups. In this context, state collapse could be understood as the breakdown of the regulative and penetrative capacity of the state, the end points of a phenomenon that Huntington popularized as "political decay," where political institutions atrophy on account of their inability to contain centrifugal forces in society (Huntington 1968: 386–430; see also Yoffee and Cowgill 1988: 12–13).

Academic depictions of the state as "fictitious," "lame," "soft," "hard," and "overextended" seem to capture problems of state-making in Africa (Myrdal 1971; Ergas 1987: 1–22; Sandbrook 1985; Marennin 1987: 65; Doornbos 1990: 179–198; Fatton 1992). The state in Africa has been characterized as weak, precisely because it lacks both social cohesion, an institutional core, and organizational capacities. State softness, Rothchild (1987: 126) says, delineates the limitation of state control over its society and the incapacity to implement regulations effectively within a given territory. Proponents of state hardness, on the other hand, have described the propensity of African regimes to deploy coercive power without legitimacy: states thereby distort the making and implementation of policy (Forrest 1988: 423–442; Rothchild 1987: 141). The "lame leviathan" is a paradox— because although the state looms large in relation to other organizations, it has limited capacity for managing society and directing change (Callaghy 1980; Zolberg 1992: 309). Rather than signifying collapse, these categories speak to the perennial discrepancy that Binder (1986: 5) has described as that between the maleficence and beneficence of stateness. It requires a particular configuration of political circumstance to obliterate stateness.

■ Amin and the Collapse of the Ugandan State

Idi Amin destroyed a state that was still being made, a state groping with rudimentary tasks of broadening its authority over an uncertain territory, against a background of scarce resources and unrefined administration. A

few years after independence from Britain in 1962, the civilian regime of
Milton Obote abandoned its grand postcolonial experiment—an attempt to
manage Uganda's cultural pluralism by harmonizing the paternalism of the
center with embryonic mechanisms of local control and participation (Kiapi
1989: 91–104; Barongo 1989: 72). The ineluctable process of state collapse
began with the unraveling of this constitutional experiment.

To Obote, the independence constitution of 1962 that allowed a measure of decentralization—dispersal of power among predominant ethnic
groups—impinged directly on his ability to consolidate state power. His
ultimate strategy was to encroach on powers of federated states through
proscription of kingdoms and the imposition of a one-party state in 1967
(Mamdani 1976; Ibingira 1980). Uganda's constitutional crises of the mid-
1960s stemmed from competing visions of state-making: the centralizing
tendencies of a state ranged against the interests of local groups, especially
the Baganda, to maintain their autonomy (Wrigley 1988: 34; Mudoola
1989: 124).

Obote managed to ride roughshod over the weak constitutional
arrangements by simultaneously increasing the power of the military. First
he courted the army, under its leader General Idi Amin, and used it effectively against his civilian opponents. Second, after consolidating power, he
attempted to undercut Amin's position by building a countervailing force to
the regular army. When military power became functionally indispensable
to his rule, Obote downgraded civilian institutions of legitimation and created conditions for Amin's overthrow. This was the backdrop to Amin's
military coup of January 1971 (Ibingira 1980). Significantly, as Mudoola
(1989: 131) has suggested, Amin was a product of the gradual disintegration of civilian institutions of statehood:

> The Amin coup and the politics Amin pursued afterwards, simply pushed
> to a logical conclusion trends already set by Obote—trends which increas-
> ingly rendered powerless any political institutions for resolving conflicts.
> By the time Amin assumed power, such institutions were so fragile that it
> needed only a simple pronouncement to have them banned.

Amin's major contribution to the collapse of the state was the militarization of politics. Stateness assumes that the instruments of rule are situated in social groupings that furnish universal reference for authoritative
action (Nzongola 1985: 536–537; O'Donnell 1988: 181). Although he initially rallied all the anti-Obote forces to create a measure of popular support, Amin subsequently relied solely on a narrow social base in the military and the administration. In addition, he sought to enhance his image at
home and abroad by embarking on an aggressive foreign policy, champi-
oning assorted radical African and international goals (Mazrui 1980: 53;
Mutibwa 1992: 104–108).

In using force to exact compliance, the Amin regime lost its organizational clarity and functional role as a social manager. In appearance, the state displayed all the features of overextendedness; in reality, it was weakened by its inability to penetrate society. This explains the paradox of the "hard" and "soft" state, underscoring, in Mann's (1984: 185–213) framework, the incongruity between despotic and infrastructural power; or, as Jeffries (1993: 32) puts it, the state was "frequently authoritarian because it [was] markedly non-authoritative." Relying solely on despotic power became counterproductive since it could not dovetail with any infrastructural objectives. Collapse under Amin demonstrated the relapse of public power into political irresponsibility, the transformation of a pivotal state institution into a source of insecurity.

The economic dimensions of collapse logically followed from the peculiar exercise of state power with consequences for production. When Amin tried to augment economic power without the support of established social groups and institutions, he exacerbated social disintegration. Economic deterioration followed Amin's initial efforts to build a power base by launching the Economic War, involving massive redistribution of property expropriated from Asian entrepreneurs (Mutibwa 1992: 115–120; Jamal 1988: 679–701). Stagnation with redistribution, Jamal (1991: 85) demonstrates, was to become Amin's singular impact on the decline of the Ugandan economy.

Of equal significance with regard to the economy was the severance of the reciprocal links between the state and its periphery. Bunker (1985: 372–373) has shown that, prior to 1971, state dependence on agricultural exports had enhanced peasant leverage considerably. The state had, in turn, developed institutions of restraint and accountability for intervention in the economy. Infrastructural decay, neglect of agricultural production, and extraeconomic coercion under Amin interrupted these experiments in responsive institution-building (Mamdani 1990: 433–434; Brett 1991: 303–309; Kayizzi-Mugerwa and Bigsten 1992: 58–75). In effect a retreat of the state from the rural areas, this led to extensive political and economic restructuring—efforts that, in some cases, strengthened the autonomy of the peasantry. Alternative rural and urban strategies for survival, however, were poor substitutes for the formal institutional structures providing regular links to the national economy (Southall 1980: 627–656; Kasfir 1983: 85–103). Green (1981: 1) described concisely the urban *magendo* (underground) economy as a "brutally exploitative system which degrades, corrupts, deprives, and routinely kills." Furthermore, with the breakdown of state-periphery institutional ties, subsequent state-builders had to work to recapture a peasantry that had lost confidence in the capacity of central authority to perform its accustomed functions (Helleiner 1981: 27–35; Adams 1981: 15–25; Rothchild and Harbeson 1981: 115–119).

Amin was forced out of power in March 1979 by a combined force of Ugandan exiles and the Tanzanian army. The liberation, however, ended a long phase of brutality without resolving the underlying questions of the means and ends of reconstituting state power. The institutionalization of violence had virtually effaced civilian institutions and made the military the sole arbiter of conflicts. Subsequent regimes predicated reconstruction on recreating civilian institutions of rule, but they could hardly maintain order without reliance on the military. This dilemma explained the instability that characterized the post-Amin period.

A quick succession of regimes showed the illusory nature of restoring the state's dual function as an intermediary between social groups and the defender of the territorial unit. Between 1979 and 1985, various groups vied for the control of fragmenting central power. With the exception of Obote, who returned through election in December 1980, all gained power through armed force. But even Obote had again to resort to segments within the military to subdue a growing opposition. As before, despotic power used without infrastructural power confirmed the vulnerability of state managers and, at most, emboldened opposition factions.

Of the opposition forces, Yoweri Museveni's National Liberation Movement (NRM), with its army, the National Resistance Army (NRA), proved the most formidable, launching a successful guerrilla war in most parts of the country, starting in 1981. When Obote was overthrown by his military in July 1985, a power vacuum ensued in Kampala that Museveni was to exploit effectively. The weak military government invited him to join a provisional government in August, but Museveni refused, opting instead for Kenya's mediated talks for a peace agreement. During the negotiations, the NRA strengthened its position on the ground by establishing control over the western half of the country. Although both sides signed a peace agreement in December 1985, the militarily preponderant NRA captured Kampala in January 1986, putting Museveni in power (Gertzel 1990: 205–208; Brittain 1986: 51–61).

■ Museveni and the Reconstruction of the State

Conceptually, state reconstruction deals with rejuvenating institutional mechanisms that formerly gave consistency to state action, legitimized power, and established social trust, returning the state to the center of political life.

In Uganda, when the new state managers began restoring statehood, they did so in a climate of diminished popular faith in the capacity of the state to provide security. The dominant trend was institutional immobilism, creating uncertainty, loss of commitment to the common good, devaluation of human life, and mistrust of authority (Ouma 1991: 474–475; Mutibwa

1992: 122–124). The first order of business hence became rebuilding the credibility of the state as a predictable instrument of order.

In assuming the primary role of rebuilding state power, Museveni's NRM reversed the military's image as a predator on society by reclaiming juridical statehood. Confronted with insurgent and sectarian movements from the north and northeast, Museveni first relied primarily on military power, depicting it as a contest between the "forces of patriotism and modernization on one hand, and colonial practices of putting vital institutions of state such as military forces in the hands of illiterate and backward elements, on the other" (*FBIS-East Africa,* August 21, 1987: B1–B2). As in Chad, however, the priority shifted to a judicious mix of coercion and incorporation, meeting the military challenge from sundry guerrilla movements with force while incorporating others into the NRM's governing structure.

From the beginning, the NRM adopted a ten-point program, emphasizing democracy, security, national unity, and the restoration of the economy. This program was to "form the basis for a nationwide coalition of political and social forces that could usher in a new and better future for the long-suffering people of Uganda" (cited in Museveni 1992: 197). A core southern alliance of the Baganda and Banyankole comprised the institutional fulcrum for interethnic mediation and mobilization. To broaden his power base, Museveni invited leading members of the old political parties into the government and granted them ministerial positions. Through this elaborate cooptation, Museveni achieved the goal of a broad-based national government that allowed him to concentrate on rebuilding a disciplined national army. In a "gentleman's agreement," political groups agreed to suspend partisan activities until the adoption of a new constitution. In 1989 Museveni established a commission to draft a new constitution.

To penetrate the rural areas, the NRM established resistance committees (RCs), organizational structures that evolved from the days of the guerrilla war. Formed to strengthen local security, these committees evolved gradually into administrative structures for state control and political mobilization (Kasfir 1991: 247–278; 1993: 603–605). By 1989, the RCs had become vehicles for grassroots participation, electing representatives into a government-controlled parliament. Fundamentally, the RCs emerged after the elections as the rural organs for Museveni's "no-party democracy," conceived as a system amalgamating all conceivable forces, irrespective of past political affiliation, within the structures of the NRM. Museveni defended this system as an antidote to past conflicts that he saw issuing from "party competition in a context in which the stakes were too high and political sophistication too low" (cited in *New Vision,* August 28, 1992).

Constituted behind Museveni's strong leadership, the emerging state institutions became the focal point for the grand project of national rehabilitation. As the operative concept, rehabilitation was to embrace communities, infrastructure, and economic and political institutions. The immediate advantage of a unified government, or what Museveni (1992: 33) billed as the "politics of unity," was to bring a measure of policy coherence and stability unknown to Uganda in over two decades. By 1992, however, this broad-based alliance was beginning to crumble, for two interrelated reasons. First, Museveni the state-maker was increasingly becoming a victim of his own success. The capacity of the state to restore security destroyed its principal reason for sustaining the essentially soft authoritarian pact with all political parties: the further he moved the country from the civil wars of past decades, the greater the support for the resumption of multiparty politics. To the opposition, a more secure environment occasioned the normalization of political life through the return of effective participation.

Second, while conceding that centralized control was crucial in the formative phases of national rehabilitation, opposition forces began to view Museveni's "no-party democracy" as a strategy to undercut their organizational abilities. They saw the NRM as delaying deliberately the constitution-making process to cement its institutional base. In the words of an opposition member:

Many governments have been coming and trying to suppress the multiparty system in Uganda, but parties resurface immediately after coups. Obote wanted to kill parties by violence. Museveni, being a tactician, wants to kill them by kindness—giving us ministerial posts (cited by *International Press Service,* September 22, 1992).

Besides, the opposition found ammunition in Museveni's own rationale for a nonpartisan democracy:

Some in Africa think if we have multi-parties we will have prosperity! This is putting the cart before the horse. If we are going to follow Europe's lead, then let us first eliminate the peasants, industrialize and achieve the same level of skilled manpower before embarking on multiparty politics. This is what Europe had to do, why should we be any different? (cited in *New African,* July 1991: 15).

This conflict took a decisive turn in August 1992, following Museveni's proposal to impose a permanent ban on opposition parties. Describing them as "divisive and destructive" to peace and harmony, Museveni asserted that he did not rescue Uganda from the spate of turmoil and mismanagement only to put other parties in power. When, however, leading members of his ruling party refused to endorse this proposal, parliament came up with a compromise that endorsed the continued restriction on party activities pending a new constitution. Parliament also advised Museveni to seek dialogue rather than confrontation with the opposition.

Strengthened by this move, opposition parties pressed unsuccessfully for representation on the constitutional commission (*New Vision,* August 12, 1992, and August 14, 1992; *FBIS-Africa,* September 11, 1992: 13–15).

The major provisions of the draft constitution, submitted in December 1992 and reviewed over the following year, embodied Museveni's views that return to a multiparty political system would destabilize Uganda. The report recommended nonparty presidential and parliamentary elections in 1994; subsequently, the president would govern for five years through a "national council of state" structured along the lines of the current cabinet. After what would in effect be a seven-year period, Uganda would then hold a national referendum to decide on a more permanent constitutional order (*Africa Confidential,* January 22, 1993: 2; *African Economic Digest,* December 14, 1992: 18). These arrangements are instituted with the approval of a constituent assembly, elected in March 1994.

In the view of Uganda's state-makers, this constitution-making, to be accomplished through the building of a national consensus on political arrangements, is a way of providing a solid foundation for democracy. This gradual approach, Museveni has stated, will "facilitate the entrenchment of norms of accountability, respect for public office, and competition into the political culture." Responding to those opposing the constitution, he said:

> There is a growing opportunistic use of mistrust. This mistrust has been applied to the making of the constitution. In the initial stages of the exercise, some people were saying that the NRM government already had a constitution up its sleeve. It is now being said that . . . [writers] of the draft constitution were doing the bidding of the government. Such mistrust is a gross injustice. It is also a pernicious form of corruption. It undermines human dignity and patriotism. Leadership of any kind becomes impossible when bad faith and insincere motives are imputed by detractors intent on making political capital" (cited in *New Vision,* January 28, 1993).

In the long run, the NRM envisages a federal constitution that would progressively decentralize political authority to allow subregional units some autonomy. In granting local autonomy, the state hopes to revert to the preindependence practice of power devolution, steps that might reduce ethnic conflicts while strengthening administrative capacity (*New Vision,* January 28, 1993; *Ottawa Citizen,* February 1, 1993: A4).

Debates on "constitution-making from above" nevertheless symbolize larger issues pertaining to the actors, pace, and direction of reconstruction. Constitution-making, Arjomand (1992: 39–40) has noted, is a central process in political reconstruction since it deliberately lays down "the normative and legal foundations of the political order"—its product, constitutions, become "monuments around which institutions can crystallize . . .

[creating] a new constellation of institutional interests, and thereby, new agendas for politics." Do the admittedly present dictates of political reha-bilitation constrain future attempts at constitutionalism; that is, limits on the exercise and differentiation of power? Should constitution-making be a hegemonic agenda, as Museveni prefers, or a shared enterprise, as some in the opposition have argued? If strengthening the state requires tactical elite autonomy from centrifugal forces in society, how can this autonomy be bal-anced with enduring institution-building?

Unquestionably, the task that Museveni has described as "Uganda's convalescence" looms large on the national agenda. In certain respects, therefore, constitutional arrangements might reflect, in the Gaullist spirit, both Museveni's imprimatur and the imperatives of reconstruction. Yet some see these arrangements as contrived to build a civilian political base for what remains, essentially, a military government (Gingyera-Pinychwa 1991: 224–229). Omara-Otunnu (1992: 460), for instance, has argued that while there has been a dramatic transformation in "Uganda's political grammar . . . the equation or formula of power has remained essentially the same: soldiers and not civilians form the backbone of those in power." From this perspective, Museveni's constitutional engineering allows him the time to restructure the RCs into formidable "people's party machines" that will ensure his future reelection.

More sympathetic critics have also noted that although Museveni has maintained high levels of popular support, he faces the danger of squander-ing a remarkable opportunity to construct a much more durable and less idiosyncratic constitutional framework (*Africa Confidential,* January 22, 1993: 2). This is a vital question since the prevailing consensus for rehabil-itation affords state-makers very wide latitude in political experimentation. If a "no-party democracy," however, becomes their sole institutional inno-vation, how will they differ from the first generation of founding fathers who destroyed the feeble state inherited from colonialism? It would appear that this second generation has enormous responsibilities and opportunities for creating a more secure political infrastructure for Uganda's statehood.

■ **Reconstructing the State Through the Economy**

No less critical in the overall resurrection of moribund state structures is revitalization of systems that allocate goods and services. When the state returns to reestablish its economic position, it does so invariably as a junior partner, pressurized on one hand by multilateral and bilateral external actors and on the other viewed suspiciously by internal actors. No longer authoritative, bereft of resources, the resurgent state largely improvises the necessary economic reconstruction. It is, perhaps, for this reason that reconstructing the economy raises more interesting issues than those of simply rebuilding the functional instruments of political rule. Contributing to the salience of these issues are contemporary debates about the trade-offs between market efficiency and state intervention (Mamdani 1990: 427–467; Mugyenyi 1991: 61–77; Ochieng 1991: 43–60).

Specifically, since state collapse was accompanied by a modicum of peasant autonomy, might the priority of recapturing it impinge on this autonomy? What happens when a formerly interventionist state returns to supervise peasant production? What are the most appropriate methods of subduing the *magendo* economy? In the Ugandan case, answers to these questions lie in the pattern of interaction between a weak state and power-ful external economic actors. Economic reconstruction has encompassed three broad components: reform of governmental institutions, rehabilitation of physical infrastructure, and economic liberalization. The general thrust of these policies has been the emphasis on the twin goals of rehabilitation and production (Jamal 1988: 679–701; Tindigarukayo 1990: 427–467; Museveni 1992: 60–65).

Just as the destruction of basic political infrastructure undermined sub-sequent efforts at rehabilitation, effective state leverage over economic policies was affected by the years of economic mismanagement and decay. Weakened by prior processes of collapse, the economic adjustment started from a very low base (Kayizzi-Mugerwa and Bigsten 1992: 58–75). The result was overwhelming dependence on external resources at every stage of economic reconstruction. Bunker (1985: 374) points out that, since the early 1980s, the state's alliance with external forces has restricted effective local intervention in policy formation and program implementation. Yet unlike previous regimes, Museveni has been more attractive to external donors because of his abilities to restore political tranquility. By projecting sufficient power, Museveni, in the eyes of donor countries, was better placed than any other civilian government to push through harsh economic policies.

Since 1986, the government has won the support of aid donors to reha-bilitate infrastructure and stimulate economic growth through diversifica-tion of agricultural exports. Central to these policies have been marked increases in producer prices for basic agricultural goods with a view to stimulating production (Tindigarukayo 1990: 349; World Bank 1991). In 1990, for instance, the state liberalized coffee trade, abolishing state-owned marketing boards and licensing private exporters. This liberalization was partly prompted by the collapse of international coffee prices, forcing authorities to decontrol producer prices. Equivalent measures to introduce a competitive environment in the agricultural industry have been extended to cotton production (*Africa Economic Digest,* January 11, 1993: 10).

In one of its major infrastructural projects, the government established the Northern Uganda Reconstruction Program (NURP), covering an area equivalent to one-third of the country. At the cost of $93.6 million, NURP involves the rehabilitation of physical and social infrastructure. In the long run, the state intends such projects to stimulate economic growth and repay the initial costs of the infrastructure (*New Vision*, July 14, 1992). Through loans from the World Bank's agricultural sector reform programs, the government embarked on projects to strengthen the delivery of extension services; i.e., improvements in training, skills, and management systems in rural areas. Similarly, the World Bank approved a $29 million credit in 1992 toward the financing of a management project designed to build greater institutional capacity in key government organizations (*African Economic Digest*, November 30, 1992: 17).

Under the direction of the International Monetary Fund (IMF), Museveni launched an economic recovery program in May 1987. It included steep devaluations, tighter fiscal policy, less state expenditure, and liberalization of trade in farm produce and foreign exchange (Ochieng 1991: 43–60; Mugyenyi 1991: 61–77; Mamdani 1990: 447–467). The centerpiece of these efforts was a divestiture campaign that was to dispose of ill-managed and heavily subsidized state concerns to help curb public spending: under the plan, public enterprises were to be sold to the highest bidder, while others would form partnerships with foreign companies. After five years of privatization, however, the parliament suspended these efforts in February 1993 due to widespread concern over the pricing of these enterprises. There was growing concern that the government, in haste to please Western donors, was selling valuable state assets for a fraction of their worth (*New Vision*, March 5, 1993).

Privatization was accompanied by vigorous efforts to downsize the civil service (a cut of 80,000 employees out of the estimated work force of 180,000 in 1992–1993). Museveni has spoken of ridding the country of "the corrupt, the drunkards and deadwood, who not only swell payrolls but also frustrate efficiency. I am tired of corrupt and unpatriotic bureaucrats who do not appreciate the value of social property" (cited by *International Press Service*, August 28, 1992).

Part of the privatization of the economy also entails attracting foreign investment through the gradual removal of all restrictions on foreign exchange. In addition, the government established the Ugandan Promotion Association and Uganda Investment Authority, bodies that coordinate foreign investment and formulate industrial policies. The World Bank's Multilateral Investment Guarantee Agency (MIGA) has been instrumental in guaranteeing foreign private-sector investment in cobalt and copper production (*African Business*, December 1, 1992: 20). In other attempts to spur private investment, Museveni invited back Asians expelled by Amin, adopting a comprehensive policy on repossession of confiscated properties (*Journal of Commerce*, October 16, 1992: 4).

Six years after the inception of economic reconstruction, Museveni's policies have produced mixed results. Economic liberalization has had a devastating impact on the social sector, primarily through increased unemployment. By 1992, reforms had rendered 30,000 people redundant in the public sector, causing widespread hardships. Moreover, as market reforms gradually decimated the magendo economy, fewer safety nets were left for a majority of urban dwellers (Kizito 1993; *African Business,* December 1, 1992: 20). On the other side of the economic ledger, liberalization has reined in inflation and brought a measure of visible growth. By 1991, the country had reduced inflation (300 percent rate in 1987) to 45 percent. The deceleration of inflation has encouraged local savings and improved the external balance (*African Economic Digest,* November 30, 1992: 17). In the same year, the World Bank reported economic growth of 5 percent in gross domestic product (GDP) and in 1992 the government estimated GDP growing to 10 percent annually by 1995 (cited in *International Press Service,* September 17, 1992). In a major reversal, the World Bank (1991) described Uganda as the third best among African countries striving to overcome structural weaknesses that constrain economic growth and development. Reform policies have in turn boosted donor assistance, with total foreign aid growing from $308 million in 1987/88 to about $800 million in 1992/93 (*African Economic Digest,* December 14, 1992: 19; *Vancouver Sun,* August 17, 1992: A6).

The partnership in economic reconstruction has also been apparent in the moves to halve the Uganda army through a three-year Western-funded demobilization plan (Kizito 1993; Colletta and Ball 1993: 36–39; *African Economic Digest,* December 14, 1992: 19). Parliament passed legislation in October 1992 creating a Veterans Assistance Program that coordinates rehabilitation policies for demobilized soldiers and between December 1992 and March 1993 some 20,000 soldiers and their families were demobilized (Colletta and Ball 1993: 38).

Like political reconstruction, questions abound about the means and ends of rebuilding the state's overall economic capacity. Having repaired the worst of the damage inflicted in the past, how does the state move beyond rehabilitation to the creation of more sturdy structures for the future? Where is the boundary between rehabilitation and reconstruction? Can the regime sustain economic reconstruction without external support? Some analysts contend that, despite economic pitfalls, the Museveni regime has, through external prompting, made pertinent reforms that form the background of strong local and national economic structures (Tindigarukayo 1990: 348–350; Kayizzi-Mugerwa and Bigsten 1992: 73–

74; Kizito 1993). Mugyenyi (1991: 75) has emphasized the links between rehabilitation and reconstruction: "Notwithstanding the intractable nature of some of the inherited problems and the NRM's inability to influence the IMF negotiations, the government is shrewdly investing in political and physical infrastructures that are unavoidable prerequisites for economic transformation."

Mamdani (1990: 463) has, on the other hand, criticized the wider framework upon which the reform program has been conducted, noting that excessive market-oriented policies sidestep the question of rural democratization and diminish the state's essential role in the economy. He argues:

> Ideal changes demand deliberate and decisive state action, for the real question about the role of the state is not its extent but its nature, not the size of state intervention but its direction. . . . The terms of the debate as cast by the IMF—state versus market—fail to capture the need of the hour in contemporary Uganda. That need is not for statization, nor for privatization, but for democratization.

■ Conclusion: State or Society?

State reconstruction in Uganda or elsewhere might not resolve questions about the relationships between state and society. Recent discussions that separate these spheres have had wider policy implications. How do African states reconcile the goals of reversing institutional collapse with equally pressing demands on them to build "civil society" and "associational life"? A number of scholars have proposed the rejuvenation of civil society as the means of creating strong foundations for African statehood (Hyden 1992; Woods 1992: 77–100). They have proffered diverse strategies, ranging from popular political and economic arrangements that "empower" the countryside through "governance" and pluralism, all united by the objective of sidestepping the state (Landel-Mills 1992: 543–567; Nolutshungu 1992: 326–329).

Proponents of "civil society" are pitted against those who stress the need for the African state to matriculate to the "developmental" status of its Southeast Asian variant by insulating itself from societal (primarily, distributional) forces (Callaghy 1990: 257–318; Jeffries 1993: 20–35). They propose the construction of elaborate bureaucratic structures that might infuse coherence in policymaking. In this view, cohesion is equated with centralization: the faith in pluralism and governance as panacea for development "is somewhat misplaced relative to the importance of first, improving the capacity, commitment, and quality of governmental administration, of developing an effective developmental state" (Jeffries 1993: 28).

Uganda illustrates that policymakers can strike a compromise between building strong state institutions and the demands of external forces intervening directly to promote their own initiatives at the grassroots. Perhaps the increasingly dominant, albeit contested, role of nongovernmental organizations (NGOs) under Museveni illustrates this dynamic (Brett 1993: 288–298; Khadiagala 1993). In the short- to the medium-terms, the urgent need for external assistance to propel economic reconstruction leaves the state with fewer choices. More critical, the partnership with heterogeneous external actors, however asymmetrical, seems to be the precise division of labor that gives state-makers a degree of maneuverability as they embark on painful political reconstruction. If this partnership eventually creates the right mix of state and society relations, it might contribute to building stable bases of statehood. If, however, reconstruction is permanently predicated on external actors protecting elites from pressures of "associational" groups, it might only weaken the capacity of the resurgent state to anchor its authority in society and establish reciprocal institutions of legitimation. Ultimately, successful reconstruction might require the state to regain its responsible and indispensable position in society. Nolutshungu (1992: 331) is correct in noting:

> In the circumstances of Africa today, it is particularly important to stress, in an answer to prevailing attitudes, some old verities. Democratization cannot abstract away or bypass, the task of state construction, the consolidation of state authority, the building of institutions and, even without a Hegelian belief in the "divine" character of the state, a certain ascendance over "civil society" that circumscribes the domain of private interests, placing it within the compass of social policy and law.

4

Rawlings and the Engineering of Legitimacy in Ghana

Donald Rothchild

In the conventional scenario involving a breakdown of the state, powerful elements in civil society grow in capacity and effectively challenge state authority (Rothchild and Lawson 1994). In countering state domination, the autonomy of the societal actors expands, seriously limiting the central government's extractive, penetrative, and regulatory capabilities. On some occasions, societal interests exhibit even greater strength vis-à-vis the state and its institutions. In this *societal conflict model,* powerful local groups overwhelm the center and undermine its ability to offer effective leadership. As the state elite finds itself isolated and marginalized, societal interests, both cut up and cut down by the center, and lacking national legitimacy of their own, fight among themselves, still strong enough to destroy central power but not strong enough to take it over themselves. In this scenario, reconstituting the state means restoring a natural center and finding leaders of local society who can be promoted to state leadership, putting the pieces of society back into a national whole.

In a somewhat different scenario, the weak state, plagued by incapacity and "immobilisme," may deteriorate from within—the *state contraction model.* Because the state is unable to offer effective leadership, it loses credibility as a political and economic manager. Its ineffectiveness or "collapse" is more a consequence of its own decline and general incapacity to govern than an inability to cope with the pressures of powerful counterelites. In this scenario, the state elite must garner new political and economic resources in order to perform the tasks associated with effective governance. The challenge is primarily one of renewal and mobilization; and, at a deeper level, the acquiring of a new base of political legitimacy.

This chapter focuses on the second scenario of state decline, examining the processes of state contraction and subsequent revitalization in Ghana in the 1980s. It starts by looking at the short-lived, polyarchical regime of Dr. Hilla Limann (September 1979–December 1981) and its steady decline in managerial capacity. This is followed by an examination of the military coup of Flt. Lt. Jerry Rawlings in December 1981, representing as it does a sharp break in the political process. In this instance, dissatisfied elements among enlisted military personnel, in alliance with lower-level civil servants, workers, students, and others, rejected existing constraints and patterns of relations and interceded decisively in the political arena to alter the state's organizing principles and its practices of political interaction.

In time, facing a crisis of legitimacy and purpose, the Rawlings regime attempted to restructure relationships in such a way as to protect its perceived interests while reorganizing state-society relations in a more satisfactory manner. The chapter analyzes the regime's search for a new basis for organizing the populace to deal with the twin challenges of economic development and legitimacy-building. The initial experience with a populist revolution is probed, as is the controversial decision to change political directions and adopt an economic recovery program (ERP). While Ghana's experiment with structural adjustment did manage to halt the economic decline and start a process of renewed economic growth, it was not sufficient in itself to ensure a political support base and validity in the eyes of the public.

To achieve this stamp of public validation (as well as international legitimacy), it became essential for the regime to adopt measures of political liberalization, culminating in regime-organized district assembly elections in 1988–1989 and presidential and parliamentary elections in 1992. There was fallout from these managed elections: further alienation and suspicion. As a result, questions arise about what new alternatives are open to the Rawlings regime in any courting of public confidence and support in postelection years.

■ Breaking with the Past

By the end of 1981, Naomi Chazan (1983: 320) concluded, the political center in Ghana had "collapsed." "Not only had the government lost what little control it held over the population," Chazan (1983: 319) stated, "but it had to contend with the veritable shadow government that took shape to fill the void left by regime inaction." As a political manager, the Limann administration had certainly lost its capacity to exert a decisive influence over the groups making up the society.

Moreover, the extent of its commitment to directing governmental affairs declined noticeably over the 1979 to 1982 period, continuing what was already a downward trend in aggregate governmental expenditures. When these expenditures are calculated as a percent of gross domestic product (GDP), a steady erosion in governmental activity becomes apparent: from 19.3 percent and 21.7 percent in 1972 and 1975 respectively, to 15.1 and 15.2 percent in 1978 and 1979, to 11.4 percent and 11.1 percent in

1980 and 1982 (IMF 1981: 243; IMF 1985: 361; IMF 1984: 293).[1] The
government continued to function, but a process of implosion had become
evident over time. Jon Kraus (1991: 121), noting that per capita GDP fell
by approximately 3.2 percent per annum in the 1970–1981 period, concluded that "the PNDC [Provisional National Defense Council] regime confronted in 1982 an economy in an advanced state of collapse." With industrial production and agricultural exports falling and the costs of imports
soaring, Ghana experienced a sharp increase in budgetary deficits. Unable
to finance the importation of raw materials and spare parts necessary to
break the cycle of increasing misery, the government found itself without
the means to halt the economic deterioration, repair the infrastructure, or
rebuild the social sector. As anticipated by the internal contraction model,
the state was in sharp decline during the Limann years, losing political
legitimacy as well as influence over the political process and the administration of public affairs.

   Why did the democratically elected regime of Hilla Limann flounder
as a political manager after a mere twenty-seven months in office? To
answer this, it is necessary to focus on the character of the regime itself and
the constraints under which it operated. Two factors damaging to regime
stability emerge most clearly: the unwillingness and inability of the Limann
government to reach out and include major societal groups within the ruling coalition, and the government's insufficient use of its fleeting opportunity while in power to make the hard decisions necessary to rehabilitate the
economy. Perceived as elitist and overly cautious, the Limann regime was
unable to exploit the initial political advantage it secured from an election
victory to lay the basis for sustained democracy.

   The Limann government came to power following an extended period
of authoritarian rule under three successive military regimes: Col. (later
Gen.) Ignatius Kutu Acheampong's National Redemption Council/
Supreme Military Council (NRC/SMC) (1972–1978), Lt. Gen. Frederick
Akuffo's reconstituted SMC (1978–1979), and Rawlings's Armed Forces
Revolutionary Council (AFRC) (1979). After undertaking a series of
"housekeeping" initiatives aimed at rooting out corrupt practices, the
AFRC, which had offered little in the way of a coherent economic policy,
decided that it had gone as far as it could with a program of economic populism and would now protect the corporate interests of the military by turning over political power to a constitutionally elected government. Its programs left the next government in a difficult economic predicament. Not
only had the disciplining of market traders, hoarders, and currency dealers
had a depressing effect on savings and petty trading, but the imposition of
price controls further accelerated the rundown of existing stocks (Rothchild
and Gyimah-Boadi 1981: 6). As a consequence, the incoming regime was

saddled with an extreme scarcity of economic goods as well as a sense of political uncertainty over the capacity of a constitutionally elected government to survive in the face of unrelieved military ambitions.

In organizing the process of a return to civilian rule, the first Rawlings regime convened a constitutional commission in 1978, followed by a constituent assembly in 1979. After lengthy debates in these bodies over the form that the new constitution would take, the regime authorized the holding of competitive presidential and parliamentary elections to select a new Ghanaian government. The voters' choice, for all intents and purposes, was in line with past political traditions, pitting a party espousing Nkrumaist principles (but with its support base in the north and west: Limann's People's National Party—PNP) against a more conservative party in the J. B. Danquah/K. A. Busia tradition (Victor Owusu's Popular Front Party— PFP—drawing its support from professional agricultural and merchant interests in Ashanti and Brong-Ahafo Regions). Clearly, the continuity with the past must not be overstated. The northern influences on the composition of the PNP and a narrowing of Akan backing for the PFP meant that both parties were reconfigurations of old coalitions. Nevertheless, allowing for a degree of adaptation and realignment, the legacy of former traditions may be said to have carried over into the 1979 elections.

In the free and fair elections that followed, Limann led the PNP to a convincing victory over the combined political forces arrayed against him. PNP candidates took 71 out of 140 seats in parliament and, in a striking display of nationwide support, won seats in all nine regions of the country. PNP candidates scored convincing victories in such ethnically and religiously disparate regions as Volta, Western, Northern, and Upper, displaying a sensitivity to local issues and sentiments that was not matched by their opponents. The PFP, its closest challenger, obtained 42 seats in seven regions (mainly in Ashanti and Brong-Ahafo), while the conservative but ethnically diverse United National Convention (UNC) of Paa Willie Ofori-Atta won 13 seats and the Fante-based Action Congress Party (ACP) of Frank Bernasko gained 10 seats. In the presidential election, Limann's victory was even more conclusive. Mobilizing broad national support, Limann defeated his main rival, Victor Owusu, by the wide margin of 1,118,405 votes to 686,132 votes.

The breadth of the Limann victory at the polls gave him a strong mandate to put his program into effect. Limann can be credited for being respectful of the opposition and generally abiding by the norms of democratic governance. However, the short boost that the election gave him in terms of public support and legitimacy proved to be very fleeting. His program of economic reform was sound and realistic but under the circumstances not sufficiently bold and innovative to build a broad support base or to encourage rapport between his rather elitist cabinet colleagues and the powerful interests (including the military) that make up Ghana's civil society. In the end, the Limann regime was caught in the vise of "immobilisme," unable to secure the domestic and international support required to surmount the daunting economic challenges inherited from the past.

In the political sphere, the Limann regime's inability to forge strong and effective linkages with civil society left the regime perilously isolated and fragile. Clearly, any civilian government elected to power after a decade of military governance lacked deep roots in society. It would have little choice but to compensate for its frailty by pursuing a strategy of inclusion; that is, attempting to bring as many of the major societal interests into the political process as possible and, above all, avoiding situations that might leave wounded tigers on the sidelines (such as the former AFRC members). The Limann administration, however, acting as if normality had been restored in full, made all too few adjustments to conciliate the powerful interest groups around it. Not only did Limann and his cabinet insulate themselves from the former AFRC leadership, financing study tours abroad for its members and generally reducing their political influence, but they failed to give adequate recognition and backing to other important groups in the society. Included in the latter category were the labor unions, farmers, students and intellectuals, and ethnic interests—most particularly, the Akan peoples who lived in the cocoa-producing areas of Ashanti and Brong-Ahafo Regions and who had voted in large numbers for the PFP in the 1979 elections.

As the regime sensed its loss of control and inability to halt the general political deterioration, it moved away from its democratic commitment and respect for the opinions of its rivals and became increasingly heavy-handed in measures directed toward these groups. This proved most calamitous in terms of its dealings with Rawlings, who remained a foreboding reality on the Accra scene and who refused to be coopted to the Council of State (Boahen 1994). The Limann government, then, remained aloof and secluded, unable to forge effective links with powerful interests in the society. The precariousness of this situation became increasingly evident once the mantle of legitimacy put in place by the elections began to wear thin.

In the economic sphere, the lift given by the election victory was also fleeting. Indeed, forward momentum in the economic realm would only have been sustainable through successful rehabilitation of the agricultural and industrial sectors. This was a very difficult task in light of the structural nature of the problems confronting the regime. Certainly, the incoming Limann government operated under no illusions regarding the dimensions of the country's economic crisis. Limann spoke of an economy "in shambles"; and Kofi Batsa, chairman of the PNP Publicity Committee, talked of the economy as being "in complete tatters": "Our voice is that of the sick old lion, its paws broken, its fangs removed. We need to be carefully tended back to health" (Rothchild 1981: A135–A145). The economic indicators highlight the gravity of the challenge facing the new administration: a steadily declining GDP; a fall in gross domestic savings to below 3 percent per year; a high rate of inflation (down from 117 percent in 1977 to 68 percent in the twelve months prior to Limann's assumption of power); a rise in food prices of 59 percent in 1978; an overall budget deficit of Cedi(C)2 billion in the 1978/79 year; and external debts, in December 1979, of C3.6 billion. Further complicating the picture, the population was increasing rapidly (2.8 percent per year), international banks were reported to be refusing further credit, and the price of crude oil jumped to $35 a barrel just as Limann assumed power.

In an effort to revive the economy, Limann sought to lay the groundwork for long-term agricultural and industrial growth. With agriculture accounting for more than 40 percent of GDP and 70 percent of export earnings, it was logical for Limann to concentrate his attention on increasing the output of cash-crop and subsistence farming (Ghana 1977: 1). Declaring that agriculture was his administration's first priority, Limann outlined a plan of giving price incentives and providing such inputs as cutlasses, hoes, fertilizers, and improved seeds and insecticides to farmers. The government affirmed its support for intensive production of such important foreign exchange earners as cocoa and palm oil and gave assurances that state agricultural enterprises would not be sold off to private interests. In the industrial sector, Limann urged policies aimed at overcoming the artificial and inefficient structure of production resulting from past import substitution industrialization strategies, calling instead for greater utilization of local inputs and the promotion of new industries linked to the country's natural resources. Invitations were extended to foreign entrepreneurs to invest in Ghanaian industries (oil, bauxite, and other natural resources) and appeals were made to foreign and domestic industrialists to locate plants in rural areas.

All in all, the Limann economic package was eminently rational. Under the circumstances, however, it was much too cautious to fulfill public expectations: the public wanted to see results immediately. Consequently, Limann's prudence was to contribute to his undoing. With his political support base limited and his economic program perceived as wanting, he became easy prey for an inspirational figure waiting in the wings, such as Rawlings. Irked and offended by the government's attack on the AFRC and fully aware of the government's ineffectual leadership, Rawlings soon emerged as a kind of irresponsible opposition. What began as barbed criticism of the ruling elite spiraled over time into a Rawlings counterattack on the Limann-controlled state. Rawlings waited for the legitimacy surrounding Limann's electoral victory to dissipate; then, on

December 31, 1981, he seized political power. Democratic governance had been replaced by a new strongman.

■ Restructuring Through Societal Mobilization: Radical Populism

It was one thing for a military leader to seize political power through a coup d'état; another for him to run the country. Military interventions inevitably raise serious questions about the legitimacy of the new government. This problem was compounded by the badly run-down nature of the Ghanaian economy and the low level of public morale. Given the very rigid constraints under which the new government had to operate, Rawlings had few readily available options. Yet against this general backdrop of discouragement and resignation, during the turbulent period following the takeover Rawlings kept his balance and sense of purpose. This inspired Ghanaians to develop a new, authentic, African formula for dealing with the country's problems.

Having overthrown an elected government, it was necessary to start immediately by constructing a new basis for legitimate governance. Rawlings had no intention of returning to the past in the form of multiparty elections. His preferred alternative in the wake of the coup was to craft a homegrown type of radical populism that sought to eliminate manifestations of elitism, class privilege, *kalabule* (corrupt practices), and external, "neo-colonial" dependency; and to emphasize such values as equality, social inclusion, broad citizen participation, and moral rectitude. Rejecting the individualism and acquisitiveness that he associated with capitalism, Rawlings made use of the rhetoric of Afro-Marxism. Society was to be transformed, wealth redistributed, and the exploitative features of the old regimes eliminated. In practice, however, Rawlings planned to do this in his own way, not by means of orthodox, scientific socialist guidelines (especially regarding the need to create a disciplined vanguard party) (Rothchild 1985; Rothchild and Gyimah-Boadi 1989: 221–224).

Rawlings's populist experiment attracted enthusiastic support during its first fifteen months, winning "sizable political space" among the lower classes at the cost of defections by the middle class (broadly defined here to include the professional classes, businessmen and merchants, large traders, higher civil servants, academics, churchmen, judges, and others) (Chazan 1991: 50). During this initial period, his supporting coalition could be found among the rural and urban unemployed, the disadvantaged workers, the lower ranks of the military and civil service, and radical university students and intellectuals. Populist slogans on "power to the people" and "social revolution" were conspicuous everywhere, appearing in newspapers, on billboards, and at public rallies. A regime founded upon an illegitimate seizure of state power sought to validate its rule through state reorganization and societal transformation.

In an effort to reorganize state institutions and carry out a populist agenda, the PNDC set up a number of defense committees and people's tribunals to work alongside and supplement the formal administrative system. Such quasilegal bodies sought to involve the public actively in the process of governance. People's defense committees and workers' defense committees were organized in the workplace and at district, regional, and central levels to mobilize the citizenry to support and defend the regime and to implement PNDC policies. Moreover, the regime established a number of extralegal institutions—the Citizens Vetting Committees, the National Investigations Committee, and Special Military Tribunals—to investigate alleged tax avoidance and fraud, accounting and financial practices, and other forms of corruption. In cases involving hoarding and overpricing, populist vigilantes confiscated goods and destroyed sheds, tables, and even entire markets. In other cases, "popular" courts meted out heavy punishments for politicians linked to the former order, including sentences of sixty years (with part of the time at hard labor).

It should not be thought that populist fervor concentrated solely on the denigration and punishment of regime opponents. In some cases, public exuberance also united the people around a variety of economic tasks: work on cocoa collection and transportation, road repair, and communal self-help projects. Nevertheless, the positive achievements of these task forces were more than offset by loss of morale in the middle class and the implications of this for the well-being of the economy. Most shocking to the leaders of civil society was the kidnap and murder of three judges of the high court and a retired army officer, a crime that many observers regarded as being linked to earlier trials involving AFRC officers. The murders were seen as an ominous blow against the integrity of the judiciary and the legal profession generally, and the Ghana Bar Association, stirred into action, criticized what it perceived as the regime's anti–civil liberties stance and threatened to refuse to cooperate with the new legal institutions. Middle-class resentment over the populist transformation taking place in the country—its criticisms, austerity measures, penalties, confiscation of assets, and abuses of civil liberties—had now surfaced. Increasingly, governmental leaders came to recognize the depth of this resentment and the need to conciliate the establishment. A gradual rethinking of populist notions took place that was to lead to a new spirit of pragmatism in mid-1983, a change of emphasis that is discussed in the next section. In a process akin to the Thermidorean reaction in France, the Ghanaian revolutionaries saw no option in light of their deteriorating situation but to turn to the right. This shift, justified on the grounds of realism but described derisively by hostile wall posters at the time as a U-turn, was costly for Rawlings. In accepting external formulas and backing, the Ghanaian strongman became an isolated and lonely figure, reproached by students, intellectuals, and others for retreating from the people's revolution and abandoning his original support coalition. Paradoxically, this detachment left Rawlings with greater space to impose economic reforms from above.

■ Restructuring Through Economic Liberalization: Structural Adjustment

Rawlings's shift toward economic pragmatism not only separated him from his original support base, it also attracted few backers in the middle class. After disclosing his intention to change policy directions, he remained suspended above society, compelled to base a claim to political legitimacy on his acumen as an economic manager (Jeffries 1991: 168). Why did Rawlings alter his course on dealing with the economy? And what were the consequences of his decision in terms of economic performance and political legitimacy?

The first indication of a change in policy direction became evident with the presentation of the April 1983 budget. Displaying a new caution on economic matters, the budget put a number of austerity measures into effect: taxing transactions that utilized foreign exchange, increasing indirect taxes and customs duties, and boosting the price of essential goods and services. The budget also established a system of bonuses that raised the effective cedi/dollar rate from 2.75 to approximately 25 (an implied devaluation of 89 percent) (Rothchild 1991: 7; Herbst 1990: 4). Convinced that there was no alternative but to go to the international community to secure the resources necessary for Ghana's economic rehabilitation, Rawlings dramatically changed course and announced structural reforms.

This was an extremely difficult decision for an erstwhile proponent of populism. Yet Rawlings, an inspirational leader with few effective rivals on the scene, was in a relatively strong position to impose his reform package on a society uncertain of its bearings and in search of a plan of action. As it became increasingly apparent that the radical proponents of populism lacked a well-conceived strategy for reversing Ghana's economic decline, there was little that the opposition could do to stop Rawlings from putting his reform program into effect (Herbst 1993: 30–33).

Following the adoption of the April 1983 budget, the PNDC formally introduced the ERP (economic recovery program). The government sought to halt the declines in industrial production and commodity exports by progressively liberalizing the exchange rate system, eliminating price controls, and raising the producer prices for cash crops. Furthermore, it made a concerted effort to restore fiscal and monetary discipline, placing restrictions on the money supply, putting new controls on expenditures, and enacting measures to facilitate the collection of taxes. The government sought to reduce inflation, generate savings and investment, and lessen the overhang of domestic and international imbalances. The Organization for Economic Development (OECD) and lender governments, as well as the World Bank and International Monetary Fund, reacted most positively to the adoption of these and subsequent market mechanisms, providing debt relief as well as gross inflows of foreign exchange amounting to $472 million in 1983, rising to $632 million in 1985 and $797 million in 1988 (Martin 1991: 253).

These inflows of foreign funds had a positive impact on economic growth performance, halting the downward slide of the 1970s and recovering some of the lost ground. Although the statistics lack precision, the trend was nonetheless encouraging. GDP grew annually by over 5 percent per annum during the 1984–1988 period; when one takes the population growth rate of 3 percent per annum into account, this means that income per capita can be expected to rise at a rate of 2 percent per annum (taking the average person in poverty twenty years to cross the poverty line) (World Bank 1993b: 10). In addition, the industrial sector showed an estimated increase in output of approximately 14 percent in the 1984–1987 period, falling to about 3.3 percent between 1988 and 1991; domestic savings rose from C62.5 billion in 1987 to C84.8 billion in 1988; inflation fell to 31 percent in 1988; and an overall balance of payments surplus of over C22.5 million was achieved in 1987 (Rothchild 1991: 10; World Bank 1993b: 44). There is evidence that the rise in cash-crop production and exports did not come at the expense of food production, for per capita food-crop output reportedly increased over the preadjustment period, at a rate of 2.7 percent in the 1980s (Jaycox 1993; World Bank 1993b: 22). By comparison with many other countries in Africa, Ghanaian economic performance seemed praiseworthy, encouraging further generosity on the part of international lending agencies and showing steady increases in aggregate growth indicators into the early 1990s. As the 1992 national election was to reveal, this ongoing achievement was indeed highly valued by the Ghanaian public.

□ *Economic Downside*

If the move toward economic pragmatism had resulted in some improvement in terms of aggregate growth, there was also a downside to the market economy approach. First, by implementing a variety of measures intended to cut back governmental expenditures, the structural reform program had resulted in severe hardships for many elements in Ghana's society. This was particularly the case for the less advantaged, who lacked the resources to cover additional expenses in the areas of education, health, and social services. The government put user fees into effect for providing water services, set new or additional levies on the use of schoolbooks at the elementary level and fees on housing and provisions at the secondary and university levels, and assessed a basic charge for consultation with a doctor or use of a clinic or hospital. The World Bank estimates that, for households at the lowest expenditure quintile, average per capita expenditures for primary education represent 12 percent of total per capita expenditures, and the figures for junior and senior secondary education are 17 percent and 41 percent respectively (World Bank 1992: 22). Moreover, the costs of these social services have continued to rise significantly, imposing a heavy burden on the poor. In September 1992, for example, Korle Bu Teaching Hospital in Accra and the Akomfo Anokye Hospital in Kumasi announced very sizable fee increases. Adult consultations with specialists rose from C200 to C500, major surgery increased from C1,000 to C10,000, and minor surgery jumped from C500 to C3,000 (*West Africa* 1992: 1537). Not surprisingly, such financial outlays—to say nothing of the long-term costs of the services foregone by people who cannot pay the fees—led to substantial public indignation. In the words of one newspaper editorial (*Ghanaian Voice*, November 2–5, 1992: 2) just prior to the 1992 presidential election:

> It is important to take cognisance of the fact that Ghana is today in a very deep crisis. The economic situation of the masses has not improved significantly after 11 years of Structural Adjustment. . . . The unemployment situation is worse than it has ever been and the people's access to social services has been drastically curtailed.

Second, as indicated by Zartman in the first chapter of this book, external reliance weakened the legitimacy of the Rawlings regime. The making of external debt relief, financial flows, and investment conditional upon satisfactory realization of the government's structural reform program has caused deep suspicion and resentment among radical intellectuals and others. These groups have long been fearful of external manipulation and some Ghanaians have expressed grave misgivings to this author over what they perceive as the World Bank's and IMF's "neo-colonialist" roles in present times. The ability to grant or withhold resources is the very essence of power and it inevitably awakens apprehensions in a formerly colonized area over the intentions that foreigners harbor in their relations with modern Ghana.

Third, structural reforms were imposed top-downward by an authoritarian government that was not accountable to the public. Although Rawlings complained on occasion about a "culture of silence" in the country, this was explained by Professor Adu Boahen in terms of the citizens' "fear" of being victimized if they spoke out against the costs entailed in implementing structural adjustment. Certainly, the controls exercised by the government over the right of free expression and the killing of the three judges (as well as numerous others during the early period after the seizure of power)[2] gave the public reasonable grounds for uncertainty when criticizing Rawlings and his entourage. No doubt, some would justify authoritarian regimes in the short term as a means of imposing unpopular policies that will leave the country better off in the long run. Such explanations are small comfort, however, for people apprehensive over their security and they cause profound suspicions of Rawlings and his policies.

As a result of these three factors, Rawlings was unable to link his short-term success in ending economic decline and achieving increases in the GNP to full political legitimacy for his regime. As the national elections in 1992 were to show, there was some spillover from economic performance to public acquiescence and even to some acceptance, but this approval was halfhearted and largely contingent on further achievements in securing and distributing resources. Thus a grudging conditionality became evident in domestic politics as well as international economics. To understand the critically important link between governance and economic reforms, we turn now to Rawlings's efforts to engineer political legitimacy.

■ Restructuring Through Political Liberalization: Managed Elections

With domestic and international donor community pressures for democratization building, Rawlings, recognizing the need to establish a new support coalition, moved cautiously to link political reform with economic reform. Elections for district assemblies were held in 1988 and 1989, followed by the appointment of a "committee of experts" and a consultative assembly to draft the constitution of a fourth republic, and then by the national referendum of April 1992, which approved the constitution by an overwhelming majority. In what was to be the crowning event, a presidential election was held in November 1992, followed shortly by parliamentary elections. What is striking in this process is the effort by Rawlings to strengthen his claim to domestic and international legitimacy while at the same time managing the process in such a way as to ensure continued PNDC control. Recognizing that the basis for his continued political survival lay in conciliating international interests, the strongman reluctantly, to the extent he deemed necessary, gave in to the demands of his foreign backers for political liberalization.

Rawlings's firm hand was quite evident throughout the process leading up to national elections in November 1992. The International Foundation for Electoral Systems report on the 1992 constitutional referendum

(Cooper, Hayward, and Lee 1992: 1) concluded that Rawlings and the PNDC "remain the obvious source of political initiatives, retaining their claim to the last word in decisions that affect the forward movement of Ghanaian policy." In the district assembly elections, those elected to office ran without party affiliation and the remaining representatives were appointed by the PNDC (and included a variety of traditional authorities, retired civil servants, and activists drawn from the ranks of local political movements and populist organizations). Not only did the PNDC appoint the members of the committee of experts and heavily influence the selection of people to participate in the consultative assembly deliberations, it also controlled the agenda and timetable leading up to the presidential elections.

According to respondents on the scene, the ability of Rawlings to create job programs and boost civil service salaries considerably just prior to the voting gave him a distinct edge over his opponents. Moreover, as one local observer notes, Rawlings gained an advantage over the other presidential candidates from his position of control. He had "state resources at his disposal for his campaign—money, government vehicles, helicopters, the press, everything. The other parties, starved of funds and resources—some had only 5, 6 or at most 12 vehicles for their national campaigns—could not simply compete" (Ankomah 1992). And the incumbent's advantages did not stop there. Opposition leaders complained that the PNDC dominated the state-owned media, influencing the way that it disseminated news (Abdulai 1992). In addition, Rawlings campaigned for months before legalizing parties; and even after the ban on political party activity was lifted on May 18, 1992, it remained difficult for opponents to get police permits for rallies.[3] Furthermore, Rawlings's refusal to open up the voting lists to those who had not registered for the earlier referendum (on district assemblies) or the partially updated register in 1991 meant, in effect, that hundreds of thousands of regime opponents were left without a chance to participate.

In the short time allowed for party politics prior to the 1992 presidential election, a number of parties and leaders came forward to campaign for the state's highest office. Rawlings's intentions remained unclear until late in the preparatory period. Then, with the public becoming impatient as to his plans, he resigned his position in the Ghana Air Force and began to campaign actively for the presidency. His position was strengthened by the alliance that he forged between his own National Democratic Congress (NDC) and the Egle Party and the National Convention Party (NCP), both Nkrumaist-oriented organizations. Opposed to this grouping were four main parties and presidential candidates: A. Adu Boahen's New Patriotic Party (NPP), the inheritor of the liberal Danquah-Busia tradition, and three parties with an Nkrumaist thrust to their programs—the former president,

Hilla Limann, with the People's National Convention (PNC); businessman Kwabena Darko's New Independence Party (NIP); and Lt. Gen. (ret.) Emmanuel Erskine's People's Heritage Party (PHP). Observers described this opposition as "unfocused" and "fragmented," and were particularly critical of its inability to forge a common front and to articulate a constructive vision of a future Ghana (Aboagye 1993).

During the election campaign, some Ghanaian reporters on the scene concluded that Rawlings was drawing larger crowds than the opposition candidates, particularly in the rural areas. Writing insightfully, Azu (1992) noted: "The NDC has support in the rural communities who see the extension of electricity, the provision of potable water, good roads as a way of improving their conditions of living." Despite such signs, many people still assumed that a close contest would take place between Rawlings and Boahen, with some giving Boahen the edge. These election watchers, therefore, were very much surprised at the result: Rawlings won a clear majority of 58.3 percent of the votes cast countrywide. This ruled out any need for a run-off election (under the election rules a candidate polling over 50 percent of the votes cast would be declared the winner). Rawlings ran particularly well in the rural areas, but also in most parts of the country (93.3 percent in Volta Region; 66.5 percent and 60.7 percent in Western and Central Regions respectively; 61.9 percent in Brong-Ahafo Region; and 63.2 percent in Northern Region). The great exception was Ashanti Region, where Boahen won 60.5 percent of the votes cast (*West Africa* 1992: 1963).

The 1992 election outcome represented a tremendous personal victory for Jerry Rawlings. Despite austerity and hard times for many brought on by the structural adjustment program, he was able to move from what was perceived as a somewhat unpopular and repressive past to become the first leader of an African coup regime to win a competitive, multiparty election. It seems likely that the lack of opposition unity combined with the relative strength of the Rawlings message proved decisive. K. Gyan-Apenteng's point that "the absence of a level playing field in a game in which the ruling junta was player, referee and linesman virtually guaranteed failure for the opposition" is pertinent (Gyan-Apenteng 1992). But an instrumentalist factor was also in evidence. The peasants appeared to be extremely wary of any shift of regimes that might lead to reduced employment, a fall in cocoa prices, or a slowdown in rural electrification. If the economic reform package caused lingering resentment and failed to establish political legitimacy, it remained the only solid proposal on the table, not something to be rejected lightly.

Despite the magnitude of the Rawlings victory the main opposition leaders questioned the voting results, alleging widespread "rigging." In some instances, opposition supporters went beyond expressions of discontent to demonstrate their strong disapproval. This happened in Kumasi, and to a lesser extent in Tamale and Sunyani. The Kumasi demonstrations led to the imposition of a dusk-to-dawn curfew in that city for several days. People whom I interviewed immediately after the rioting in the Kumasi area refused to accept the validity of the election outcome. Some expressed anger over alleged incidents of intimidation, ballot stuffing, and impersonation. In the words of one person, the election represented a "big fraud."

In the days that followed, opposition spokespersons continued to hammer away at the alleged irregularities in the voting process. In a press conference held in Accra, Boahen issued a joint statement on behalf of his NPP and the PNC, PHP, and NIP expressing shock and dismay over what they depicted as widespread abuses, fraud, and the rigging of the election results (New Patriotic Party 1993). To some extent these charges of irregularities were externally validated by the Carter Center Election Mission, which raised serious questions about the dated nature of the voter register, the absence of a reliable and consistent procedure for identifying eligible voters, inconsistency in determining what should be regarded as spoiled ballots, the improper sealing of the ballot boxes, the undue influence exerted by some polling agents, and the inability of security officers to control the crowds. The election was less than "free and fair," the Commonwealth Observer Group (1992: 1) determined, but the Carter team did not doubt that Rawlings had won.

The showdown was not long in coming. Some days after the presidential election, the opposition parties jointly announced their decision to boycott the parliamentary elections (rescheduled for December 29 to allow for several efforts at mediation) unless the government agreed to compile a new voter register and to issue voter identification cards. When the government refused to meet these demands, the four opposition parties, now united into an Inter-Party Coordinating Committee (ICC), refused to contest the parliamentary elections (Amihere and Ankomah 1993). The result was a one-sided victory for Rawlings's NDC—189 out of 200 parliamentary seats, the rest going to its two allies, the NCP (eight seats) and the Egle Party (one seat), and to two independents. The damage caused was mutual: both the government and opposition lost credibility and effectiveness. The Rawlings government again emerged isolated and suspended above the political process, and the opposition stayed outside the legislative body, unable to act as a major influence on such issues as the controversial 1993 budget, the allocation of equal time to various parties on television, and relations with Togo following the violence in that country. Although the ICC did urge its supporters to give the new Rawlings government a chance to prove its commitment to a democratic restoration, tensions between government and opposition parties remained high.

■ Conclusion: The Continuing Search for Legitimacy

Military interventions, and especially coups against a legitimately elected civilian government, represent sharp blows against the valid exercise of authority. In Ghana, it was easier for Rawlings to intercede against the internally contracted state than to preside over a transition back to generally accepted and democratic rules of the game. Rawlings tried various strategies aimed at securing the moral legitimacy to govern, only to find that legitimacy engineering is a highly complicated process, involving multiple actors. It is not easily managed from above. To this point, his reach has exceeded his grasp, creating anger and uncertainty in a country beset by heavy burdens and limited resources.

After seizing power in December 1981, Rawlings used three strategies to gain political legitimacy for himself and his regime: the adoption of a radical populist ideology and program, an effort to restructure the economy through structural adjustment, and an attempt to restructure the political arena by liberalizing the electoral process. Each of these initiatives ran into difficulties, for diverse reasons. Radical populism antagonized important "supports" of the political and economic system—the Ghanaian middle class and the international donor community—leaving Rawlings with few options other than to build a new constituency of backers. Economic reforms strengthened by foreign patronage achieved impressive results in GDP growth rates; however, their accompanying austerity measures imposed substantial costs on many citizens, leading to considerable resentment in many quarters. Finally, the managed transition to multiparty elections left the ruling coalition isolated and the opposition parties convinced that the national elections were contested on an uneven playing field. Clearly, skewed elections led to deep animosities, as the defeated candidates refused to be coopted into a political system they deemed unresponsive and lacking in accountability.

In such a situation, legitimate governance cannot be imposed by a strongman from above. It requires agreement between state and society on a new social contract acceptable to the major actors. Such an implicit social contract is not an event but a process of renegotiating the terms of interaction upon which constructive and legitimate governance can be based. Accordingly, if the dominant leader is to avoid turning multiparty elections into "a meaningless ritual" (Ottaway 1993: 3), that person must initiate conciliatory moves and accede to a neutral oversight of the process leading up to and including the elections; otherwise, rules of encounter are not likely to surface that encourage defeated candidates to accept defeat at the polls and their subsequent role as members of the loyal opposition.

What incentive do defeated candidates have for accepting such rules of the game? In part, the answer lies in their desire to preserve and promote the norms of a system they value; also in part, the possibility that in a fair election process they will have a reasonable chance to win high office in the years ahead. In this respect, the shadow of the future is important to the observance of norms in the present. To facilitate these expectations a new social contract is likely to prove critical, for it sets the basis on which the norms of fair play can evolve.

■ Notes

1. I am indebted to Carol Lancaster for suggesting this line of analysis.

2. In 1993, Justice D. K. Okyere charged that soldiers were responsible for killing some 207 civilians in the first six months after the coup (*West Africa,* January 11–17, 1993: 13).

3. Information from an interview conducted by the author, Accra, October 31, 1992.

PART 2
CURRENT COLLAPSE AND FUTURE RESTORATION

5

Somalia:
A Terrible Beauty Being Born?

Hussein M. Adam

When a candle is about to flicker out, it tends to shine more brightly for a while. For a decade or more the military regime headed by Mohamed Siyad Barre manifested a strong Somali military state that extended its influence into both urban and rural areas. Its legitimacy and functioning receded during the 1980s, ending in violent collapse in January 1991. The Siyad regime's concentrated power fell into a vacuum created by years of violent oppression of Somali civil society.

Postcolonial Somalian history dates from 1960, when the former Italian colony of Somalia and British Somaliland, in the north, united to form the Somali Republic. Through the 1960s, irredentist attempts to unite Somalis in northern Kenya, eastern Ethiopia (Ogaden), and Djibouti failed (Laitin and Samatar 1987; Zartman 1989). As a consequence of border and nationality tensions with the Ethiopian Empire under Emperor Haile Selassie, which had base and military agreements with the United States, Somali parliamentary regimes sought military aid and training from the USSR.

In these early years, Somalia's multiparty politics degenerated into greed and corruption. During elections, parties multiplied, as organizations and clans splintered; and following elections, there was a rush to join the leading party in order to obtain ministerial positions and other official perquisites. The parliamentary and ministerial edifice, built on sand, was bound to collapse. The military, headed by General Mohamed Siyad Barre, grabbed state power on October 21, 1969.

■ **The Clans**

The Somali population of 8 to 10 million is made up of five major clan-families (Hawiye, Darod, Isaq, Dir, Digil-Mirifle); each one is subdivided into six or more clans and each clan is subdivided into subclans and sub-subclans, all the way down to lineages and extended families. Within the series of concentric and interconnected circles, with kaleidoscopic and diffuse attachments, the most stable subunit is the lineage segment, consisting of close kinsmen who together pay and receive blood-compensation in cases involving homicide. In general, the Somali people share a common language (Somaale), religion (Islam), physical characteristics, and pastoral and agropastoral customs and traditions (Lewis 1969).

Clanism is the Somali version of the generic problem of ethnicity or tribalism: it represents primordial cleavages and cultural fragmentation within Somali society. After World War II, politicized clanism among Somalis favored nationalism and a Greater Somalia concept. At other times, clanism has assumed a negative aspect—the abandonment of objectivity when clan and local/parochial interests must prevail. Clan consciousness is partly a product of elite manipulation, the cooptation and corruption of politicians claiming clan leadership (Saul 1979: 391–423), but at times it is the elite themselves who are manipulated by politicized clanism.

On the other hand, aspects of clan consciousness, transcending false consciousness, reflect a plea for social justice and against exploitative relations among ethnic groups. Uneven class formation has led certain groups to utilize clan formation as embryonic trade unions. In such cases, affirmative action–type policies are the best way to overcome discrimination against clans and groups. Clan consciousness tends to rise during periods of extreme scarcities—drought, famine, wars. Clan conflicts are also instigated by memories of past wars for resources or for naked prestige. However, such disputes take place only between neighboring clans and intricate mechanisms have been evolved for conflict resolution, for clan territory is often extensive and sometimes even noncontiguous. By far the greatest damages brought about by clan conflicts spread over large geographic areas have resulted from elite manipulation of clan consciousness.

■ What Brought About Somali State Collapse?

At first, the Siyad military regime seemed destined to strengthen the Somali state. Financial and administrative incapacity had limited the scope of Somali civilian governments: they ventured into rural areas only during elections. The military regime, unencumbered by the costs entailed in the parliamentary bargaining process, seemed to divert such energies to mobilizing resources for the expansion of the modern socioeconomic sector. The government conducted campaigns against urban and rural illiteracy (after scripting the Somali language), expanded health and education services, resettled drought victims, and encouraged self-help community projects.

Meanwhile, Siyad was consolidating his personal power and building an autocratic regime. He framed and executed those among his colleagues whom he considered to be key opponents. In 1975, he executed ten relatively unknown religious leaders for opposing his new family law on the grounds that it was contrary to Islamic teachings.

The era of creative sociocultural experiments lasted until 1977–1978, the year of the Ogaden War with Ethiopia, the abrogation of the USSR/Somali Treaty of Friendship, and the search for a Somali-American alliance (Samatar 1988). Thereafter, as the regime became more self-centered and vindictive, the opposition began to rise, first in the north and then as widespread dissidence throughout the country. Why did the Somali state collapse? Below, under eight headings, I list the main factors. Seven of the eight are essentially internal. The eighth considers external factors.

□ *Personal Rule*

Like other African rulers, Siyad installed a personal rulership: his lasted from 1969 to 1991 (Jackson and Rosberg 1982). Over time, he was able to manipulate and modify his rulership style, from being a prophetic ruler advocating "scientific socialism" (1970–1977), to an autocrat (1978–1986), and finally a tyrant (1987–1991). During his earlier years, Siyad utilized mediatory mechanisms that postponed final confrontations, but his prolonged dictatorial rule damaged and distorted state-civil relations. Later, as an outright tyrant, he applied absolute principles of governance, irrespective of human cost.

□ *Military Rule*

Siyad's dictatorial rule did not function in an institutional vacuum. The Somali military structure was considered to be one of the best in sub-Saharan Africa and Siyad also understood the importance of controlling other state sectors and civil society, through institutions and organizations such as the military, security, paramilitary, an elitist vanguard political party, and so-called mass organizations. As a personal ruler, he had the autonomy to operate above institutions.

Soon after independence, the Somali army numbered 3,000. The USSR agreed to train and equip an army of 12,000 and by 1977 an army 37,000-strong entered the Ogaden War. By 1982 the Somali army had grown to a suffocating 120,000 (Adam 1993). The army of liberation had been converted to a huge army of repression.

□ *From Nomenklatura to Clan-klatura*

Essentially, nomenklatura involves appointing loyal political agents to guide and control civil and military institutions. The introduction of nomenklatura to Somalia by the Soviets involved politicization of institutions that were beginning to function well, relying on education and training, technical competence, specialization, and experience. As early as

1972, the military regime began to appoint political commissars for the armed forces, administrative institutions, social organizations for workers, youth and women, and cooperatives.

Siyad soon substituted clanism for ideology as criteria for such appointments. Foreign aid provided the glue that held the system together in spite of internal waste and corruption ("selective misallocation"). Clanklatura involved placing trusted clansmen and other loyalists in positions of power, wealth, control/espionage. It also involved creating clan-klatura organizations. One such organization, Hangash, conducted military intelligence; the *Dabarjebinta,* literally, *the backbone breakers,* was military counterintelligence; then there were the military police, identified by their red berets. The majority of these forces were drawn from the president's clan, the Marehan of the Darod. In such a situation of divide and rule, state institutions were thrown into gridlock, jealousy, confusion, and anarchy.

From its inception, the Siyad regime rested on three clans from the Darod clan-family. Lewis (1988) describes how this background was "reflected in the clandestine code name 'M.O.D.' given to the regime. M (Marehan) stood for the patrilineage of the President, O (Ogaden) for that of his mother, and D (Dulbahante) for that of his principal son-in-law, head of the National Security Service. . . . [Although] no one could utter the secret symbol of General Siyad's power openly, the M.O.D. basis of his rule was public knowledge and discussed and criticized in private" (Lewis 1988: 222).

□ *From Class Rule to Clan Rule*

Once he dropped "scientific socialism" as his guiding ideology, Siyad did not resort to Islam, as did Numeieri in the Sudan. Atavistically, he resorted to clanism. Hardly any members of his clan gained strong bourgeois roots during his long reign—neither educational qualifications, economic knowhow, nor professional competence. Promising clan members were plucked out of educational institutions to fill clan-klatura posts. Siyad systematically sought to destroy the bourgeois elements of other clans—sending them to jail or to exile abroad. The damage done to the Somali elite class partly explains both the total state collapse and the delay in Somali state renewal. On this point, Frantz Fanon noted in 1968:

> We no longer see the rise of a bourgeois dictatorship, but a tribal dictatorship. The ministers, the members of the cabinet, the ambassadors and local commissioners are chosen from the same ethnological group as the leader, sometimes directly from his own family. . . . This tribalizing of the central authority, it is certain, encourages regionalist ideas and separatism. All the decentralizing tendencies spring up again and triumph, and the nation falls to pieces, broken in bits (Fanon 1968: 183–184).

Virtually writing a script for Somalia, Fanon went on to observe that the actions of a tribal(clan)-minded dictator provoke the opposition to demand regional and ethnic distribution of national resources. However, the tribalist dictator, "irresponsible as ever, still unaware and still despicable, denounces their 'treason'" (Fanon 1968: 184). Siyad went beyond shouting about treason to bombing villages, towns, and cities, destroying water reservoirs vital to nomads in what he called enemy territories, indiscriminate jailings, utilizing terror squads and assassination units, and intensifying interclan wars. He allowed no space for a nonviolent opposition movement. When one such group—the "Manifesto" opposition group—appealed, at the last moment in 1989, he jailed and harassed its leaders instead of negotiating with them in good faith.

☐ Poisoning Clan Relations

The clan-klatura havoc within state institutions was exported into rural civil societies. After the Ogaden War (1977–1978), Siyad practiced brutal divide-and-rule, encouraging clan warfare. At first he used his army to conduct punitive raids, similar to those under early colonial rule. Later his troops armed so-called loyal clans and encouraged them to wage wars against "rebel" clans. The damage caused by elite manipulation of clan consciousness contributed to the inability of civil society to rebound when Siyad fell from power. It will take years to heal these societal wounds.

☐ Urban State Terror

Young people began to disappear in regional cities like Hargeisa in the north, considered to be rebel territory, during the early 1980s. This phenomenon, reminiscent of Argentina, continued in other towns, then spread to the capital city, Mogadishu. During 1989 and 1990, Siyad's clan-klatura forces massacred hundreds of religious protestors. Following killings in July 1989, one of Siyad's former ministers observed:

> What has shaken the Somali people has been the slaughtering of 47 young men in Jasiira Beach a couple of days after the prayer shootings. Taking a page from the book of Death Squads, an area of Mogadishu known to be inhabited by people from the North (Isaq) was selected. At least 47 individuals, taken out of their homes in the middle of the night, are confirmed to have been shot in cold blood and put in a mass grave. This is a crime not only against the grieving Somali people, but also against humanity (Galaydh 1990: 26).

A similar vendetta awaited Hawiye clans, raising a rebellion across the country. Siyad's vindictive terror-state laid the basis for wars of revenge that postponed civil society's ability to create a successor state.

☐ *Neofascist Campaign Against the North*

Northern Somalia (formerly British Somaliland) came to resent the south for various reasons. At independence and unification in 1960, the south monopolized all key posts: president, prime minister, commander of the army, head of the national police, and so forth. The former prime minister of the north, Mohamed Ibrahim Egal, merely became minister of education in the union government. Popular resentment was manifested in an overwhelming negative vote among northerners during the constitutional referendum of 1961. Late in 1961, northern officers trained at Sandhurst, Britain's officer school, unsuccessfully attempted a secessionist coup. The judge sentenced them lightly, because a legal act of union had never been passed. In 1967, northern leader Egal had managed to emerge as prime minister by manipulating the multiparty system. The conflict between the north and the south generated low-intensity demands for distributional benefits within the political system, which, when unsatisfied, escalated into the current high-intensity demand for separate statehood and independence for Somaliland once the Siyad Barre state collapsed.

Once Siyad had taken over and armed opposition to his regime grew, he singled out the northern region, inhabited by the Isaq clan-family, for extraordinary punishment. Some say he hoped to unite the south by punishing the north and the (Isaq) Somali National Movement (SNM). Lewis (1990) observed:

> Male Ogadeni refugees [from the Ogaden War, who fled to Isaq territory] in Northern Somalia, who have long been subject to illegal recruitment into Somalia's armed forces, have been conscripted as a paramilitary militia to fight the SNM and man checkpoints on the roads. Ogadeni refugees have been encouraged to take over the remains of Isaq shops and houses in what are now ghost towns. Thus, those who were received as refugee guests have supplanted their Isaq hosts, many of whom—in this bitterly ironic turn of fate—are now refugees in the Ogaden (Lewis 1990: 59).

These Isaq refugees and displaced persons, almost a million of them, returned to their devastated villages, towns, and cities in 1991. Thousands more await the removal of mines before they can return. Their bitter experiences and what they saw of their remnant towns led them to support the northern secession in May 1991.

□ External Factors

Military, technical, and financial foreign assistance played a key role in prolonging the life of Siyad's regime. Somalia's geographic position on the Red Sea and Indian Ocean has long attracted foreign interests. Early in Siyad's rule, the USSR provided substantial military and economic assistance, including fuel, supplying financing for project local costs that helped cushion the Somali economy from international economic conditions. After 1977, the United States replaced the Soviets in providing armaments— unlike the Russians, sending mostly defensive arms—and during the 1980s, about $100 million of economic aid per year (Foltz and Bienen 1985: 100).

Italy provided the regime with bilateral aid, and was also a conduit for other European (EEC) assistance. During the mid-1980s Italy launched a 1 billion lira project in the Bari (northeast) region of Somalia. Italian parliamentary investigations later showed that Italian officials and the Siyad family siphoned off most of the funds (Galaydh 1990: 23).

China invested in a series of remarkable projects, including the north-south tarmac road, a cigarettes and matches factory, a sports and theater complex, and rice and tobacco farms. China also provided light arms and spare parts.

The military regime also benefited from significant financial assistance from the United Nations system and the World Bank. Siyad maneuvered Somalia into the Arab League in 1974 and the regime received generous Arab petrodollar assistance. There was, for example, "an alleged unofficial transfer of substantial sums of money from Saudi Arabia to the Somali government in mid-1990 to ensure that [Siyad] Barre did not side with Iraq" (Drysdale 1992: 4).

As long as resources did not dry up, Siyad was able to hold on to power. But U.S. congressional criticisms of Siyad's human rights record, made dramatic and visible by the war in the north, led to the suspension of U.S. military aid in 1988. In 1989 economic aid, too, was blocked and other states and international organizations began to follow suit. The regime collapsed in January 1991.

In the world after the Cold War, internal protests and external donor pressures can facilitate nonviolent regime transitions, *without engendering state collapse*. In Somalia, an abrupt stoppage of all aid followed a history of too much aid. Modest assistance might have facilitated formation of flexible interim administrations. To cite examples, in providing pressure for multiparty elections in Kenya and Malawi in 1993 and 1994, the major donors backed up internal protests. Their unambiguous message in suspending economic aid could not be ignored. In Somalia, on the other hand, international intervention missed the window of opportunity that was

framed by the rising rebellion in the north in the 1980s, the outbreak of
urban opposition in 1988, and the immediate post-Siyad clan warfare in
1991.

■ The Clan-based Armed Oppositions

Siyad's clan persecutions obliged the opposition to utilize their own clans
as organizational bases for armed resistance, echoing the Swahili proverb:
dawa ya moto ni moto (The medicine for fire is fire). The first clan-based
armed opposition group seemed to have stumbled into existence. After failing in an anti-Siyad coup attempt in 1978, Col. Abdullahi Yusuf fled to
Ethiopia where he established the Somali Salvation Democratic Front
(SSDF). The front attracted support mostly from his subclan of the
Majerteen clan (another part of the Darod clan-family that spawned Siyad).
The SSDF, following a burst of cross-border activities, atrophied as a result
of heavy reliance on foreign funding from Libya, Abdullahi Yusuf's dictatorial leadership, and Siyad's ability to appease most of the Majerteens as
fellow cousins within the Darod clan-family. Eventually, with funds and
clan appeals, he was able to entice the bulk of SSDF fighters to return from
Ethiopia and participate in his genocidal wars against the Isaq in the north
and later against the Hawiye in the south, including Mogadishu. More
recently (following Siyad's fall) the SSDF has claimed control of the Bari,
Nugal, and parts of Mudug (northeast) regions of Somalia, under the new
leadership of Gen. Mohammed Abshire.

The major opposition clan grouping was the Somali National
Movement (SNM), which derived its main support from the Isaq clan-family of the north (see appendix at end of this chapter listing political factions). The SNM was established in London early in 1981 but soon decided
to move its operations to the Ethiopian Somali towns and villages close to
the border with former British Somaliland. Because Qadhafi disliked SNM
leaders and so would not finance their movement, they were obliged to
raise funds among the Somali Isaq communities in Saudi Arabia and the
Gulf, in other Arab states, in East Africa, and in Western countries. This
decentralized method of fundraising gave the movement relative independence: it also enhanced accountability to its numerous supporters. The
SNM evolved democratic procedures. Between 1981 and 1991 it held about
six congresses, during which it periodically elected leaders and evolved
policies. In 1988, the SNM conducted several raids and a major military
operation in northern Somalia following a peace accord between Ethiopia
and Somalia that removed Ethiopian restraints on SNM operations. They
were able to block Siyad's huge army barricaded in towns and bases for the
next two years. The SNM played an indirect role in the formation of the

United Somali Congress (USC), an armed movement based on the Hawiye clan-family that inhabits the central regions of the country, including Mogadishu.

□ Enter Aidid and Ali Mahdi

The USC was founded in 1989 at a contested congress held partly in Ethiopia, partly in Rome. A third faction of the USC continued to exist in Mogadishu—a nonviolent opposition called the Manifesto Group. The weakening military power of the Siyad regime had allowed a narrow space for a so-called loyal opposition that issued a manifesto during his last year. However, the rapid success of the Mogadishu USC facilitated by this political opening left them without a developed, politically mature, party program and organization.

The charismatic journalist founder of the group, Jiumale, died in mid-1990, leaving a bitter conflict between the USC's military wing leader, General Aidid, and its Manifesto representative, Ali Mahdi. In a typical example of elite manipulation, once Siyad was expelled from Mogadishu, conflict between the two for USC and national leadership led to internecine wars, in June and September 1991 and March 1992, between their sister clans. Large parts of the capital city were destroyed and the way was paved for creeping warlordism in southern Somalia.

□ Proliferation of Factions

A group of Ogaden clan soldiers and officers defected from Siyad's army in 1989 and formed the Somali Patriotic Movement (SPM). A splinter SPM faction, headed by Umar Jess and based in the Kismayu area, became allied to the Aidid faction of the USC.

After Siyad fell, a number of other protopolitical clan organizations were formed, much less well-armed than those that formed during the struggles to overthrow Siyad. The Rahanwiin (main branch of the Digil-Mirifle) and related clans around Baidoa formed the Somali Democratic Movement (SDM), which divided into two factions, one allied to Aidid's USC branch. The Somali National Alliance (SNA) provides a general title for the USC–SPM–SDM–SSNM alliance (see appendix). The Southern Somali National Movement (SSNM) represents Dir clans. Somali farmers of Bantu origins, normally outside the clan system, have recently formed the Somali African Muki Organization (SAMO). Another group outside the clan system, dwellers in the ancient coastal cities, have established the Somali National Union (SNU).

More needs to be said about the Somali National Movement (SNM), mentioned earlier, which attended the January and March 1993 Addis

Ababa reconciliation conferences with observer status (the fifteen protopolitical groups that signed the agreement are listed in the appendix). Under conditions of peaceful political transitions, opposition parties are able to uphold state structure, authority, law, and political order so as to ensure state continuity; and mature and united armed political movements are able to develop experienced cadres and parallel structures facilitating their eventual control of state power. In Somalia, the SNM decided to concentrate on the northern region—more or less as did the EPLF in Eritrea (described by Keller in Chapter 8 of this book). But the SNM did not have the will or the means to pursue the EPLF path of establishing a new state. Ethiopia is agrarian: pastoral Somali society is much more deeply divided along clan lines and a protopolitical clan movement is little able to project its power beyond its natural clan territory. On the whole, the Somali opposition movement was weak, inexperienced, decentralized, clan-based, and unable to provide capable national leadership and vision. As Nietzsche said: "Those who set out to destroy monsters must beware they do not become monsters themselves" (Nietzsche 1966 edition: 89). This seems to be what happened in southern Somalia. Chaos, anarchy, and famine engulfed the country.

■ State Collapse and Beyond

The visible collapse of the Somali state has lasted half a decade. In some respects the country appears to have reverted to its status of the nineteenth century: no internationally recognized polity; no national administration exercising real authority; no formal legal system; no banking and insurance services; no telephone and postal system; no public service; no educational and reliable health system; no police and public security services; no electricity or piped water systems; weak officials serving on a voluntary basis surrounded by disruptive, violent bands of armed youths.

Unlike in Liberia, where the capital at no point fell into rebel hands, chaos and anarchy engulfed Mogadishu. In most of Africa, countries with weak but nominal authorities in the capital city endured civil wars that caused state retraction—but not total collapse.

As in Chad (analyzed in Chapter 2 by Foltz) factional war erupted among the victors over the previous regime, in this case, the USC. Fought mostly in Mogadishu, the war brought the capital city to the center of the civil wars, destroying all institutions and records of central government. Dictator Siyad fled Mogadishu in January 1991; unlike Mengistu in Ethiopia, he did not leave the country but established himself with loyal followers in his clan homeland near the Ethiopian and Kenyan borders. Less than a month after he left, his followers launched an attack on

Mogadishu, but they were soundly defeated, returning to their homeland.

Siyad continued to pursue ReNaMo-type tactics (see Chapter 7) for most of 1991 and 1992. His military raids devastated the clan-family situated around Baidoa, between his home base and Mogadishu. The agropastoral Rahanwiin had to flee into the bush, abandoning farms and livestock, an exodus that led to the manmade famine so intensively covered by the media. Operation Restore Hope followed. This amounted to a Bosnia-type of situation, posing a choice between military intervention or arming the Rahanwiin to protect themselves. Operation Restore Hope had a positive impact in south-central Somalia (Oakley 1994).

Many Somalians, especially unarmed farmers and coastal city inhabitants, made desperate escape attempts, creating a "boat people" problem. Refugees sought asylum in Yemen or Kenya; many perished at sea. The punishment meted out in the north led the Somali National Movement (SNM) in May 1992 to opt for independence as the Somaliland Republic, adding another complicated layer to the Somali crisis: an Eritrean-type situation. Putting the Somali state back together involves the possibility of renewing two states, rather than one. Somalis in the self-declared Somaliland Republic argue that their economic and social ties are closer to Somalis in nearby Ethiopia and Djibouti than those in Mogadishu and southern Somalia. Whether a new Somalia should be made up of one or two independent states, or perhaps a confederation of two autonomous states, is left to the Somali people to decide, hopefully with guarantees from the United States, the United Nations, and other external actors that the process be based on peaceful, political means, involving referendum and negotiation.

One urgent task involves disarmament. Somalia was armed in the Cold War in quantities not witnessed in other African crisis areas, and these arms are still available, often at prices cheaper than food. The political factions must be induced to give up their arms—especially heavy arms. This must be done fairly and simultaneously. Factions should not be permitted to import arms, as is done especially across the Kenyan border. International force is required to disarm bandits and criminal gangs (peaceful rural nomads have traditionally reserved the right to carry a gun to protect their livestock).

■ Prospects for Reconstitution

There is a growing strength in Somali civil society—essentially because the state has collapsed so absolutely (Rothchild and Chazan 1988).[1] In the north, and practically in areas of the country that did not require the intervention of foreign troops, the role of "traditional elders" (both secular and religious) has been both visible and positive. Women leaders have also been active, and women and children constituted a majority in demonstrations for disarmament and peace. Throughout the crisis, professionals, especially doctors and nurses who stayed in the country, have served as positive role models. Teachers have begun to revive rudimentary forms of schooling in urban areas.

As an aspect of civil society strength, the private sector has become revitalized. Gone were the so-called socialistic restrictions imposed by the dictatorship. The thriving small-scale private sector (in both the north and Mogadishu) has moved far ahead of embryonic regulatory authorities. In most parts of Africa, the state pulls or constrains civil society; in Somalia the state is challenged to keep up with a dynamic small private sector. In 1988 there were eighteen Somali voluntary development organizations (VDOs); now the number of such organizations has grown and they need help from international VDOs to enhance the nonprofit private sector.

There is a palpable spirit of anticentralism, an atmosphere favoring local autonomy, regionalism, and federalism—and in the north, self-determination and secession. As as corollary, there is a preference for locally controlled police forces over a large standing central army. In Somaliland, and to some extent northeast Somalia, there are embryonic manifestations of consociational democratic mechanisms involving consensus, proportionality, and avoidance of winner-take-all situations. Somali irredentism has collapsed with Siyad and in its place one finds broad cooperation and relative harmony between Somalia and Ethiopia. There is also a vibrant emerging free press—about six papers in Hargeisa and over sixteen in Mogadishu. Printed in Somalia, they are produced by computers and mimeograph machines. Upon my return from my last visit to Somalia, in 1991, a friend asked me to summarize what I saw in one sentence. With fresh images in my mind, and with the potential development of a more indigenous state, I paraphrased a line from W. B. Yeats (1983 edition: 182): "I think I saw a terrible beauty being born."

Operation Restore Hope and the UN have played critical roles in rebuilding Somalia's infrastructure, including ports, airports, roads, and bridges. Operation Restore Hope undertook a number of transitional measures, such as providing food for famine-stricken zones. The United Nations is to continue food aid for Somalis, but it must ensure that this policy does not damage the agricultural private sector. Food aid needs to be carefully targeted: as food-for-work to strengthen the voluntary sector, the purchase of locally produced food can help monetize the economy and strengthen local markets; however, vulnerable groups should receive food through NGO/VDO-supported local health and maternity services. Somalia needs assistance to evolve a public sector that is accountable to local taxpayers. Foreign aid helped facilitate corruption in the previous regime: the country needs to be assisted to get back on its own feet, without being put on the dole.

Attempts to reconstruct the state in Somalia have taken various forms.

☐ Top-Down Negotiations

In May and July 1991, the Italian and Egyptian governments backed the USC faction of Ali Mahdi and the Manifesto Group in organizing two conferences in Djibouti with the objective of forming a national government. The Aidid USC group and the SNM refused to attend. This top-down approach was intended to confirm Ali Mahdi as interim president and reject Somaliland's independence. The July conference advocated reviving the 1960 constitution and its 123-member parliament for an interim period of two years. The parliament would elect a president nominated by the USC.

This attempt at parachuting state power from Djibouti to Mogadishu proved unworkable. Ali Mahdi was too impatient to await the parliamentary nomination process—he had himself sworn in soon upon his return. The method of filling parliament seats was never spelled out. Ali Mahdi renominated the northerner (Isaq) politician Omar Arteh as prime minister, but his eighty-three ministerial appointments could not obtain parliamentary and USC approval. The two leaders hoped to obtain quick injections of foreign aid and to be able to function. They ignored the realities of post-Siyad Somalia: open warfare and banditry had made Mogadishu ungovernable.

☐ The Islamic Temptation

Post-Siyad Somalia manifests a tangible Islamic revivalism involving traditional Somali Sunni Islam. The chaos has, however, encouraged groups of youthful Islamic fundamentalists, who offer politicized and distorted Islam as a solution to Somalia's problems. All the protopolitical, clan-based groupings—SNM, SSDF, USC, SDM—have pockets of Islamic fundamentalists among their fighters. Some of them feel that their chances of capturing state power are in the long term, while others want to take immediate risks. They have not yet evolved significant leaders and the clan factor tends to check the fanatic Islamic element. The movement has been relatively strong in the northeast (Bari, Nugal, and Mudug regions). In July 1992, a fundamentalist faction took over the port town of Bosaso for over a month, but the SSDF and clan supporters fought back. The fundamentalists retreated to the port of Las Khore on the Somaliland border. Some of them received help from Saudi Arabia; others have links with Iran and Sudan. Islam will play a significant role in the post-Siyad era—the question is, how much and what kind of Islam? But an Islamic state (or states) is not likely to arise out of the present turmoil and chaos.

□ *Northern Grassroots*

In the north, Somaliland is groping toward a grassroots approach to state formation. In 1988, following SNM attacks, Siyad's army pushed northern populations across the border into refugee camps in Ethiopia where they were organized by the SNM. Clan and religious elders played crucial roles, distributing food aid and other relief, adjudicating disputes, and even recruiting fighters for the SNM. A council of elders (*guurti*) will be incorporated under the new constitution as a second chamber of the National Assembly; indeed, elders meeting in Erigavo recommended stronger powers for the guurti than for the elected lower house.

The SNM called a congress of Isaq and other elders in Berbera in February 1991. A second, larger, popular assembly was convened in Burao in May the same year and it was there that the self-determination decision was taken, renouncing the union with southern Somalia. In four years, no state recognized the Somaliland Republic and this has posed serious problems for relief, reconstruction, and development assistance. Somaliland experienced clan and factional-related warfare between December 1991 and April 1992. Although the situation did not degenerate to the warlordism of the south, it paralyzed the evolution of public institutions. The elders and other elements of civil society launched a peace and national reconciliation conference in Sheikh in November 1992, followed by local peace conferences throughout the north. Non-Isaq clans inhabiting Sanag, Sool, and Awdal regions have emerged as key participants in what was previously mostly SNM territory. Many northerners believe that Siyad's wars brought conflicts to civil society that, unless healed, will inhibit the trust necessary to reestablish state organs.

The northern grassroots peace and reconciliation movement culminated in a "grand conference" in Borama (a non-Isaq town) from late February to May 1993. The conference brought together elders from all clans and subclans, SNM leaders, professionals, young people, women, and veteran politicians from the parliamentary and Siyad era (including Omar Arteh, former Prime Minister Egal, and former Interior Minister Jama Mohamed Ghabib, who were originally opposed to the independence declaration). Omar Arteh has since gone back to his homeland to be involved in Somaliland activities. He ran for president in the May 1993 Borama elections but lost to the former northern independence prime minister, Mohamed Ibrahim Egal. An intellectual non-Isaq participant assessed the Borama conference as follows:

Responsible traditional elders, drawing upon the salutary mediums and wisdoms of clan conflict resolution are continuously attending to alleviate the suffering of their nation. Increasingly the traditional elders are emerging as the spiritual government of Northern Somalia, and supplanting the legally installed government which is fast losing credibility and legitimacy. . . . The politics of consensus and compromises seems to be foreign to the existing ethical standards, with unabashed confrontation and total success over the opponent being the motto of the existing leadership, whether in power or in opposition. Though my optimism of success in Borama outweighs my hunches of its failure, the reverse could happen (Ali 1993: 4–5).

□ *The Addis Ababa Compromise*

Prior to 1993, the United Nations had lost prestige among many Somalis with its clumsy evacuation and abandonment of Somalia in 1991 and its slow, bureaucratic methods and lack of financial muscle. The UN had also been criticized for the unceremonious firing of UN representative Mohamed Sahnoun, who had begun to win Somali cooperation by advocating a gradual approach, in harmony with traditional mechanisms of conflict resolution. Sahnoun became convinced that establishing a national government from the bottom up was the best approach, even though that might take two or more years. He attended local peace and reconciliation gatherings, believing that Somali civil society needed strengthening before the pressures of state structures were imposed on it.

In January and March 1993, the UN called meetings of Somalia's clan-based protopolitical organizations in Addis Ababa. Those within the UN who expected to see the immediate formation of a juridical Somali state were disappointed. The fifteen protopolitical organizations that attended (listed in the appendix to this chapter), plus a large number of civil society representatives (secular and religious elders, women delegates, professional, business, and VDO representatives) called for a fair, simultaneous ceasefire and disarmament, and the establishment of regional police forces. The Addis Ababa conference agreed on a two-year transition period during which "emphasis will be put on the rehabilitation and reconstruction of basic infrastructures and the building of democratic institutions" (Addis Ababa 1993: 3). The conference adopted a regional autonomy approach based on Somalia's previous eighteen regions, each with a regional administrative council, police force, and judiciary, as well as district councils, leading Somali observers to comment that the conference decided to turn Somalia into eighteen Somalilands!

Avoiding the issue of forming a central government, the conference recommended the formation of a transitional national council (TNC), to be made up of three representatives from each region (including one woman), with five additional seats for Mogadishu, and one representative from each of the fifteen political factions. The TNC is to serve as a legislative body that appoints administrative heads to resurrect ministries. It will also appoint a transitional charter drafting committee and a national committee to bring about reconciliation with the SNM and Somaliland. Its main task is to prepare for democratic elections and a constitutional government by March 1995. The participants pledged "to abandon the logic of force for the ethic of dialogue" (Addis Ababa 1993: 3).

In order to deepen the process of peace and reconciliation, the Addis Ababa group needs to learn from the northern experience. At the meeting in Sheikh, for example, reconciling the Habar Yunis and Issa Musse clans, religious ceremonies were accompanied by "peace marriages": fifty women from each clan married fifty warriors of the opposite clan, a traditional trust-enhancing mechanism. Nothing similar has taken place between Hawiye and Darod clans in the south and Mogadishu has ceased to exist as a multiclan Somali capital. Warfare, banditry, and looting have chased clan members to their homelands. Obviously, multiclan, statewide institutions must be based in a neutral, federal-type capital. It will take time, in wartorn Mogadishu, to revive mutual trust between clans.

The United Nations mobilized $142 million at a donors' conference organized just before the Addis Ababa political conference, to be spent for relief and rehabilitation, mostly in the Triangle of Death and similar war zones in southern Somalia. Somaliland, and the nearby northeast zone, excluded from UN efforts because unrecognized, also deserve their share, lest their stable situation unravel. Resources alone will not bring peace: steps have to be taken to heal civil society and build mutual trust.

■ The United Nations vs. General Aidid

The UN was mobilized to provide humanitarian assistance under UN Operation in Somalia (UNOSOM 1). For the United States, former Ambassador Robert Oakley negotiated UN approval for Operation Restore Hope (ORH). Oakley favored Sahnoun's style and encouraged grassroots and regional approaches. Restore Hope supported local peace efforts and the establishment of local police forces approved by and accountable to local administrative committees led by prominent members of civil society. Oakley encouraged Somali factions to disarm themselves, beginning with heavy armaments. He worked hard to reconcile General Aidid and Ali Mahdi in an effort to reunite the capital city, avoiding overt political actions aimed at choosing sides among Somali political factions. ORH lasted from December 1992 until May 1993. At that point the United States ceased to play a leading role, although it continued to give significant support under UNOSOM 2.

The policies and practices of the United States and the UN changed radically with the appointment of Admiral Jonathan Howe to head UNOSOM 2, with a former U.S. ambassador to Iraq, April Glaspie, as his special political adviser. The new UN strategy was to isolate and confront Aidid while supporting General Abshir of the SSDF, who controlled the northeast regions.

In late May and early June 1993 Aidid's faction held surprising reconciliation meetings with SSDF leaders. A reconciliation of the two hostile organizations and clans would facilitate early departure of UNOSOM 2 from Somalia. Aidid felt that UN Secretary-General Boutros Boutros-Ghali was "tainted" by his previous experiences with the Siyad Barre regime. He was unhappy with the Egyptian government for having joined the Italian government in holding the Djibouti conferences that favored Ali Mahdi as the new interim president. During Boutros-Ghali's March 1993 visit to Mogadishu, Aidid organized demonstrations that humiliated the Secretary-General, preventing him from even visiting UNOSOM headquarters in Mogadishu. Then in June 1993 a confrontation between a UNOSOM unit and Aidid's militia left twenty-four Pakistani soldiers dead. Aidid was declared guilty, airpower was brought in to destroy his positions, and Admiral Howe placed a $20,000 reward on his head—a ridiculous (as well as humiliating) gesture in clan society! The Italians recommended isolating Aidid but recognized (and dealt with) his clan and his protopolitical organization—the Somali National Association (SNA)—as bona fide Somali political actors. Boutros-Ghali and Howe rejected the Italian suggestions, rebuked them for their initiatives, and deployed them out of Mogadishu.

Elders and prominent personalities from Aidid's Habar Gedir clan met on July 12, 1993, to explore their options: without warning U.S./UNOSOM helicopters strafed the building and over fifty respected leaders and supporters died. The clan decided to solidify behind Aidid, taking heavy casualties but also inflicting serious damage, paralyzing the UNOSOM operation. They began to shoot down U.S. helicopters and in one battle in August eighteen U.S. elite soldiers were killed and one was taken hostage. President Clinton immediately reversed Boutros-Ghali's policy of militarily hunting Aidid. Not, he said, at the expense of U.S. troops. Ambassador Oakley was sent back to Somalia to pursue a policy of energetic diplomacy involving regional actors such as Ethiopia and Eritrea.

It is too early to draw comprehensive lessons from these events, but two points stand out. First, in assisting a country devastated by primordial conflicts and state collapse, it is important for international intervention to avoid overt political activities that favor one side at the expense of others.

The murder of U.S. troops attests to the fact that Aidid's hunted clan came to see the U.S. and UN troops as simply another rival clan. Second, Aidid's example shows that, should even one segment of society decide to reject foreign interventionism, recolonization, or absorption into a larger state, and is willing to pay the heavy price demanded in waging a determined guerrilla war, they can cause radical policy reversals. There is, after all, an empirical reality in the resistance of African societies. Somalis laugh to tell how the United States and the United Nations were "defeated" by only one Somali clan. In a society imbued with warrior traditions, Somalis point out that Somalia has at least fifty clans and if even half of them had risen in armed rebellion simultaneously, the U.S. and UNOSOM forces would have been forced to evacuate the country in forty-eight hours or suffer unacceptable losses!

■ The Way to Restoration

How to revive the Somali state/states? Following the U.S. intervention in December 1992, many Somalis felt that staying the U.S. course and deeping Operation Restore Hope, facilitating the empowerment of civil society and pursuing vigorous, creative diplomatic efforts would have put the United States in the best position to play midwife in the process of state renewal. Once the United States declared a halt to the Aidid hunt, Aidid supporters flew U.S. flags, to the applause of crowds. Mistrustful of the UN, Aidid insisted on using a U.S. plane to fly to the third Addis Ababa conference in late November 1993. Practically all the Somali factions that waged war against the Siyad regime reflected pro-American attitudes, even though, paradoxically, the United States supported the Siyad regime from 1978 to its overthrow. Aidid has called upon the United States to replace the UN as Somalia's main patron.

It is extremely important for the United States to remain committed to Somali development even after its troop withdrawal in April 1994. The United States can continue to play a pivotal external role, supporting the renewal process through diplomacy and resources, including assistance to U.S. NGOs in Somalia. President Clinton has appealed to Ethiopia, Eritrea, and other regional nations to mediate the Somali conflicts; these states can be effective only if they receive adequate U.S. encouragement and the provision of logistics and related services.

The United Nations had an excellent second chance in mid-1993. It could have built on the solid base created by Operation Restore Hope, initiated within a few days of UNOSOM 2 taking over. But the political outlook for the UN is full of question marks. Three options are under consideration: (a) to ask member states to maintain UNOSOM levels of troops

(28,000) with some capability to undertake disarmament; (b) to maintain a force of 18,500, including logistics forces; and (c) to deploy only 5,000 troops with emphasis in assisting UN agencies and NGOs in the delivery of humanitarian aid and in undertaking development projects (*Horn of Africa Bulletin,* November/December 1993: 13). Disarmament would be entirely voluntary, under options (b) and (c), but Security Council support for option (a) is unlikely. Other industrial countries (France, Belgium, Italy, and Germany) have left with the United States. The future role of UN troops in Somalia presupposes that the local authorities would be prepared to cooperate with UNOSOM operating under UN peacekeeping rules (Article VII) rather than the enforcement provisions (Article VI). Somali state renewal still needs UN humanitarian and development assistance, including support for local and international NGOs.

There are numerous precedents for strongmen establishing and renewing states; but the basic structures of Somali society preclude Aidid's being able to play the role of such a strongman in Somalia. He was not able even to exercise hegemony within his own clan-family, the Hawiye, let alone over all six Somali clan-families. The 1991–1992 intra-Hawiye civil war between his Habar-Gedir and Ali Mahdi's Abgal clan led to a stalemate and the Beirut-like division of Mogadishu into north (Ali Mahdi) and south (Aidid) zones. What could still emerge in southern Somalia is an era of warlords or strong regional leaders, especially if such leaders would be willing to assure minimum cooperation with each other to avoid famine and related catastrophes as occurred in 1991 and 1992. Such a scenario could evolve positively or degenerate into embattled rulers and internal border wars. The UN war against Aidid served only to strengthen him, especially psychologically, but it was not sufficient to assure him overall prominence.

There is a democratic option for Somalia, where democracy can find indigenous roots. Historically, Somalis have lived in societies with rules but without rulers, as portrayed in I. M. Lewis's classic study, *A Pastoral Democracy* (1969). The democratic state renewal option has several advantages for Somalia/Somaliland: it is compatible with traditional consociational structures and mechanisms; it offers a real antithesis to the detested Siyad military dictatorship; and it situates Somali struggles within the global democratization movement, making the country more amenable to the international assistance necessary for rapid renewal, reconstruction, and long-term development. Other traditional African democratic or semidemocratic polities (e.g., the Kikuyu in Kenya and the Ibo in Nigeria), juxtaposed with centralized, hierarchical traditional polities (Nigeria's Hausa-Fulanis), cannot easily rely on traditional structures to construct a modern polity. Somalia, however, like Botswana, is relatively homogeneous and can hope to evolve a modern consociational democracy from its traditional consociational practices, moving from local, district, and regional finally to national levels. The UN has moved to encourage the empowerment of district and regional councils in southern Somalia. UNOSOM personnel helped to set up forty representative district councils in Somalia's seventy-seven districts (Somaliland not included) by September 1993. Three regional councils had been formed in Garowe, Bakool, and Baidoa by mid-October. This kind of activity will probably mark the most significant UN contribution to Somali renewal (*Horn of Africa Bulletin,* September/October 1993: 16).

Consociational democracy (modern versions of which are practiced in Switzerland and other smaller European societies) recognizes and acknowledges ethnic, clan, or religious cleavages in constituting membership of governments, parliaments, and national commissions. In such societies, army, police, and civil service recruitment are based on the combined principles of merit and proportionality. Somaliland appears to be evolving along these lines and whether it rejoins the south or not, offers an excellent blueprint for Somalia. Somaliland cabinets since 1991 have striven to include modern elites and yet reflect clan diversity and representativeness. The interim National Assembly consists of a house of secular and religious elders (guurti) and a second house is made up of modern elites. Somaliland has sketched out the stages in this activity: peace *and* reconciliation; formation of local and regional bodies; and then national representative institutions. Somaliland President Egal, in proposing a peace mission of seven elders each from Somaliland, Ogaden, and Djibouti, spelled out the alternatives.

> This would be a formulation of peaceful settlement originating from the grassroots and projected in a native indigenous framework recognizable and familiar to every member of the society. . . . The role of the United Nations in my proposed process would be one of support, encouragement and the provisions of logistics and services. . . . With all due respect to the conveners of the Reconciliation Conferences in Addis Ababa, men of whose sincerity and good-will there is no shadow of doubt, these conferences become forums where faction leaders tried to score points against each other. The rest of the participants were only confused by the alien surroundings and the foreign chairmen and other organizers of the conference whose speeches and languages they could not even understand" (*Horn of Africa Bulletin,* November/December 1993).

■ Appendix: Somali Political Factions

Somali African Muki Organization (SAMO)
Somali Democratic Alliance (SDA)
Somali Democratic Movement (SDM)

SDM (SNA*)
Somali National Democratic Union (SNDU)
Somali National Front (SNF)
Somali National Union (SNU)
Somali Patriotic Movement (SPM)
SPM (SNA*)
Somali Salvation Democratic Front (SSDF)
Southern Somali National Movement (SSNM)
United Somali Congress (USC)
USC (SNA*)
United Somali Front (USF)
United Somali Party (USP)
(SNA* denotes affiliation with the Somali National Alliance, described in text of this chapter.)

Some of the most acrimonious debates arose around the question of representation. General Aidid (USC/SNA) and his allies felt that too many Darod clan political factions were registered by the UN: SSDF, SNDU, SNF, SPM, and USP. They claimed that some of these, for example, did not represent Somalis who were substantially within the borders of the Somali Republic. The groups that waged war against Siyad wanted more influence than those that had formed recently in order to appear at the peace table. The leaders of some of the groups were accused of being puppets of some of the other groups. As of mid-1994, the farming communities were represented by SAMO and the ancient coastal cities populations by SNU. Factions of non-Isaq clans participating in Somaliland were partly represented by SDA, USF, and USP.

The major group, the Somali National Movement (SNM), adopted observer status during the the first two Addis Ababa conferences but boycotted the third, held in late November and early December 1993.

■ Note

1. About five months after Siyad was chased out of Mogadishu in 1991, I spent three weeks in northern Somaliland and three weeks in Mogadishu.

6

Liberia:
Putting the State Back Together

Martin Lowenkopf

In Liberia, not only is "the state as a legitimate functioning order"[1] absent, but society in general has been shattered, the nation fragmented, the population dispersed, and the economy ruined. In addition, in the absence of a state, neither order nor power nor legitimacy has devolved to local groups (although several existing organizations could evolve in that way). Both the reality and the symbols of power are up for grabs among the several Liberian armed factions fighting one another. To complicate matters, the struggle has been internationalized, involving Liberia's West African neighbors, the UN, the United States, and France. Most remarkably, an active, perhaps determining, foreign armed force is involved, acting on behalf of the Economic Community of West African States (ECOWAS). In mid-1994, no one could tell how this cluttered, near anarchic, situation would come out.[2]

While this chapter is not about how to end the conflict, it is obvious that conflict resolution and reconciliation must take place before Liberia can be put back together. A democratic outcome, however desirable, is remote. Even if the warring parties agree to stop fighting and to seek a political solution through powersharing or elections (or both), new, volatile forces would almost certainly emerge that would further rend the already tattered political fabric. And if one side were to "win," whether on the battlefield or through the ballot box, and thus be able to impose its will on the others, the heritage of violence, hatred, and vengeance would so burden a new government that it would have great difficulty in holding the country together. And if at all, probably not for long.

This chapter, then, seeks not, first, the political kingdom, but looks to the people of Liberia to bring their country together again—from the bottom up. I do not propose a millenarian grassroots democracy: simply the revival of the bases of economic life and, hopefully, development, and the reconstruction of a social order upon which a new political system might be established to serve the needs of the people.

■ The Crisis of Collapse

While efforts have been under way for over three years to reconcile the several contenders for power, armed struggle persists. At least 20,000 people have died and over half the population has been displaced since the conflict began in December 1989. Ben Okari (*New York Times,* January 29, 1993), could have been writing about Liberia in his passage about soldiers.

> They fought among themselves eternally. It didn't seem to matter to them how many died. All that mattered was how well they handled the grim mathematics of the wars, so that they could win the most important battle of all, which was for the leadership of the fabulous graveyard of this once beautiful and civilized land.

In the latest in a series of efforts to resolve the conflict, the Cotonou Agreement (see below), the warring parties agreed in July 1993 to a ceasefire, disarmament, the establishment of an interim government, and the holding of elections in early 1994. With explicit UN backing and support, and a substantial new U.S. financial commitment, Cotonou produced fresh hopes for peace in Liberia. It also brought non–West African participation in the form of peacekeeping troops from Uganda, Tanzania, and Zimbabwe. But in the absence of progress on disarmament and the relocation of each party's fighters to supervised "encampments," by the end of 1993 the ceasefire had begun to unravel and prospects for early elections had faded. Bickering among and within the parties to the agreement over portfolios in a new transitional government threatened to abort the latest peace process.

Of the three signatories to the Cotonou Agreement, the most powerful is the National Patriotic Front of Liberia (NPFL) of Charles Taylor, which overthrew the government of Samuel Doe in 1990. Taylor's original force of some 250 men crossed Liberia's northeast border into Nimba County from Côte d'Ivoire in December 1989. Members of the Mano and Gio tribes of Nimba County, harshly treated by Doe since a 1985 coup attempt by citizens from that area, flocked to the NPFL. Doe's forces responded with brutal assaults on the civilian population; these were eventually matched by NPFL atrocities committed against members of Doe's tribe, the Krahn (see George 1993: 10–24 for a detailed and harrowing description of the war). By June 1990, Taylor had occupied all major towns and Robertsfield International Airport and was at the gates of Monrovia, the capital city. The offensive stalled; and in August, West African forces entered Monrovia to put an end to the slaughter of civilians being committed by both sides.

The NPFL is estimated to have over ten thousand people (many of them children) under arms and occupies nearly three-quarters of Liberia (until early 1993 it held 90 percent). The United Liberation Movement of Liberia (ULiMo), the next leading claimant, is a several thousand–strong guerrilla army of ex-president Samuel Doe's Krahn tribe and their Mandingo allies. ULiMo has won considerable territory from Taylor's forces. ULiMo's gains have been along the border with Sierra Leone, from which it launched operations in early 1992, to the gateway to Monrovia on the Atlantic Ocean.

The reconstituted Armed Forces of Liberia (AFL) is made up largely of the Krahn-dominated army of former President Samuel Doe. Its approximately three thousand soldiers have occasionally done battle with the NPFL, but more often have engaged in marauding actions around the capital. The AFL remains capable of serious mischiefmaking and terror. A new armed force emerged at the end of 1993. Named, ironically, the Liberian Peace Council, it harasses Taylor's NPFL in southeastern Liberia. Small in numbers, it is yet another Krahn organization, drawing supporters from ULiMo and the AFL. In early 1994, another local group, the Lofa Defense Force, crossed the northern border from Guinea to attack ULiMo and NPFL positions.

Under the Cotonou accord, the Interim Government of National Unity (IGNU), the only internationally recognized body in the Liberian equation, has been formally superseded by a new Liberia National Transitional Government. Since the NPFL had not, as of January 1995, taken its place in the executive Council of State, IGNU continued to run the government with most of the same personnel. IGNU was an alliance of seven political parties. Mostly Monrovia-centered, it came into existence in the late 1970s and prior to the 1985 election under Doe. It has been governing perhaps four-fifths of Monrovia and formally administering the AFL (through the Ministry of Defense). IGNU invited ULiMo to join it and has fielded an elite force of its own (the Black Berets—some five hundred troops trained in Guinea). Led by Interim President Amos Sawyer, a former political science professor at the University of Liberia and a long-time leader of the opposition to the late President William Tolbert and to Doe, IGNU has been a *Who's Who* of Monrovia-based political aspirants (among them Bacchus Mathews and H. Boima Fahnbulleh, Jr.).

Whatever else may be said about Taylor's rule over what came to be called Greater Liberia (under the name, Government of the National Patriotic Reconstruction Assembly, based in Gbarnga, ninety miles from Monrovia), he has, in three years, consolidated enough control to establish a rudimentary administrative system (although coercion, pillage, and rape by an armed rabble seem more the order of the day, particularly in Grand Gedeh County, Doe's home area). With help from UN and voluntary agencies, Taylor had begun to restore some basic infrastructure and social services and to arrange with foreign corporations the resumption of rubber, logging, and mining operations.

Until a two-year-old ceasefire broke down in late 1992, trade and communications between Greater Liberia and Monrovia were opening up. But after 1993, with ULiMo's expulsion of Taylor's forces from northwestern Liberia and the imposition of a UN arms embargo, plus an economic blockade enforced by ECOWAS, economic life and the NPFL's administrative control have been severely hampered.

■ Displaced Liberians

The resumption of fighting in October 1992 sent a new wave of refugees into neighboring countries and Monrovia, which was already overcrowded. As many as 700,000 citizens live outside Liberia as refugees, mostly in Sierra Leone, Guinea, and Côte d'Ivoire, but also in Ghana, Nigeria, and the United States. In Monrovia and its immediate environs, the population by 1993 had swollen to 1 million. Half of these people had sought refuge there in the past three years. Thus, of the country's population of some 2.5 million, now well over half have been displaced from their homes. Many of the people under Taylor's or ULiMo's control probably are not living in their original homes. Most of these displaced persons are subsisting on the international dole. Only shared misery and fear of all the armed factions (and a 7 P.M. to 7 A.M. curfew) keep Monrovia's population quiescent, but the city has not been spared from lawlessness and violence.

■ The Foreign Factor

The principal armed factions at various times were supported by different West African neighbors of Liberia. Taylor, at the outset, was assisted, if not sponsored, by Libya; then he enjoyed Burkina Faso's and Côte d'Ivoire's support. Until the imposition of the UN arms embargo and an ECOWAS trade ban in late 1992, Taylor had been exporting and receiving supplies through his neighbors' porous borders. At the same time, European and U.S.-based businesses operated within Taylor's territory, taking out iron ore, rubber, timber, diamonds, and gold. These activities provided an estimated $8 to $9 million in revenues per month for the NPFL's purchase of supplies and arms.

Whatever their distaste for Samuel Doe, Sierra Leone and Guinea, for internal reasons, maintained relatively friendly relations with his government. In 1991, each had a hand in forming ULiMo, and ULiMo's leadership is currently divided between factions in Freetown (the Sierra Leone capital) and Conakry (the capital of Guinea), the first being the dominant one.

Chance and the-lesser-of-evils would seem to characterize the choices Liberia's neighbors have made in aligning themselves with one faction or another. Ivoirian President Felix Houphouet-Boigny, whose daughter had been married to the late President William Tolbert's son, was quick to support any effort to overthrow Doe and his Liberian son-in-law's murderers and to see a friendly regime in Monrovia: Taylor's was only the latest and most successful of the rebel groups assisted by Houphouet and another of his sons-in-law, President Blaise Campore, of Burkina Faso.

Sierra Leone and Guinea were inundated with Liberian refugees, many of whom had been Doe allies. NPFL elements, some possibly rogue, had been marauding inside Sierra Leone and, following an army coup in 1992, Taylor was seen to be supporting an antijunta guerrilla movement. This probably was cause enough for the new Sierra Leone government to arm and assist Krahn and Mandingo elements to fight the NPFL. Guinea has its own substantial Mandingo population as well as a vestigial distrust of Côte d'Ivoire. It seems farfetched to suppose that any of these countries harbors territorial or economic ambitions in Liberia or immutable preferences for one or another element in the Liberian morass (hence, Guinea's covering of its bet by training an IGNU paramilitary force). A peaceful and stable Liberia would seem best to serve all their interests, but they are all, for the moment, stuck with earlier attachments.

ECOWAS first got involved in Liberia when, in August 1990, it sent in several thousand troops, under a Ghanaian commander, to put down the violence Doe's nearly defeated army was wreaking in Monrovia, in effect putting the capital to the torch ("No Doe, no Monrovia"). Some fifty to sixty persons were dying each day from disease and starvation; the first relief supplies in five months arrived from the United States in October 1990. ECOWAS was concerned about member-country citizens, particularly Nigerians and Ghanaians, living there.

The West African force, called the Economic Community of West African States Monitoring Group (ECOMOG), by mid-1993 had grown to some 16,000 (somewhat reduced in 1994) and its mandate had evolved from peacekeeping to outright intervention against the NPFL. ECOMOG's role in the war, and on behalf of IGNU, has brought into question its neutrality, not only from Taylor but from the United States as well.

Disproportionately manned and commanded after 1991 by the Nigerian armed forces, smaller contingents from Ghana, Senegal, Sierra Leone, Guinea, and the Gambia made up the rest of the ECOMOG force (Senegal withdrew its contingent in early 1993). Since October 1992, when Taylor's forces broke a nearly two-year ceasefire by mounting a major assault on Monrovia after ULiMo had taken over territory with ECOMOG assistance, ECOMOG has undertaken a naval blockade of ports shipping goods from Taylor's territory. ECOMOG also occupied Buchanan, Taylor's principal port, and has engaged in air attacks on major NPFL positions and NPFL-occupied towns (with many civilians also being killed). In repulsing NPFL offensives, ECOMOG from time to time has facilitated ULiMo operations against Taylor and worked with the AFL.

Usually under ECOWAS auspices, and involving most of the West African chiefs of state, a number of initiatives aimed at bringing peace to Liberia were launched between 1990 and 1992. The most important were:

- Banjul, Gambia, August 1990, at which representatives of most ECOWAS member-states, six Liberian political parties, and a number of Liberian civic groups elected Amos Sawyer president of an interim government of national unity (IGNU). Taylor's group did not attend and did not recognize IGNU, though it later entered into agreements with it. ECOWAS recognizes IGNU and the OAU has seated it (as has the UN).
- The Bamako Accord, November 1990, agreed to by all the warring factions (but not ULiMo, which did not then exist) and by IGNU. This accord established a ceasefire that lasted until October 1992.
- A series of meetings in 1991 in Côte d'Ivoire, culminating in the Yamoussoukro 4 Accord of October 1991, which spelled out a time frame for disarmament and elections. Houphouet-Boigny's participation apparently ensured Taylor's compliance (George 1993: 93–98), but the agreement fell apart with ULiMo's August 1992 entry and NPFL's October 1992 offensive.

Prodded by the international community, Liberians also have searched for a political solution. An All Liberia Conference was held in Monrovia in March-April 1991, attended by IGNU, the NPFL, and civic, professional, and religious groups. Taylor demanded that representatives from each of Liberia's counties (most of which he then controlled) be seated and that a three-person ruling council (i.e., Taylor, Sawyer, and a neutral figure) run the country until elections could be held. The conference rejected these conditions, reelected Sawyer (who vowed not to seek the presidency), and offered Taylor one of two vice-presidencies. Taylor declined. The NPFL convened a similar conference in May 1992, leading to the preparation of a meeting of Taylor and Sawyer in Harbel. ECOMOG canceled the meeting as it was set to begin.

■ The Cotonou Accord

Internationally supported efforts to find a settlement and the relative peace in the country under the Bamako ceasefire disguised the deep differences between the principal antagonists and produced undue optimism about disarmament and early elections under the Yamoussoukro Accord. In brief, IGNU and the Monrovia political leaders saw Liberia's salvation—and their political futures—in the dismantling of Taylor's armed forces. Taylor, in turn, saw disarmament, which would leave only ECOMOG in the field, as a threat to the territory he occupied as well as to his claim to leadership, which he seems to have equated with Liberia's salvation. Hence, he went for it all—Monrovia and the destruction of ECOMOG—in his October 1992 offensive. He nearly succeeded.

The reversal of Taylor's fortunes—a UN arms embargo and the ECOWAS-enforced blockade; his defeat in Monrovia in 1992 and subsequent expulsion by ECOMOG from his principal port at Buchanan; and pressure from ULiMo nearly to the gates of Gbarnga—apparently played a critical role in taking him to Cotonou. But the Cotonou accord did not bring peace, either. Taylor's military string had not yet run out and he may well be one of Africa's most watchful students of Nigeria's current political problems. If Nigeria's internal uncertainties cause it to reduce its role in, or to pull out of, ECOMOG, the balance of power could shift again to Taylor.

Further armed conflict might also figure in the AFL's and ULiMo's calculations. Just because neither had yet found a political voice did not mean they would go along with any political deal hatched by ECOWAS, the UN, or contenders in the Liberian struggle—not so long as they retained their arms. The three warlord groups—NPFL, ULiMo, AFL—met in Akosombo, Ghana, under UN auspices and on September 12, 1994, signed a new agreement for a council of state of the three parties plus two civilians, in yet another attempt to find a solution.

■ The Non-African Roles

The United States has played a low-key role in Liberia since Doe's fall, which it helped precipitate when it finally withdrew its support for his government in 1988. Reluctantly at first, Washington has supported ECOWAS's dispatch of troops to Liberia. It helped finance ECOMOG operations (having subsidized Senegal's now-terminated participation), is the largest donor of emergency aid to Liberia, and continues to press all players to reach a peaceful settlement. Even while inadvertently publicly casting doubt on ECOMOG's neutrality, the neutrality and determination of the United States itself are in question owing, in part, to its earlier support for Doe, its aversion to Taylor (because of the Libyan connection, and, later, a massacre of U.S. nuns by NPFL elements), and its failure to act more forcefully in the face of Liberia's suffering and self-destruction. The myths attending the historical "special relationship" between the United States and Liberia have by now been more or less dispelled, to the satisfaction of some in Washington who wish to pass the cup to ECOWAS and the UN, but less so to Liberians, who continue to hope for a greater U.S. role in their country.

In spite of its ambivalence about its responsibilities, the United States remains an important player in the peace process and the largest financial contributor to ECOWAS operations and to relief efforts (in December 1993 it committed $31 million to finance the deployment of Ugandan and Tanzanian peacekeepers). But, apart from money and diplomatic pressure, the United States appears to be unwilling to become more deeply involved in the Liberian morass, especially after the shock of the Somali and Rwandan debacles.

The French have played a shadowy role in Liberia's crisis. France's objective may simply have been to support its old friend, Houphouet-Boigny, and, in turn, Houphouet's protégé, Blaise Campore of Burkina Faso; or it may be trying to protect its source of Liberian timber and minerals. France was a leading importer of the estimated 343,000 cubic meters of timber that came out of Taylor's territory in 1991–1992 (Germany, Britain, Italy, the Netherlands, Spain, Greece, Portugal, and Turkey being the other importers [*Independent,* November 23, 1992]). Thus, when the UN Security Council imposed an arms embargo on Liberia, France and several other members tried, unsuccessfully, to get the council to apply it equally to ECOMOG (George 1993: 57–58). The French gambit could also be seen as being aimed at reducing U.S., and possibly Nigerian, influence in the region.

The United Nations belatedly began to assert its interest in Liberia in late 1992, having determined that "the deterioration of the situation in Liberia constitutes a threat to international security, particularly in West Africa as a whole" (Security Council Resolution 788—Liberia: November 19, 1992). The Security Council threw its weight behind ECOWAS and the Yamoussoukro 4 Accord and called for an arms embargo, excepting ECOWAS forces from the ban. The UN resolution also called on the Secretary-General to dispatch a special representative to Liberia. Following Trevor Gordon-Sommers's first visit, the Secretary-General issued a report (March 8, 1993) that did little more than endorse continuation of ECOWAS's efforts to find a peaceful settlement, avoiding any greater role for the United Nations. This deference to ECOWAS has caused some critics to challenge United Nations impartiality (Ankomah 1992).

As cosponsor with ECOWAS of the Cotonou Agreement, the United Nations finds itself more deeply involved in Liberia. Under Cotonou, the United Nations is to oversee the disarmament of the antagonists and to supervise elections. Several UN agencies are active in relief and refugee operations both in Liberia and in neighboring states.

■ Why Did Liberia Collapse?

By the title of this chapter, "Putting the State Back Together," I imply that we understand or can agree on what held the state together before and, then, what went wrong to cause its collapse. If we can do that, presumably we can fashion a formula for its reconstruction.

The broadly accepted notion that repressive and exploitative Americo-Liberian rule over the mass of tribal peoples carried the seeds of its own destruction is too facile an explanation for Liberia's collapse. Reactionary oligarchies are holding on to power in a number of countries throughout the world today; and they may continue to do so if they are repressive enough, or if they cleverly manage a salami-slicing type of reform, as the British did in the nineteenth century. In that case, the ruling class may well be replaced, but the state need not be destroyed.

Liberian history has been marked by sometimes cruel repression of the tribal peoples, but that was not the case after World War II. Rather, the second scenario seems to have been under way, although one may question how cleverly reform was managed in President W.V.S. Tubman's last years, when retrenchment replaced the fading leader's earlier modernizing innovations (Lowenkopf 1974: 162–169). Things did begin to fall apart, however, under William Tolbert, who became president on Tubman's death in 1971.

In an effort to affirm his own claim to leadership, Tolbert undertook some modest reforms, apparently without much conviction and certainly without much skill. His timing was wrong, for Liberia was in the throes of an economic downswing. But it was more than poor timing when the government announced a 50 percent increase in the price of rice in April 1979. Mishandling by police of a protest march in Monrovia, led by one of the new parties Tolbert had allowed to form, resulted in rioting and looting. Hundreds, mostly students, were killed or wounded, and soldiers and police joined the looters.

Tolbert, who had been uneasy about the new, populist political parties that opposed the old order (he had outlawed several of them) responded to these threatening signals as halfheartedly as he had to the need for reform. He permitted the army to fester in poor living conditions and did little to revamp the security services. A few strikeleaders and politicians were jailed, freedom of the press was further curtailed, the university was closed, and the 700 Guinean troops Sekou Toure had sent to help restore order were sent home.

Tolbert's vacillating policies had weakened the already fragile political system. Thus, few Liberians rose to defend it when a handful of enlisted men assassinated Tolbert and other government leaders in April 1980. Liberia then suffered for nearly ten years under a more ruthless, more narrowly based regime, and then experienced a "liberation" that was more devastating than the injustices it had known in the past.

□ *"Same Taxi, Different Driver"*

To understand why this happened, it is necessary to reexamine the objectives and effects of Master Sergeant Samuel Doe's coup. Was Doe's seizure of power *consciously,* or even indirectly, conceived of as a way to overthrow the existing order? So it seemed to some analysts at the time, and to many of Liberia's people, who danced in Monrovia's streets and in the villages (as did comparable groups in Uganda when Idi Amin took power in 1971). It became clear quite early in Doe's reign that he had no idea how to transform Liberia's political system into a democracy or to advance economic and social equality. Even when Doe's government experimented with rural development, based on community-owned farms, these degenerated into government-run operations supervised and exploited by the military. "In the unlimited exercise of military control, every institution that formerly imposed social and cultural constraints on the exercise of power was destroyed or severely weakened" (Sawyer 1992: 295, 298).

Doe had crushed the previous regime only to replace it with his own followers, largely from his own ethnic group. The former patron-client system was turned upside down, with Doe's cohorts as the new class of "honorables" and many members of the former elite serving as their retainers. Within months of the coup, the words in Monrovia's streets were: "Same taxi, different driver."

Doe's tribe, the Krahn, who had been at the bottom of the social hierarchy—as one long-time student of Liberia observed, they were "the one-at-a-time cigarette sellers, prostitutes, and enlisted men"—and who were the last to enter Liberia's modern sector, quickly grabbed the rewards and symbols of high office. As we now know, the revolution never happened. It did not happen because Doe and his cohorts had no greater vision of power than something that could be used for their own enrichment. Pathetic attempts by progressive (and opportunistic) Liberians, plus generously funded official U.S. prodding, to steer Doe on to a constructive path had no chance (notwithstanding some academics' delusional hopes).

Since then, studies of military coups invariably refer to "the Sammy Doe factor." For Doe became a standard or a symbol of unpredictable events . . . an unlettered, noncommissioned officer who was in the right (or wrong) place at the right (or wrong) time, and who, with a handful of equally unlettered comrades overthrew a regime that was basically unlucky, unprepared for such an inside job, and was exceedingly feckless in the bargain.

Doe's April 1980 seizure of power was neither a military coup nor was it a revolution against Americo-Liberian domination of the indigenous peoples. Rather it was a coup *within* a marginal institution (the military had no power and low status under Tubman and Tolbert), by a socially marginal element, the Krahn. It had first to purge the military before its own claim to leadership was secure, which is precisely what Doe did. Doe and his ilk were simply the first generation of warlords. They introduced interethnic rivalry, not unity; did little to liberate and develop the so-called tribal people (except the Krahn and some of their ethnic allies); and spawned the vicious progeny who now stand in the way of putting Liberia back together.

Among Doe's other destructive accomplishments was his handling of the 1985 election that supposedly was aimed at restoring civilian rule. The throttling of the promise and the hope it conveyed probably did as much as anything else to make his violent overthrow inevitable. The "election campaign was characterized by more severe repression than any time (sic) in recent memory" (Lawyers Committee for Human Rights 1986: 17). Nevertheless, some 750,000 Liberians, nearly one-third of the population, cast ballots, only to see the election stolen by Doe's electoral commission and a clearly larcenous vote count that gave Doe 50.9 percent of the electorate. Declared outright theft by all observers (with the notable exception of the U.S. government) Doe's "victory" ended any pretense of observing the rule of law and was followed by an even more brutal campaign to entrench his power.

While Doe's nine-year reign and what followed (four years of guerrilla war, armed occupation of most of the country, and near-anarchy) did destroy the previous order, it left in its place only more corruption, interethnic hatreds, rule of the gun, and fear and physical destruction. It also severely discredited rule from Monrovia and the electoral process. If this chapter's examination of the roots of Liberia's collapse points anywhere, it is that all the kings' horses and men may not want to put Humpty together again—at least not in the way it was. Indeed, it is the kings' men who are tearing Liberia apart.

■ Can Liberia Reconstruct?

It is useful to cite African examples of failed efforts to put collapsed countries back together (e.g., Angola and Somalia) and to warn of the pitfalls of winner-take-all competitions for a powerful presidency; of premature elec-

tions; of the failure to disarm old armies before constructing new ones; and
of inadequate neutral arbitration. But simply to offer in their place such
concepts as empowerment of local groups, powersharing, decentralization
through local and federal forms of government, and the like, begs several
questions: Who does the empowering? Who are the powersharers to be?
Who and what will carry the legitimacy-bestowing symbols of the nation
and the state?

Interestingly, a glimmer of an answer has been revealed among the
refugees subsisting in Monrovia. Because their survival depends upon UN
and NGO relief operations, some neighborhoods have organized block
committees to handle the requisitioning and distribution of food and cloth-
ing (there were 175 such distribution centers in 1992). Under the name
SELF (Special Emergency Life Food), their spokespersons are chosen by
some form of election. When I asked a UN informant: Who gets elected?
he answered: "The best, most honest person on the block." With computer-
ized records of the number of residents in each house in the city, SELF's
primarily volunteer force is distributing food to over 600,000 people in
Monrovia. A group similar to SELF was formed in NPFL territory
(Liberians United for Self-Help, LUSH), and has met with SELF leaders to
receive technical advice (Ruiz 1992).

An ancillary, but essentially autonomous, arm of SELF has also
emerged: the Community Welfare Team. Some six hundred teams, whose
leadership is elected semiannually, go beyond supporting SELF's relief
operation: they assess each community's reconstruction and development
needs in order to enlist UN and NGO support for self-help projects
(Martone 1993). One wonders if people so involved will ever again accept
politics as usual. The important thing is to allow this type of grassroots
organization to flourish, without political interference, and then to examine
the ways it can be given expression in a national format.

Near the close of the colonial era, social scientists spent a great deal of
time on such concepts as nation-building and state-building. When the
seemingly popular nationalist movements took over the state, most pretend-
ed—even to themselves—to be using their new positions to mobilize the
people for the purpose of nation-building. What they succeeded in doing in
many cases was to aggrandize the state and their own power.

Liberian leaders and opinionmakers, as well as interested and involved
foreigners, seem to be in a great hurry to reconstitute the state in Liberia.
But, given the current roster of political aspirants in Monrovia and the
ambitions of the leaders of the armed groups in the country, such a hasty
process would likely be a ticket to political impasse, or to deals and
alliances that would cede power to the dealmakers at the expense of good
government and the people. Much more sorting out of the question of who

shall represent the people is necessary before the state apparatus is reestablished.

Prospects for a stable powersharing government are even less attractive, as the situation since Cotonou illustrates. Apart from their own mutual hostilities, the armed factions are themselves often bitterly divided. The loyalty of Taylor's minions, who have been living off the land and lording it over a defenseless population in a sort of institutionalized anarchy, is hardly monolithic. Rumors abound of deadly purges within NPFL ranks. One must question how much control Taylor would have over his followers in a powersharing arrangement in which he has less to offer them in material or political goods than they have been able to obtain with their guns.

ULiMo's power struggle between Krahn and Mandingo elements and between the Sierra Leone and Guinea factions already has spawned a new military faction, the Liberian Peace Council. Led by George Boley, an official in the late Doe government, it has attracted elements from the AFL and ULiMo. ULiMo itself has degenerated into a vicious exploiter of the territory it controls and some elements have attacked Liberian refugee camps in Guinea and Sierra Leone. The AFL, while nominally subservient to the IGNU, is a rogue army at best, determined to get even with former and current enemies, and to take what it wants in the meantime. A hideous example of the AFL's violent propensities was revealed in a June 1993 massacre of over five hundred refugees (mostly women and children) at Harbel, the former headquarters of the Firestone plantation.

The parties that made up IGNU are, in most cases, essentially instruments of the political ambitions of their leaders. The government portfolios they held were often exploited for material and political gain for their followers, although there was little largesse to spread around with an annual budget of only about $18 million, obtained largely from the licensing of ships under the Liberian flag and the registration of overseas paper corporations. In such an environment of all against all and each for himself, the powersharing idea doesn't stand a chance.

How then can Liberians determine who will form a government? Modern nations have not yet come up with better means to answer this question than through broad-based elections. And that is what is prescribed for Liberia, by Liberians themselves, Yamossoukro 4, Cotonou, ECOWAS, and the United Nations. Apart from a general skepticism about the promise and legitimizing qualities of most elections in Africa, even if unchallengably free and fair (see Ottaway in Chapter 15 of this book regarding some of the reasons for such skepticism), the case for early elections in Liberia that would establish a government of and for the people is feeble and technically unmanageable.

As noted above, well over half the people are not living in their home

areas. They are unlikely to be able both to return and be prepared and registered for elections in the short period that most prescriptions envision
(Yamossoukro 4 called for elections in 1992; Cotonou by February 1994).
The UNDP consultant charged with setting up the 1992 elections optimisti-
cally estimated 800,000 eligible voters, even while observing that most displaced citizens would be excluded (Lopez-Pinter 1992). More important,
the enormous task of resettlement and the resumption of economically
viable lives will blot out most Liberians' political concerns, apart from
those for their security. Since neither an interim nor a newly elected government will be able to respond to these basic concerns, why should
Liberians care much about elections in the near future? If elections are to
be used to free the United Nations and ECOWAS from further responsibilities in Liberia, they will leave a vacuum in precisely those basic areas of
Liberians' concerns, law and order.

     As for the question of a strong executive (i.e., strongman rule), as
Ng'ethe discusses in Chapter 16, Liberia's historical experience with a
powerful presidency is unremittingly sour (see Sawyer 1992: 278, on the
"cult" of the presidency). However the Liberian state is rebuilt, the exercise
is bound to be an authority-aggrandizing one, and the people most likely to
end up in charge are precisely the ones who have been willing to lay waste
their country and kill and maim their own people in order to win power.
Even some of those intellectuals and politicians in Monrovia who claim to
be noncombatants have made deals with gun-toting elements, as did some
of them with Doe in the naive hope that they could direct or control, and
hopefully eventually supplant, the unlettered master sergeant (a similar
class tried the same tactics in Uganda with Idi Amin, and ended up either in
the boot of an army death squad's automobile or had to flee the country for
their lives, as Khadiagala documents in Chapter 3 of this book).

     The reconstruction of Liberian society, the economy, and the develop-
ment of political entities below the national level should be the first order
of business in Liberia. Then comes rebuilding of the state. But how is even
this to come to pass unless the prerequisites of a civil order—effective laws
and their enforcement, security of self, property, and one's labor, to begin
with—are established? Who will provide the infrastructure—roads, markets, water, and electricity—and a legal system that will bring Liberia's
dispersed masses back home?

     Most refugees living abroad are believed to want to return to their
homes, though not until their safety is reasonably assured. Past experience
suggests that few of the people now living in urban areas will do so. Liberia
had already been in the grips of uncontrolled urbanization—some 38 percent of the population in 1985 (Liebenow 1987: 161). The million or so
people in and around Monrovia live almost completely on the dole, with
their daily bread provided by the United Nations, the United States, and

NGOs. What conditions must pertain before they accept the authority and the institutions of a reconstituted central authority? What social contract would they now respect and adhere to?

Further complicating this issue is the savagery that has been unleashed over the past thirteen years. In the not so remote past, *book* (i.e., education) was the route to influence, affluence, even a share of power. In this way, so-called tribal people (i.e., non–Americo-Liberians) had begun to find their ways into the elite class. But since Samuel Doe took power in 1980, a generation of young people has learned about the power of the gun, not the ABCs. They may know little else, or be unwilling to exchange that cheap and readily available way of making a living for a life of hard work and learning. Taylor told one correspondent: "We keep them armed as a means of keeping them out of trouble" (Berkeley 1992). A new Liberia must offer relief from the fear of kids with guns, and its kids a reasonable alternative to the rewards of a violent way of life.

If the military factions are not disarmed, what recourse have the politicians in Monrovia? They have neither the capacity nor the financial base to run even the most basic public services, let alone maintain security, particularly outside Monrovia, nor the popular mandate to do so. And from where will Liberia get the $200 million that the UN/ECOMOG joint committee chairman, Trevor Gorden-Somers, says will be required for its reconstruction? (The estimate, it seems to me, is low.)

In outlining the paramount problems facing Liberia before a new political order can be constructed, and in perhaps too harshly contending that Liberians alone cannot overcome them, I may seem to be stacking the deck in favor of foreign intervention. But as much as we may argue—and protest as the Liberians undoubtedly will—that it is not for outsiders to set the terms for, or to arrange and oversee, a "solution" to Liberia's dissolution, outsiders already have made an irreversible impact on the situation. For there to be a successful outcome—instead of continued conflict and partition, or military victory by one side or another, or a soon-to-be-breached compromise peace settlement—outsiders will have to play a significant role, along the lines discussed in the concluding chapter of this book. As Francis Deng put it in addressing the Somali situation,

> tragic situations of that magnitude cannot be left to local actors when the extent of human suffering and destruction of life and property far exceeds what should be tolerable even by minimum standards of human dignity and global responsibility (*Brookings Review,* spring 1993).

Who the mediators are likely to be, and what roles they will play as conciliators, supervisors, or peacekeepers, at this point is far from certain. The United Nations, thus far, for all its recent activism, appears to want to stand firmly *behind* ECOWAS. But ECOWAS, in spite of its relative unity on ending the fighting in Liberia, is divided to some extent on Anglophone and Francophone lines, and several of its members have competing agendas. Among the *devil* theories that exist is one that portrays Nigeria as a potential regional imperialist, with designs on the wealth of Guinea, among others. One might say that ECOMOG is as Nigeria does. In any case, the neutrality of ECOWAS, given the interventionary role of ECOMOG, is at issue, particularly for Taylor. ECOWAS, nevertheless, must play a role, but one that is part of a broader international effort, if only on the grounds of the sheer cost of rehabilitating Liberia.

Once it is determined who will oversee the peace and rehabilitation processes, early agreement is necessary on how much and what duration of foreign intervention is acceptable to the various Liberian contenders, as well as to those who are not represented either by the armed factions or by the politicians in Monrovia. The answers to both these sets of questions may be found in the broadest and most neutral form of intervention, that of the United Nations. For, in spite of its alleged partiality during the conflict (Ankomah 1992), and scapegoating in Somalia, the United Nations is the only international organization with the capabilities of pressing a political agenda once peace has been established. (See Deng, Chapter 13 of this book). Will it be a Somali-type arrangement, where outsiders decide how long to stay (or, rather, one that reflects the lessons of Somalia's difficulties)? Or will it be a more limited, Angola-type (and demonstrably insufficient) UN overseeing of the peace process?

■ How to Rebuild Liberia

The following recommendations are set primarily in terms of economic and social programs, but they reflect as well Liberia's need for political reconstruction. In this light, the most immediate objectives—following disarmament (see below)—would be (1) to resettle the former armed elements, in jobs or job-training for the adults, back to school for the children; and (2) to create the conditions that will bring the dispersed refugee populations back from abroad and as many as possible out of Monrovia and other urban centers, which cannot support one-third of the population without a real economic base. To this end certain public "goods" are required:

Security. Separating, disarming and demobilizing the several armies will require a neutral security force, one that has not engaged in fighting in the past. Cotonou's plan to assign east and southern African troops to this task, under UN and ECOWAS auspices, and keeping Nigeria's writ limited to Monrovia and Buchanan, seems to meet this requirement.

Economic and social infrastructure. UN agencies and NGOs have experience in Monrovia and up-country in starting up electric power production, water supplies, medical clinics, and schools. The UN High Commission for Refugees (UNHCR), which has been responsible for Liberian refugees abroad, already has begun resettlement planning and, with other aid donors (particularly the United States) a fairly quick start in rehabilitating the country is possible.

Land. A macroeconomic approach to agriculture and land use will be among the first orders of business. To reconstruct the Liberian economy, it will be necessary to

- determine through consultation with the people involved the appropriateness of communal ownership by lineage chieftaincies or kinship descent groups with usufruct rights to households and individuals, or of a system of private property and rights of transfer to enable family-based farming on the basis of long-term leases or ownership (Sawyer 1992: 308)
- provide rural credits to compensate for farmers' limited capacity to acquire such things as fertilizer and equipment, which are needed to increase production

Foreign investment and banking. Among the initiatives that must be considered at an early stage, if Liberia is to produce jobs for its urban and educated peoples, are

- selective opening of the banking systems to foreign banks in order to foster competition, thus to hold down interest rates
- legislation to allow the private sector to participate in joint ventures with foreign investors
- incentives, such as lower costs for power and land rents, to encourage investment in less developed parts of the country
- standardization of the monetary system: Monrovia and Taylorland each has its own currency

☐ The Political Structure

Some form of agreement on interim powersharing almost certainly will be necessary to bring the fighting to an end, get the armies to disarm and demobilize, and to give Liberians a renewed sense of participation in building their nation. But such power must be carefully circumscribed if the old divisions and hatreds are not to suffocate at birth a new political system. Hence, executive power must be at least partially insulated from partisan politics. The Cotonou Agreement provides for a "neutral" chairman of a five-person Council of State but leaves the rest of the process to dealmaking and odd marriages of political expediency, such as one that took place in November 1993 between the NPFL and ULiMo on the question of cabinet assignments.

A more appropriate way to delink Liberia's difficult transition from partisan politics would be to establish, alongside Cotonou's Ruling Council, an advisory council directed by a representative of the UN Secretary-General and consisting of representatives of UN agencies, the IMF and IBRD, ECOWAS, the United States (which still has the longest experience in Liberia, and should remain the principal aid donor), and a number of Liberian "unofficials" (from churches, educational, voluntary and professional organizations, and chiefs) as advisors. It would share with the Liberian transitional government control of the financial resources and security forces, through international donors, voluntary agencies, ECOWAS military personnel, and what hopefully will come to be a large array of Liberian and international technical advisers, and to arbitrate the demands of the several factions comprising the transitional government.

It may be argued that such an arrangement practically gives the advisory council control of the principal instruments of governance (security and finance) and, in consequence, a veto over Liberian government enactments. So it does, but only temporarily, until meaningful elections can be conducted. One of the arguments for early elections is that powersharing will be precarious, hence it must be brief. But because I believe that elections should come much later, this would be another reason for an international advisory council with real power during the interim. As for the argument that only an *elected* government can contract official business, including loans and grants from international financial institutions (e.g., the IMF and the IBRD), I would note that a hastily elected, hence feeble, government is not a more reliable financial partner than an interim one.

This blueprint is by no means a literal prescription. Once a clearer picture emerges of what the situation will be after a ceasefire truly takes hold and disarmament is effected, such a governing structure may be seen to be not appropriate at all. But the idea of *parallel* authorities does try to address the immediate problems facing Liberia: its need for both external arbitration and Liberian participation in the rebuilding process. Perhaps, after the country is peopled again, the economy running, and the polity restored, elections can be held.

■ Note

1. Zartman in the Introduction to this book.
2. The author is indebted to Kevin George of the Friends of Liberia and Charles Gurney, former Liberian desk officer, U.S. Department of State, for their assistance. Neither, of course, is responsible for the judgments or shortcomings in this chapter.

7

The Heritage of Revolution and the Struggle for Governmental Legitimacy in Mozambique

Barry Schutz

States collapse, or fragment, when their foundations of legitimacy, reposing in civil society, become frayed and torn. New states that have recently acquired independence are especially vulnerable to collapse because the principles of governmental legitimacy have yet to be fully espoused or understood, due to an inchoate sense of nationhood.

Mozambique's fledgling revolutionary government diligently cultivated a sense of Mozambican nationhood in its fourteen-year armed struggle against Portuguese colonialism. But because of the expanse of the country, the ethnic diversity of the population, and the peripheral location of Maputo, the capital city, the goal of nationhood was able to be subverted by externally charged internal resistance. Such counterrevolutionary resistance and terrorism ultimately caused the revolutionary Humpty Dumpty to fall from his wall of legitimacy.

States that have been formed from armed struggle against oppressive rule share the legacy of revolutionary legitimacy. However, they also share the curse of relative deprivation. More than other new regimes, they must sustain the glory and romance of heroic commitment. Governments of people's revolutions and national liberation movements must satisfy more people with greater expectations than governments that have come to power through nonrevolutionary means, by election or transfer of power. They also face the task of transforming their revolutionary legitimacy into governmental or civic legitimacy. How this is accomplished depends on circumstances of history, culture, ideology, and geographic context. Resistance by the government to pressures to meet popular expectations and admit popular responsibility for policy ultimately leads to popular resentment and demands for change. In the case of the Soviet Union, it took more than seventy years for such resistance and demands to flower. In Mozambique it took only five. Both its colonial past and its regional setting accelerated and accentuated the contradictions in the transformation from revolutionary to civic legitimacy.

■ Defining Legitimacy

Legitimacy is a concept, not a fact. It refers to popular belief in or acceptance of an authority's right to rule. However, this definition is so broad that it includes any leader who can achieve popularity in any given moment.

The current interest in the concept of democracy and its utility in Africa has tended to refocus the argument from the legitimacy of government to the preference for a specific political system. There is no doubt that democracy, in its most general and generic sense, manifests the fundamental principle of electoral legitimacy. This principle has dominated global political culture in the twentieth century. Fascism has actually been the only serious challenge to the democratic principle. Marxism-Leninism, as we shall argue later in this case study of Mozambique, was a hybrid of the democratic principle and tried to retain the legitimizing aura of democracy without actually employing its core political attributes.

These remarks are important because much of the argument in Mozambique today is about legitimacy. The consensus of the population—and certainly that of its emerging elite—is that the grand commitment to programmatic (Leninist, if not actually Stalinist) policies by FreLiMo (Front for the Liberation of Mozambique) in 1977 at its Third Party Congress sacrificed the possibility of achieving democratic legitimacy to be built on the basis of the movement's successful (and legitimate) revolutionary struggle. There must now be a turn toward "democracy"—*democracy* (in the rest of Africa as well as Mozambique) being used as an unwitting code word for *legitimacy*.

Legitimacy, however, is not a singular concept. The late historian, Gugielmo Ferrero (1942), distinguished between prelegitimacy, legitimacy, and postlegitimacy, with the first stage signifying the condition whereby the initial government tests itself in the process of establishing the principle of legitimacy. Even more central to the case of Mozambique is the distinction between internal and international legitimacy. As Jackson and Rosberg (1986) have argued, African states have received international legitimacy but generally have not been successful in establishing internal legitimacy.

A final distinction, between revolutionary and civic legitimacy, provides the most relevant contrast for undertaking the case of Mozambique. Revolutionary movements succeed primarily on the basis of their effectiveness in combating illegitimate regimes (Schutz and Slater 1992). However, they are unprepared for the problem of transforming revolutionary "movement" legitimacy into the more permanent condition of civic or governmental legitimacy. Revolutions emerge as deliverers of popular and legitimate government but their principles tend to be submerged by the expectation of perpetual rule by the revolutionaries themselves. The revolution, therefore, becomes institutionalized and eventually memorialized as the system to end all systems. However, revolutions generally fail to install or activate the very principle of popular participation and choice that they claimed to represent. Instead, the revolutionary government becomes responsible for all subsequent events in the society and, by its monopolization of responsibility in their name, prevents the people from joining that responsibility. People tend to have short memories about revolution and eventually condemn the revolutionary government for the same reason that they condemned the previous illegitimate government. Subsequent hardships, real or imagined, are blamed on the revolutionary government.

Popular responsibility for government is critical for its effective legitimacy. The problem, of course, is that people generally are not inclined to political action. They become political only when socialized into such action as a part of civic responsibility and they become revolutionary only when their capacity to improve their own lives is blocked by structural impediments (thus, the significant message of Marx's theory of revolution in the face of dominant socioeconomic impediments). But after the revolution, people revert to their fundamental cultural conservatism and become more attuned to the predominance of their own group interests.

Thus the revolutionary government needs to open itself up to popular interest. In most cases this subjects the revolution to reactionary influences, posing a most difficult choice for that government. Indeed, the revolutionary government occupies the same tentative, limiting niche as that of the newly independent nonrevolutionary government. Facing a hostile and dominating external environment and an expectant and relatively deprived internal population, the new government needs either to "deliver the economic and political goods" or else to reform the structural basis of government so that the people can quickly learn to have a political impact on their own lives (Djilas 1959).

If the revolutionary government (no longer revolutionary at this point) retrenches, it forfeits its claim to legitimacy. If it opens itself to intrinsic, programmatic modification (or outright change), it risks forsaking the perceived historic rationale for its struggle to come to power in the first place. It is a monumental moment with awesome implications. Coerced perpetuation of the revolutionary government and program threatens to transform the government from a state of prelegitimacy to one of illegitimacy. On the other hand, if the revolutionary government chooses a commitment to an elective-republican foundation of legitimacy, it runs the risk of losing power, or at least its programmatic rationale.

The cardinal point here is that revolutionary governments are quite fragile. Despite their legitimate foundations, they cannot achieve legitimacy without altering their self-perception of legitimate authority. Such authority derives from the people, not merely from revolutionary propaganda. That belief pervades the revolutionaries as they assume power. But in their desire to create the new revolutionary society, they forget the fundamental beliefs and expectations of the people on whose behalf they took power. Prelegitimacy, as defined by Ferrero (1942), points to a government that is expected to fulfill the expectations of the people. However, it rules *on spec*. The revolutionary government can only build a legitimate government; it cannot become one by self-anointment. Prelegitimacy can beget legitimacy, but it does not do so inherently. It can just as easily fall into illegitimacy. And this can either terminate the whole revolutionary process or reignite it.

■ Conditions for Legitimacy in Mozambique

Too often we assume the existence of a state. The international community is presently enmeshed in a struggle to maintain the existence of states whose legitimacy (as states) has crumbled. All states are creations of conflict, consensus, and contrivance, but perhaps the states of Africa are the most contrived of all. In very few circumstances were the states formed on the basis of internal dynamics. Most of them were configured by the imperatives of European power politics at the end of the nineteenth century. As a result, African states are especially subject to fragmentation and reconfiguration based on the claims and consequences of internal dispute and conflict and external ambitions and operations.

Mozambique is no exception to this pattern. It was created by Portuguese interest, expanded by Portuguese appetite, and, territorially configured by the interests of the international community of states, notably Portugal and Great Britain. Mozambique's present borders were internationally legitimized by Cecil Rhodes's refusal to annex Mozambique to the (then) Rhodesias after his deputy, Starr Jameson, led an unauthorized Rhodesian expedition into Mozambique in 1893 in order to claim it for the British Crown. Rhodes did not believe it was necessary to annex Mozambique formally in order to dominate it. This pattern of global and regional hegemony over Mozambique persists to the present.

Portugal did not try to settle its citizens or acculturate the people of Mozambique until after World War II, after more than two centuries of colonization. There is a very thin national veneer of Portuguese language and culture throughout Mozambique. Unlike other European colonial powers, Portugal had no real policy or rationale for "advancing" the development of the people within Mozambique. It treated the people of Mozambique as instruments of the Portuguese national economy. When it finally did arrive at a rationale for its "possession" of Mozambique—after World War II—it did so through the settlement of relatively large numbers of Portuguese.

Thus, there is not much of a foundation, even in hegemonial colonial terms, for the existence of a distinct Mozambican civil society. It is very difficult to establish political legitimacy when there is virtually no civil society. What the Portuguese did leave was the Portuguese language as the lingua franca of Mozambique, in a region dominated by an equally colonially imposed English language.

Given the underdeveloped transportation and communication links in Mozambique, the establishment of Portuguese colonial rule was restricted primarily to the provincial capitals. This has left much of Mozambique in its precolonial social forms and a serious social and political void thus preceded the successful revolutionary struggle of FreLiMo. Although FreLiMo did rely on popular rural support, and achieved that support wherever it fought against Portuguese colonial rule, when it assumed power in 1975 as a popular, successful movement, it was still one that had not reached most of the country. FreLiMo's message remained obscure, unheard, unanticipated, by the majority of the population of Mozambique. FreLiMo therefore could not assume that it had at that time achieved civic legitimacy. In order to achieve that legitimacy, it had to reach more people and to convince them that they, FreLiMo, were the legitimate government. On this count, they fell short.

It is unlikely that much international concern would manifest itself if Mozambique fell apart. With the increasingly internal focus of South African politics, there is no regional hegemon to come to the help of a unified Mozambican state. Thus, the territorial legitimacy of the Mozambican state is not only no sure thing; it has become increasingly vulnerable to potential separatist/secessionist movements. Indeed, a major concern for FreLiMo is that ReNaMo (or any other potential insurgency) accept Mozambique as a state in its present geographic contours. A major issue of peace talks in Rome in the late 1980s was not only the legitimacy of government but of the territorial integrity of the state itself.

■ FreLiMo's Claim to Legitimacy: An Assessment

FreLiMo came to power on a crest of popular domestic support and goodwill. It also enjoyed general support from the international community. Unlike Angola, Mozambique had a single government-in-waiting. There could be no doubt as to the essential prelegitimacy of the nascent FreLiMo government. There were no alternatives, at most only scattered dissidents.

FreLiMo had to mobilize popular support and to ensure "the greatest economic good for the greatest number of Mozambicans" as quickly but effectively as possible. Because it stood inalterably opposed to any elements of tradition (i.e., descent) as the principle of government, it had to espouse and incorporate an elective-republican set of principles. The general principles for which FreLiMo stood during the days of guerrilla struggle were popular, populist, and heroic. Its leader, Samora Machel, was a popular and, indeed, charismatic leader. FreLiMo had become more ideologically Marxist-Leninist in 1968 when the power struggle for succession on the death of its founding leader, Eduardo Mondlane, was settled. Relations with Moscow and Havana were solidifying, especially after 1971. But there was no hint in 1975 of a radical revolution-from-above. General popular participation was articulated through the *grupos dinamizados* that exercised elective processes at the grassroots level. The government itself responded to these *grupos,* thus preparing for a fundamentally representative (i.e., republican) form of government.

Initial government programs focused on extending the benefits of education and health care to the whole population. The popularity of this primary thrust generated tremendous domestic support. Moreover, the broad range of sympathetic governments (e.g., Sweden, the Netherlands) and NGOs gravitated to the support of the new regime. Relations within the then white redoubt of Southern Africa were also stable, if tense. South Africa maintained a wait-and-see attitude, with the hope that it could influence Maputo away from Marxism. The situation in white Rhodesia was chaotic and conflict-laden but at that point hopeful: the United States and Britain were working hard to resolve the question of majority rule in that country.

So what went wrong? Certainly the pervasive change in the international community at both the global and regional levels contributed greatly to the destabilization of the fledgling FreLiMo government. Excellent scholarship has clearly indicted the governments of Rhodesia and South Africa (Hanlon 1986). Some scholarship, although not nearly enough, has pointed to the destructive role of the United States after the installation of the Reagan regime in 1981. But problems had begun to develop before that—as early as 1977. That was the year FreLiMo made its fateful decision to adopt a hard, radical Marxist-Leninist approach and to enlist the support of the Soviet Union and its bloc in the process. FreLiMo did not at all discourage Western support (indeed, Joaquim Chissano, the new foreign minister under Machel, made an earnest and effective visit to the United States in October 1976). But the decision to impose a radical, collectivizing, rapidly industrializing policy with no room for gradualism initiated a series of events that alienated the population, dried up the availability of consumer goods, created greater dependency on the Soviet bloc, and, worst of all, elicited fear and provocation in the governments of Rhodesia, South Africa, and, ultimately, the United States.

On an internal, cultural level, the new government faced a problem of reconciling the bulk of the Portuguese settlers to the reality of FreLiMo rule. While a distinct minority of these Mozambicans of Portuguese descent rallied to support FreLiMo against the decrepit fascism of the Salazar and Caetano governments in Lisbon, the majority felt economically and politically threatened. A botched attempt in 1977 to seize the radio station in Maputo by a group of these revanchist settlers convinced Machel and his cohorts that the Portuguese presence had to be severely reduced, if not eliminated. The consequent departure of these Portuguese contributed to the evisceration of the nascent Mozambican economy under FreLiMo. Reminiscent of the French departing Guinea in 1958, the Portuguese of Mozambique grabbed or destroyed everything they could before their exit, dismantling the material base of the state as well as depriving it of their needed skills. Machel's advice to Robert Mugabe during the Lancaster House talks on Zimbabwean independence in late 1979 (that he opt for a governmental structure and social policy that would persuade the white Rhodesians to stay on in black Zimbabwe) suggests that FreLiMo had already concluded that it could have done more to retain at least some of the Portuguese. But in Mozambique in the 1970s, unlike Zimbabwe and Namibia in the 1980s, there was no internationally negotiated transfer of power and there was also no moderation of the drive to expel the Portuguese from the economy and, indeed, from the country.

Ultimately, FreLiMo was confronted with the need for a model to restructure and regenerate the economy and to organize the political system and the presumed civil society. There were not many models on the shelf. Julius Nyerere's program of cooperatives, *ujamaa,* modeled on the Chinese and Israeli concepts of rural organization, was too oriented toward agriculture to suit FreLiMo. At FreLiMo's Third Party Congress in Maputo in 1977, the party chairman, Machel, was persuaded by his closest advisers that the classical Soviet model of the vanguard-driven revolution-from-above was the optimal method for organizing and developing the country, and for rapidly legitimizing FreLiMo authority in Mozambique (those advisers, it was reported, had in turn been influenced by more romantic Western supporters—Britons, Americans, and Canadians). Following from the momentous decision to follow such a policy, FreLiMo embarked on a program of rapid rural collectivization, replete with forced resettlement, intense urban mobilization, and pervasive (and intrusive) internal security. The move from revolutionary populism to highly centralized control and collectivization was not welcomed by the populace. Repeatedly, as Geffray (1990) points out, rural Mozambicans were cut off arbitrarily from their traditional structures and beliefs. Rather than coopting people and their beliefs, as they tended to do during the struggle in the countryside, FreLiMo tried to convert and punish.

The policy of forced resettlement and collectivization began to irritate and eventually to alienate both those who had been resettled and those who anticipated resettlement. Although production figures during this 1977–1979 period reflected an improving economy, the social cost in terms of popular support was to prepare an environment favorable to a counterinsurgency. This was intensified by active South African involvement. Soon rural peoples began to adjudge FreLiMo authorities in the same light as their Portuguese predecessors, with the result that elements opposing FreLiMo were welcomed as the newest liberators. In a way similar to the Ukrainians enthusiastically greeting their Nazi "liberators" from Soviet Stalinism in the early years of World War II, rural Mozambicans began to hail the ReNaMo operatives as liberators from FreLiMo.

The Third Party Congress program of 1977 promoted a series of structural and situational developments that had a delegitimizing effect on FreLiMo and a destabilizing effect on Mozambique. The most salient factor was that Mozambique decided to join the Cold War and, therefore, created an unfavorable perception of itself in some quarters on both the global and regional levels. These two responses were neither immediate nor orchestrated. The Carter administration in the United States was far more concerned with change in Rhodesia/Zimbabwe, Namibia, and South Africa to react strongly to the Mozambican trend, and South Africa was still trying to work out its policy of a constellation of African states. However, Ian Smith's Rhodesia faced a more immediate threat from the direction of Mozambique and, as early as 1977, the Central Intelligence Division (CID), under Ken Flower, decided to retard operations of the Zimbabwe African Nationalist Union (ZANU) in neighboring Rhodesia from Mozambican sanctuary through the organization and supply of an armed, internal Mozambican opposition to FreLiMo. By 1978 it was called the Mozambique National Resistance (MNR), which in its Portuguese acronym became ReNaMo. ReNaMo had relatively little effect on the FreLiMo government at that time, compared with its impact when South Africa took over the operation (in 1980, after the Smith regime gave way to independent Zimbabwe). South Africa's interests in destabilizing operations burgeoned after P. W. Botha replaced Vorster as South African president in 1979 (Hanlon 1986). South Africa embarked on an extensive military campaign to destabilize Maputo through direct military attacks, enhanced training, and support for ReNaMo, operating from South Africa, and actively involved in tactical intelligence operations inside Mozambique.

The hostility of the United States toward FreLiMo between 1981 and 1984 accelerated the impact of ReNaMo terrorism. The Reagan doctrine of that period included support for "freedom fighters" and political harassment of any regime considered supportive of the Soviet bloc and Marxism-Leninism. Because Mozambique was probably the weakest state on this list, a modest U.S. role could accomplish the task of "turning around" Maputo. Indeed, this mission was accomplished with the culmination of the

Nkomati Accord, managing the conflict between Mozambique and South Africa in March 1984, brokered by the United States (Zartman 1989: 219–222; Crocker 1992: 236–244).

In addition to these critical external effects, there were a series of internal political ramifications. The first was primarily geographic. FreLiMo took over the southern-situated Portuguese capital of Laurenco Marques, renamed Maputo, as the site for its government. In so doing, it reinforced a perception that it was a southern, Shangaan-dominated organization. Increasingly put off by the FreLiMo government were not only the peasants of the northern Cabo Delgado and Nampula Provinces, who had been the principal base of support for FreLiMo during the struggle, but also the peoples of central Mozambique, mostly Shona and Ndau, who generally had not been part of the conflict. These groups became the natural recruiting ground for the ReNaMo campaign. Compounding the ethnic perception was the increased visibility of a privileged party/government elite. Not all of the FreLiMo ministers and functionaries were corrupt, but more than a few began to behave publicly with visible arrogance and privilege. The creation of hard currency shops allowed them to purchase Western-produced items that were too expensive to be available to most people. To many Mozambicans, these new socialist elites were all too similar to the departed Portuguese. The differences in policy orientation between the old and new leaders tended to go unnoticed in their similar means of transportation and, occasionally, lifestyle.

But perhaps most grating and delegitimizing to the recently liberated people of Mozambique was FreLiMo's absence of a cultural policy. Ignoring, even rejecting, the traditional cultures and beliefs of the variegated rural peoples of Mozambique opened the floodgates of external subversion and manipulation by ReNaMo. The antitribalist aspect of this policy led to the proscription of rights and powers on the vast range of traditional chiefs, healers (*curandeiros*), judges, and other notables. With no transition and no explanations, FreLiMo officials in the rural sectors violated the traditions and preferences of the very peasant peoples for whom they had ostensibly carried out the revolutionary struggle and for whom they were now ruling. They were carrying out the policies of FreLiMo as proclaimed at the Third Party Congress, varying only their own excesses of zeal.

Finally, FreLiMo's lease on legitimacy was vitiated by the failure of its military to fight and to protect its citizens. ReNaMo's tactics throughout its period of rebellion under South African patronage were singularly brutal, insensitive, and pointless. Under the pervasively painful conditions of seemingly anomic civil war, it was imperative that the FAM—the Armed Forces of Mozambique—carry out an effective defense of the Mozambican people. Part of the Third Party Congress "syndrome" (also referred to as "the Socialist Project") was total military dependency on the Soviet Union and its supporters. This relationship led to a rigidification of the FAM and its decreasing ability to stop ReNaMo. This demoralized the Mozambican population and, in turn, further demoralized the FAM. Without popular confidence in its own military, FreLiMo began to fail the ultimate test of legitimate government, the capacity to defend the state and its population.

It was at this point that FreLiMo became the de facto government of Maputo and the district capitals alone. Even with the help of the Zimbabwe National Army (ZNA) in removing Casa Banana, ReNaMo's headquarters in the Gorongosa section of Manica Province, the FAM could not function in any acceptable way. Six months after the impressive ZNA operation, ReNaMo was back in business in that same area. There were explanations for the weakness of the FAM military performance:

1. Soviet bloc training was inappropriate if not awful.
2. The government had fewer and fewer resources to pay or feed, let alone supply, their forces, and in inverse ratio to their proximity to Maputo.
3. The FAM's loss of support and morale led to their corruption and criminalization.

Increasing numbers of FAM personnel augmented their military roles with vagabondage. They looted and mugged to survive, often killing their victims and witnesses in order to avoid punishment from the government. FAM vagabonds, deserters, and even uniformed regulars took part in these activities. So, of course, did ReNaMo.

Increasingly massive amounts of Soviet bloc–supplied small arms, principally AK-47s, were shipped into Mozambique at the beginning of the 1990s, just as southern Africa was gripped by a massive drought. By the apex of the drought, in June 1992, the value of an AK-47 fell below that of a meal. FreLiMo's utter inability to control this flow and distribution of weapons to all sides throughout the country further eroded their ability to govern.

■ Major Trends in the Struggle for Legitimacy

This list of governmental malfeasance, error, and misjudgment might lead one to assume that FreLiMo has lost any semblance of legitimacy. However, this is not the case. We have thus far covered only one side of the ledger. As Alex Vines (1993) reported on his 1992 visit to Mozambique, "the people still cannot see any alternative to Frelimo." Mozambicans might not love FreLiMo but they considered it to be the government of Mozambique and the only government the people have. Indeed a virtually silent agreement has evolved between FreLiMo and a broad consensus of this battered and fragmented population of Mozambique: If FreLiMo could achieve a successful outcome to the peace process that opened in Rome in 1990, then it would be given an opportunity to compete for legitimate popular support in a general election.

In October 1994, FreLiMo passed the test in an internationally supervised election, with President Chissano collecting about 54 percent of the vote and challenger Afonso Dhlakama of ReNaMo getting about 34 percent of the vote. In the vote for the legislative assembly, FreLiMo received 45 percent and ReNaMo 38 percent. Because of the distribution of the vote, FreLiMo was able to form a majority with 129 of the 250 seats allotted. Thus, FreLiMo found itself confronted with a modest mandate to establish a legitimate government with broad inclusion of ReNaMo and other participating parties.

□ *The Peace Process*

The present password to legitimacy is *peace*. It has been spoken and understood throughout the country—before the election, during the campaign, and as FreLiMo forms the new government. FreLiMo needed to reach four distinct steps toward achieving that peaceful end:

• The first condition, to conclude the war, has been achieved. Although the signed agreement of October 4, 1992, by both FreLiMo and ReNaMo terminated all armed hostilities, weapons on both sides still needed to be pooled and secured by the 6,500 troops of the UN Operation in Mozambique (ONUMOZ) who were deployed in mid-1992.
• Second, ReNaMo had to be defused, defanged, and coopted into the emerging political system. This objective has apparently been achieved with the ReNaMo acknowledgment of the October 1994 election results. It is now clear that ReNaMo's inclusion in a new political arrangement or, at minimum, their acceptance into a competitive party system would have the effect of eliminating or reducing ReNaMo's desire to commit violence and mayhem against FreLiMo or the general population. Two models might have been applied. The first, that of the governing party coopting the insurgent party—as ZANU did with ZAPU in Zimbabwe in the late 1980s—has, for the time being, been rejected by FreLiMo. The second model derives from the cooptation of Al Capone's mob into the ruling Democratic Party of the city of Chicago in the 1930s. Mostly unwritten, this development brought fundamental peace to the streets of the city while offering some of Capone's cronies legitimate status in the city government. As of late 1994, this model does have some resemblance to the unfolding political process. Consequently, ReNaMo has subordinated its "bandit" image and has gained

credibility as an opposition party—especially in the central provinces of Manica and Sofala and the northern provinces of Nampula and Zambezia. However, Mozambicans—even many of those who voted for ReNaMo— are still holding back acceptance of ReNaMo's legitimacy, even as an opposition party. One of the humorous popular references during the campaign was that the contest was between "thieves" (FreLiMo) and "murderers" (ReNaMo). Such perceptions are hardly the stuff of legitimacy.

• Third, the military on both sides had to be reformed and reduced in size. Part of the Rome Accord allotted 30 percent of the positions inside the military to ReNaMo. However, the reorganized and partially retrained Mozambican Armed and Defense Force (FADM) has not reached anything close to its designated size of 30,000. By late 1994 there was considerable mistrust by both sides regarding a new armed force. Attempts by FreLiMo to convert many of those demobilized out of the FAM into a rapid response police force has sown ReNaMo suspicion without effecting a reliable police force.

• The final requisite, the pacification of the countryside, has been a relatively pleasant surprise. Despite Mozambique's size; its lack of effective roads and communications; the extreme social dislocation that has resulted from the prolonged war; and, not the least, the proliferation of small arms and land mines that has become part of the Mozambican way of life (or, rather, death), the return to the land of steady numbers of refugees suggests that this problem may be well on the way to solution. However, this whole process will probably take considerably more time, especially without the presence of the ONUMOZ personnel. Recent trends indicate that the states of the Southern African Development Community (SADC) are in the process of establishing a "neighborhood watch" to prevent emerging conflicts within the region and the unravelling of positive developments such as those in Mozambique. As an example, just as the voting began in Mozambique, ReNaMo stated that they were pulling out of the election. Within eight hours, President Mugabe of Zimbabwe and Deputy President Thabo Mbeki of South Africa played significant roles in reversing ReNaMo's withdrawal.

Even with progress on the above requisites and the successful outcome of Mozambique's first election, FreLiMo's status remains pre-legitimate. The onus of proof remains with this newly elected FreLiMo government to establish its legitimacy by performance, process, and inclusion of the substantial opposition rather than by program and propaganda. Ultimately, effective legitimacy emerges only when a second successful election occurs, thus confirming the legitimacy of the constitutional process rather than the specific government.

□   The Pillar of FreLiMo's Claims to Legitimacy: Executive Leadership

Despite their enormous problems of governance, FreLiMo's capacity to generate a plethora of strong and dynamic leaders has been remarkable. Such leadership has kept the Mozambican state from utter collapse. The consecutive leaders, Eduardo Mondlane, Samora Machel, and Joaquim Chissano, have each possessed superb and critical abilities to lead. Mondlane (party chairman from 1962 until his assassination in 1968) was an intellectual of the first rank who was, nevertheless, capable of practical thought and action.

Machel (party chairman from 1970 and first president of Mozambique from 1975 until his untimely and not totally explained death in an air crash in 1986) was the warrior-leader. He had all of the charisma of the dashing guerrilla but with the flexible demeanor of a pragmatist. Because he was no intellectual, he was easily persuaded to implement the disastrous policies that emerged from the Third Party Congress. However, his great sense of balance and flexibility allowed him to begin to move away from this "Great Socialist Project" from 1983 on. Machel knew a mistake when he saw one.

Finally, Chissano (foreign minister from 1976 until 1986 and president since 1986) reigns as the cool-headed pragmatist. Chissano may lack the charisma of the previous two FreLiMo chiefs, but he possesses a sharp, cautious sense of the practical. His attributes are many. He is an effective delegator of authority (not always successful in a party with such weak middle management as FreLiMo); he is a superb conciliator, both within FreLiMo and in Mozambique's regional and global relations; and he is an outstanding synthesizer of diverse ideas and traditions. If anyone can sustain the Mozambican union, it is Chissano. However, in a rather bizarre development, after the Peace Accord with ReNaMo in 1992, President Chissano became a devotee of the Maharishi Mahesh Yogi's Transcendental Meditation (TM). In his espousal of this belief system, President Chissano began to consider providing an official grant for popular land development to the TM organization. This project reportedly still remains under consideration in late 1994 with evident concern expressed by many of those who would be deprived of the right to occupy their land.

Despite this development, Chissano remains a relative beacon of light. His presence continues to be effective and popular despite the deplorable conditions which have dominated the country, and despite the ongoing TM imbroglio. Because of him and his predecessors, FreLiMo remains a salient actor at the international level and the continuing party of choice at the troubled domestic level.

■ Lurking Sources of Illegitimacy

Because of a number of conjoining factors, FreLiMo faces multiple challenges which could further delegitimize its rule. Government-related issues include rising crime; increasingly pervasive corruption; deadening bureaucratic incompetence and red tape; and the looming involvement of the Maharishi in governmental affairs. The war more directly engendered extreme social dislocation and economic devastation, conditions that portray any government as helpless and its actions as futile. The present sense of hope for sustained peace in the population could easily ignite high expectations for improvement in their quality of life. Such unfulfilled expectations could leave FreLiMo as the continuing government with the blame for failed expectations, returning it to "square one" in its pursuit of legitimacy.

These increases in crime, corruption, and material expectation are not the sole derivative of the war against ReNaMo. As a result of the reformed economic system, FreLiMo maintains its international legitimacy through an established co-dominion with the representatives of international development finance. Economic structural adjustment allows FreLiMo the margin to maintain its international legitimacy while, concomitantly, freeing FreLiMo elites to transform their political privileges into economic ones. As is also the case in Eastern Europe, when the spoils of political victory meet a freed market, the result is characterized by heightened levels of crime, corruption, and chaos. The cost of greater individual freedom to speak, write, and act politically is higher prices for goods, higher expectations for material fulfillment, and, therefore, more corruption and crime. The benefits of this trade-off are seen through the eyes of the beholder.

■ Beyond the Settlement and the Election

This brief overview of FreLiMo's struggle to achieve political legitimacy suggests contrasting perceptions. FreLiMo has been and remains the only option for legitimacy, but its foundation for such legitimacy rests on a set of revolutionary principles which, however noble, were abused and distorted by subsequent government policies. The legacy of FreLiMo is that of a party that has been anything but pragmatic but which is now trying to redefine itself through pragmatism (although the TM factor deals a blow to this trend). The task has been made more difficult by an internal condition which has wreaked unimaginable suffering on the population. Although FreLiMo contributed to this condition, it did not cause it. Because it cannot be blamed for ReNaMo's senseless destructions, FreLiMo stands to gain from the existing internal settlement. However, the jury of civil society will be out until FreLiMo can demonstrate effective government without war and can stem the fragmentation exacerbated by the war.

The favorable confluence of external factors (the end of the Cold War, a negotiated settlement in South Africa, and the stabilizing support of Italy, the United States, Britain, Scandinavia, and other Western countries) and internal ones (the debilitating impact of the 1992 drought and the crystallization of a popular consensus for peace) forced the actors, and especially ReNaMo, into a negotiated settlement. In one of my earlier versions of this analysis—written in July 1992—I projected a signed settlement some time in early 1993. However, the forces of resolution were accelerated by the active intervention of regional interests, especially from Zimbabwe, and by the less noticeable withdrawal of the regional behemoth, South Africa. The year 1992 was the "ripe" moment for resolution. But this remains only the beginning. The need to ensure the cessation of hostilities (absent in Angola); to provide political "space" for ReNaMo; to tame and reshape the military (already initiated by a joint British-Zimbabwean training operation); and to pacify the countryside remains. These daunting tasks suggest that the relief and possible euphoria of the Mozambicans will be frustrated by recurring banditry and terror, albeit at lower and less organized levels; confusion in revamping the government and military; and chaotic conditions for external and internal refugees attempting to return or relocate. These conditions, particularly threatening because of the departure of ONUMOZ in December 1994, would likely cause a sense of deprivation and discontent among a population that would justifiably expect concrete improvement in their lives after long enduring the scourge of war.

The current condition of Mozambique is highly expectant because of the successful electoral process. As ONUMOZ departs, the electorate will be waiting to see if FreLiMo stalwarts will press for a return to the short-sighted authoritarianism of the late 1970s. The electorate also may be waiting to see if FreLiMo will give ReNaMo or any other minority parties a role to play in the new government commensurate with their electoral performance. This participation would be necessary to moderate FreLiMo much as it has with SWAPO's government in Namibia.

Much of the impending confusion would derive from the millions of refugees returning from Malawi, Zimbabwe, and South Africa, and from Maputo and other district capitals. Competing claims for former lands could create a bureaucratic nightmare which could trigger violence. This type of situation would serve only to exacerbate the existing corruption. Corruption is a byproduct of social disorganization, extreme inequality, and the free market. It invariably starts at the governmental level and works its way down. The pursuit of profit and the concept of corruption may be discernible to Western eyes but such a distinction is not so clear in the Third World.

In such circumstances the government will be the target of continuing criticism. If a constitutionally organized representative government exists in which political parties have acquired the credibility of vehicles for change, then the system has a chance to achieve legitimacy. However, those in power are never anxious to give it up and those out of power with claims against the existing government do not often wait to see if they can try their luck in a distantly forthcoming election. Indeed, those with such claims and with guns in their hands, and perhaps with external sources of financial support, can take such concerns into their own hands. The result of these actions can be the coup d'etat, thus leading to illegitimate government, or secessionist movements and a return to civil war. The emergence of ReNaMo was an external development but the perpetuation of ReNaMo became an internal condition.

The election demonstrated ReNaMo's transformation to a more constructive role. The question now exists whether FreLiMo can accommodate that transformation by recognizing an opposition whose accepted role can lead to a more permanent cessation of hostilities and the emergence of a legitimate government.

■ **Note**

1. In addition to the citations in the body of the chapter, the following references provided influence on my analysis: Davies 1991; Geffray 1990; Haulon 1984, 1991; Schneidman 1991; Schutz 1992; and Vines 1991.

8

Remaking the Ethiopian State

Edmond Keller

On May 25, 1991, the revolutionary regime of Ethiopia's Mengistu Haile Mariam collapsed under the weight of a civil war that had begun to intensify four years earlier. A coalition of opposition groups under the leadership of the Tigre People's Liberation Front (TPLF), calling itself the Ethiopian People's Revolutionary Democratic Front (EPRDF), marched triumphantly into the capital city, Addis Ababa, and assumed complete control of the reins of central political authority with limited bloodshed. Ethiopia's army of more than half a million was completely demoralized; it had all but lost its will to fight. Whole military units disbanded, and troops fled with their weapons into Kenya, Djibouti, Somalia, and Sudan. The central government, which at the height of the consolidation of Ethiopia's Marxist-Leninist state had effectively penetrated virtually all aspects of social life, lost its ability to govern (see Clapham 1988).

Days before the EPRDF takeover, President Mengistu had fled to exile in Zimbabwe, creating a power vacuum and leaving the government in the hands of a powerless prime minister who was charged with finding a political solution to Ethiopia's civil war. It was too late. Events overtook the U.S.-brokered peace talks taking place in London. What resulted was the negotiation of the complete abdication of the Ethiopian government, and the relatively peaceful assumption of power by the EPRDF.

Once again, the Ethiopian state had collapsed. This had occurred numerous times in history, and each time, although the road to reconstitution was long and difficult, it was able to reconstitute itself. The Ethiopian state traces its history back over two millennia, reaching early prominence as the ancient city-state of Axum that flourished between the sixth and tenth centuries A.D. (Keller 1988). Throughout its history, the state expanded and contracted depending on the relative military power of state leaders. By the late eighteenth century, in the Era of the Princes (Abir 1968), the state had all but ceased to exist. Political power became decentralized as the state regressed into feudal, regional compartments. Ethiopia (Abyssinia) was then only figuratively a unified state, nominally ruled by puppet emperors—fifteen of them between 1769 and 1855. Central authority was not effectively constituted until the reign of Emperor Tewodros II, beginning in 1855, and present geographic boundaries were not established until 1908. Thus began a period of state growth and power consolidation under four successive emperors, ending with the overthrow of Emperor Haile Selassie I by a military coup in 1974. The rule of Haile Selassie was interrupted by the Italian Fascist occupation of Ethiopia between 1936 and 1941. The imperial state administration was almost completely destroyed, to be replaced by Italian colonial administration. However, in 1941 Haile Selassie reassumed the throne, and with the aid of the British he was able quickly to reconsolidate and even strengthen his authority. In 1952, Ethiopia was joined in a federation with the Italian coastal colony of Eritrea, but the emperor abrogated the federation ten years later and sought to unify the whole country under his control. However, by 1974 the imperial regime had again lost its legitimacy, and there was a military takeover. The military leaders of Ethiopia over a seventeen-year period then attempted to build and consolidate their power and authority according to a revolutionary Marxist-Leninist blueprint (Ottaway 1990). The experiment failed, bringing the state again to the brink of collapse (Keller 1993).

The purpose of this chapter is to focus on the establishment, consolidation, and fall of Ethiopia's first revolutionary regime. The questions to be addressed are: Why did Ethiopia's first revolutionary regime fail to build a coherent and cohesive nation-state? and, What progress has been made thus far by the EPRDF government toward reconstituting the state?

■ Background to State Collapse

Ethiopia was not immune from the winds of change that began to blow throughout Africa following World War II. Although it shares with Liberia the distinction among African states of never having experienced European colonialism, under Emperor Haile Selassie it faced some of the same problems as did European colonialists during the anticolonialist era. Until his removal in 1974, Haile Selassie had worked skillfully in international circles to project an image of Ethiopia as a multiethnic but unified state; but beneath the surface, ethnic claims to self-determination were being suppressed. In the course of imperial expansion between 1855 and 1908, successive Ethiopian emperors from the Amhara and Tigre ethnic groups had systematically secured through conquest and diplomacy territories occupied by other ethnic groups. Ethiopia today consists, in all, of more than forty different ethnic groups, some of whom (such as segments of the Oromo, Afar, and Somali peoples to the south and east) continue to claim that Ethiopia, by incorporating them into the empire, violated their right to self-determination.

The empire-state maintained control of territories incorporated since the mid-1800s by force of arms and exploited both the land and the people of these areas. In the periphery, imperial authority was initially exercised by the emperor's army and through *ketemas,* garrison towns. Ketemas were erected throughout the country, but they became particularly important in administering Oromo and Somali areas. These towns housed soldiers dispatched to act as "watchmen" for the crown, as well as to maintain law and order as necessary. The contrast between the indigenous populations and the agents of the state, who were for the most part foreign to them, and who resided in and around ketemas, was exceedingly sharp. There were no meaningful efforts to integrate the broad masses of subject peoples into the expanded political system, except to forcibly impose the Amhara-Christian culture upon them and to extract economic resources from them. This in large measure inhibited the development of a sense of Ethiopian national identity among the people of the southern periphery.

Under Haile Selassie, Ethiopia's economic development was heavily dependent on coffee production. Most of the coffee was produced in peripheral areas occupied by the Oromo people and characterized by landlord-tenant relations, mostly between Amhara-Tigre or "Amharized" (assimilated) settler-landlords, and Oromo tenants (Holcomb and Ibssa 1990). Very little state effort and few resources were devoted to delivering social services to these areas. The same pattern was repeated in the Afar area, targeted by Haile Selassie for the development of large-scale agribusiness enterprises, as well as in the Somali-inhabited Ogaden, valued mainly for the potential of its oil deposits. For the most part, Haile Selassie was able to repress sentiments for self-determination among the Oromos, Somalis, and Afar throughout his reign, largely with the aid of military and economic assistance from the United States.

By the early 1960s, however, ethnic and class contradictions began to manifest themselves. Significantly, at the same time that the new leaders of African states were throwing off the yoke of European colonialism and attempting to implement independent rule, Haile Selassie was being challenged to modernize the Ethiopian state in order to address such challenges as nation-building, state-building, legitimacy, and development. He pursued each of these objectives simultaneously, with varying degrees of success.

In the end, worldwide economic crisis came to exacerbate the domestic problems the emperor was trying to address. By 1973 the legitimacy of his regime was being widely called into question; the country's economy was severely underdeveloped and in a shambles; and the Eritrean nationalist movement was proving that it was now a military force that could not be taken lightly. In large measure, the regime of Haile Selassie collapsed because it could not effectively address the multiple challenges it faced, particularly in times of economic and political crisis.

When Haile Selassie was overthrown, nationalistic sentiments seemed to be unleashed. The new military government at first held out hopes that it would work hard to find an acceptable solution to the claims of Ethiopia's various nationality groups; that is, with the exception of the claims of Eritrean nationalists. Rather than extend the hand of conciliation, peace, and friendship toward Eritrea, the new regime attempted to crush the Eritrean liberation movement once and for all. Initially, the military government tried to win over dissident nationality groups through social and economic reforms, but this strategy soon failed. Between 1976 and 1978 the country was nearly torn apart as serious challenges to the state were being waged, not only in Eritrea, but also in the Ogaden and at the center, by groups opposed to the regime on ideological and political grounds.

In a climate of escalating violations of human rights, and internecine warfare, Ethiopia's superpower patron, the United States, attempted to force the increasingly radical regime to moderate its policies, but the move failed. Relations between the two countries were completely severed in April 1977, Ethiopia turning to the Soviet Union in its search for an alternative source of military assistance. This aid was crucial, as it allowed the now Marxist-Leninist regime of Mengistu Haile Mariam over the next decade to consolidate its power (Harbeson 1988; Halliday and Molyneux 1981).

Following near state collapse in the late 1970s, the Mengistu regime set about attempting to harmonize its policies with its ideology. Central to this effort was the creation of an effective state apparatus—a party-state—comprised of disciplined cadre and effective instruments of control and coercion that penetrated every corner of society. After initially questioning the necessity for a civilian vanguard party, the Mengistu regime seems to have been convinced by the crisis of the late 1970s that state survival required such a party. The Workers' Party of Ethiopia (WPE) was inaugurated in 1984, both to control politics and to legitimize the regime and its policies.

The WPE was supposed to be committed to people's democracy and broad popular participation in party affairs. In reality this was not the case; for example, of the 123 members of the WPE's Central Committee, 79 were military or police officers, and overall, party memberships consisted at most of 50,000 "committed communists" (Brooks 1987). What was striking about these developments was the fact that, despite serious efforts by the Mengistu regime to create an aura of legitimacy for itself through the party, it continued to avoid dealing forthrightly with the "national question." No ethnic groups were represented among the mass organizations that made up the WPE. In fact, anyone who raised nationality issues was branded as a "narrow nationalist" and "anti-revolutionary."

The Mengistu regime realized that it would have to demonstrate a commitment to economic development in order to enhance its legitimacy and neutralize the claims of various ethnic groups to self-determination. After a rocky beginning, the regime made some slight improvement in the quality of life, the opportunity structure, and the economy during its middle years. The feudal land tenure system was swept away, and all rural and most urban land became the property of the state, with rural usufruct distributed to meet family basic needs or to satisfy market demands as determined by the state (Keller 1988: 213–244). However, the situation of the peasantry remained far from ideal. Land fragmentation was a problem, and plots of land were often too small or too poor for family needs.

The nationalization of urban property had almost as profound a social impact as the takeover of rural land. Income from confiscated urban property became a significant part of the state's budget. Hundreds of thousands of low-cost housing units were built. Severe curbs were placed on the free market and individual entrepreneurship as the state attempted to establish a command economy.

Impressive gains were made in some areas of social policy. Over the first thirteen years of the revolution, the illiteracy rate dropped from 90 percent to less than 40 percent; and there was dramatic improvement in formal educational opportunities and access to professional health care and health-care facilities. But in the end, the patterns of inequality that had characterized the imperial era persisted to the last days of the Mengistu regime. This is not to say that the regime did not attempt to reverse the tide through economic reforms; only that it failed.

In November 1988, President Mengistu announced a package of reforms intended to promote private sector investment in industry, mineral exploration, agriculture, and tourism. He acknowledged agricultural production had declined by 0.4 percent per year between 1980 and 1988, even though the agricultural sector had received almost 25 percent of public investment over the period. He pledged the continued commitment of his government to socialism, but admitted drastic measures were necessary in a time of crisis (Workers' Party of Ethiopia 1990).

A New Economic Policy was unveiled at the 11th Plenum of the Central Committee of the WPE in March 1990. Under its terms, Ethiopia would have a mixed economy of state, private, and cooperative sectors. State enterprises were to be given managerial autonomy, to allow them to operate much in the manner of private enterprises (*Yekatit Quarterly* 1990). The controversial villagization program, designed to move the majority of the rural population into nontraditional clustered villages, was scrapped, and laws were passed guaranteeing farmers legally recognized land tenures, the right to hire private labor, and the freedom to invest private capital in commercial farming ventures. This signaled the end of the regime's attempt to develop a centrally planned economy.

These were dramatic reforms, but the Mengistu regime was unable to vitalize the economy. Foreign investors did not rush into Ethiopia and the domestic economy continued to be devoted mainly to food production and distribution. War had come to dominate Ethiopian life: defense took 50 percent of the annual state budget.

Mengistu also pledged to open up the political system, but little progress was made in this direction either. The government, by default, had lost its ability to control social life. Mengistu's pronouncements, instead of leading to a rapid return of former exiles or to the creation of political parties, resulted only in the removal of Marxist-Leninist icons from public places and the changing of the name of the WPE to the Ethiopian Democratic Unity Party. Systematic plans were not spelled out for a movement toward multiparty democracy. And the country's several internal wars raged on.

■ **Causes of the Collapse of the People's Democratic Republic**

Like the Haile Selassie regime before it, the Mengistu regime failed effectively to address the "national question." It attempted to downplay the issue by introducing a new social myth based upon the principles of "scientific socialism" (Keller 1988: 191–212), which hold that ethnicity is not a legitimate organizing principle; instead, people are grouped into mass organizations based upon their economic or social roles and positions. At the same time, it was clear to the Mengistu regime that a solution had to be found to the nationalities problem. Their answer: to found the Institute for the Study of Ethiopian Nationalities, an organization to draft a new constitution that would enhance the legitimacy of the regime and lay the groundwork for resolution of the nationalities question.

In early February 1987, the new constitution, a hybrid that resembled the Soviet and Romanian Marxist-Leninist constitutions, was submitted to the populace and received a reported 82 percent approval from 96 percent of those eligible to vote. The constitution established the People's Democratic Republic of Ethiopia (PDRE), with an 835-member national Shengo (assembly) and gave strong powers to the president. Once the Shengo was elected and held its first sessions, in September 1987, one of the main pieces of enabling legislation had to do with the administrative reorganization of the country. In an effort to defuse nationalist discontent, the Shengo created twenty-four administrative regions and five so-called autonomous regions—Eritrea, Assab, Dire Dawa, Tigre, and Ogaden. By granting autonomous status to Assab and Dire Dawa, the regime separated the two economic cores from the regions of Eritrea and the Ogaden respectively.

Despite this gesture of regional reorganization, the response of most nationalist movements fighting the Mengistu regime was swift and threefold. They rejected the PDRE initiative, increased their military activities, and began to cooperate among themselves. The Eritrean People's Liberation Front (EPLF) perceived the move to be nothing but "old wine in new bottles," a continued effort by Ethiopian "colonialists" to deprive the Eritrean people of their right to self-determination (EPLF 1987); it continued to call for a UN-sanctioned referendum on independence. The Tigre group (TPLF) and the Oromo Liberation Front (OLF) also dismissed the reforms as insignificant, stepping up military pressure on the regime. At the same time, the EPLF and the TPLF agreed to coordinate military strategy, and the TPLF began to organize a coalition of forces opposed to the Mengistu regime: the EPRDF (Dagne 1992b). Two years later, the OLF also coordinated some of its activities with the EPLF and the EPRDF. However, it is important to note that the OLF did not formally join the EPRDF coalition, maintaining its separate identity throughout. The EPRDF created its own Oromo affiliate, the Oromo People's Democratic Organization (OPDO), from soldiers who had either defected from Mengistu's army after an abortive coup in 1989 or were prisoners of war captured in past battles against Ethiopian forces. The EPRDF also created similar organizations to include other ethnic groups.

Meanwhile, the Mengistu regime, rather than having enhanced its legitimacy by the creation of the WPE, the PDRE, and the regional structure, had exposed its vulnerability. In late 1988, with Ethiopia in the throes of yet another major drought and the regime under pressure from the nationalist movements, the Soviet Union informed Mengistu that it would soon cease to provide military assistance (Perlez 1989). Mengistu declared a state of emergency and ordered "everything to the warfront." Workers were assessed one month's salary to augment the defense effort and all males between the ages of thirteen and fifty-five were subject to national conscription. The ranks of the Ethiopian military swelled to more than five hundred thousand by 1990.

The beginning of the end for the Mengistu regime—and also signaling the state's collapse—was an abortive coup in May 1989, while Mengistu was on a state visit to East Germany in search of military aid. He hastily returned to the country and the coup was brutally put down in short order (Battiata 1989). However, in the process his army began to collapse from within. Whole military units defected, taking their arms and equipment with them to join opposition forces. Over the next two years, the TPLF and its umbrella organization, the EPRDF, came to control all of Tigre and large segments of Wollo, Gondar, and Shoa. In Eritrea, the EPLF took over all but the major towns of Asmara, Massawa, and Assab. By 1990 the rapidly declining military position of the Ethiopian forces on both the Eritrean and home fronts, and the loss of political will on the part of Mengistu himself, had overtaken U.S. attempts to broker a peace between Ethiopia and the EPLF (Henze 1992) and Italian efforts to do the same with the TPLF. Even as plans were being made for an all-parties peace conference in London, the EPRDF tightened its encirclement of Addis Ababa, and the EPLF overran Ethiopian garrisons at Massawa and closed in on Asmara. Finally, on May 21, 1991, the U.S. assistant secretary of state for African affairs, Herman Cohen, secured the departure of Mengistu from Addis Ababa to exile in Zimbabwe. Before he left, Mengistu had appointed a new prime minister, Tesfai Dinka, to lead the Ethiopian delegation to the London peace talks. Even though EPRDF forces were poised less than one hundred miles from the capital city, ready to enter at any time, the Ethiopian government seemed still to feel that as a sovereign state it held the upper hand in negotiations with dissidents. When the talks opened on May 27, they were almost immediately suspended. Accusing the U.S. delegation of not acting in good faith, the Ethiopian delegation contended that the United States had ordered the EPRDF to advance on the capital and take it over, after previously agreeing that this would not happen until a transitional government had been agreed to. The U.S. delegation countered that they had asked the acting president of Ethiopia, Tesfaye Gabre Kidan, to arrange for the EPRDF to enter the city.

When the talks in London convened, the die had already been cast. The week following Mengistu's flight there was a massive airlift of some 16,000 Ethiopian Jews (*Africa Watch* 1991: 373–375), and on May 28 the stage was set for the triumphant entry of the EPRDF forces into Addis Ababa (*Africa Watch* 1991: 255–256). Law and order had broken down in the city and soldiers in the Ethiopian army defected in droves. One city garrison after the other on the road to Addis Ababa fell as the rebels advanced. The country was thrown into near anarchy.

■ Putting the State Together Again?

Any regime that attempts to restore state effectiveness must be guided by competent, politically committed leaders, working systematically to establish legitimacy and develop trust among society's disparate groups. The EPRDF regime initially attempted to present the public image that it had the political will effectively to reconstitute the Ethiopian state, but it demonstrated that the autocratic tendencies of the revolutionary movement continued to predominate in the thinking of the EPRDF leadership. At first, continuing its wartime efforts, the EPRDF sought to form a broad-based political pact involving most, if not all, of the political groupings that seemed to matter, except for those seriously opposed to EPRDF leadership (these included former members of the WPE and the government of the deposed regime). Consequently, radical leftist groups such as the Ethiopian People's Revolutionary Party (EPRP), and the All-Ethiopian Socialist Movement, and several conservative Ethiopian nationalist groups such as the Coalition of Ethiopian Democratic Forces (COEDF), were left out. At the same time, the OLF, the Afar Liberation Front (ALF), and several Somali organizations agreed to be a part of the pact. By the summer of 1992, the number of registered political parties had grown to more than two hundred, but only a couple of handfuls had significant numbers (Joint International Observer Group 1992; Dagne 1992a).

The leadership of the EPRDF moved quickly after their victory to establish a transitional government. A national conference for this purpose was convened in July 1991—an attempt on the part of the EPRDF rapidly to secure widespread acceptance. It resulted in the signing of a transitional charter by representatives of some thirty-one political movements, the creation of a Council of Representatives with eighty-seven members, and the establishment of the Transitional Government of Ethiopia (TGE). The TGE was composed of the president's and prime minister's offices and an ethnically mixed council of seventeen ministers representing seven ethnic groups. The EPRDF had the largest single bloc in the Council of Representatives (National Democratic Institute 1992: 15), with thirty-two seats, and the OLF, until its withdrawal from the government in late June 1992, was the second largest, with twelve seats.

The charter declared that the transitional period was to last no more then two and a half years. The Council of Representatives was given the authority to "constitute" a commission to draw up a draft constitution. In November 1993 the commission published a discussion paper of constitutional concepts, and in April 1994 a draft constitution was distributed for public consideration. The revised constitution will be submitted to a constituent assembly for ratification. This assembly was selected in a June 5, 1994, election that was boycotted by non-EPRDF parties. The TGE suggested that it was committed to broadening the voices represented in the constituent assembly to include many groups left out of the discussions leading up the charter agreement. Key groups such as the Amhara and Oromos continue to be poorly represented.

In a bold and controversial departure from the policies of past regimes, the national conference committed the TGE to honor the outcome of an internationally monitored referendum on the future of Eritrea. From this starting place, the TGE and the Provisional Government of Eritrea (PGE) developed close working relationships in both economic and political areas.

Cordial and cooperative relations between the two governments continued after Eritrea's declaration of independence following the referendum in April 1993.

Significantly, the charter articulates the TGE's commitment to the fundamental principles of the Universal Declaration of Human Rights of the United Nations. Individuals are accorded freedom of conscience, expression, association, and peaceful assembly, as well as the right to engage in unrestricted political activity, provided these activities do not infringe upon the rights of others. However, human rights violations on the part of the TGE continued into 1994.

Perhaps the two most important provisions of the charter are articles II and XIII. Article II asserts the right of all of Ethiopia's nationalities to self-determination, the preservation of the national identities of each group, and the right of each nationality to govern its own affairs within the context of a federated Ethiopia. Article XIII states that "there shall be a law establishing local and regional councils defined on the basis of nationality." The provision represents a dramatic departure from the policies of previous regimes on the "national question." The new policy has prompted protests and demonstrations among Ethiopian nationalists both at home and abroad. Moreover, the EPRDF government, despite its best intentions, seems to have acted too fast, without thinking this issue through and carefully planning for the implementation of the new policy. The result has been widespread misunderstandings that have led in some places to low-intensity civil war.

In its efforts to implement the terms of the charter with respect to establishing autonomous regions based upon ethnic identities, the TGE issued a law creating fourteen new regions, of which two—Addis Ababa and Harar—were designated chartered cities.

All of the regions except the chartered cities were established to conform to a census determination of the predominant ethnic groups within the particular region. The two chartered cities are treated as special cases because of their multiethnic character and their particular cultural histories. The nationalities able to command their own distinct regions were the Oromo, Tigre, Amhara, and Somali. Smaller and somewhat less homogeneous regional entities dominated by one or two ethnic communities include Wolayta, Kaffa, Afar, and Gurage-Hadiya. A region consists of a collection of districts (*woreda*). By far the largest region is Oromo, consisting of some 220 woreda out of 600 for the whole country, followed by Amhara (126 woreda), Tigre (62), and Somali (47).

The basic unit of national/regional self-government is the woreda, whose administration is to be elected according to democratic principles, and all nationalities, no matter what their size within the woreda, are to be guaranteed representation. Although the central government remains

supreme, particularly in matters of defense, foreign affairs, fiscal and economic policy, and citizenship, the law gives local regional governments
broad executive, legislative, and judicial powers.

Contrary to the EPRDF's expectation, this new approach to dealing
with the national question did little to placate the yearnings of various
nationality groups for their assumed rights to self-determination. In fact,
the initiative had the opposite effect, broadening and deepening ethnic tensions. In part this was due to the pace at which administrative reform was
implemented. Some among the Oromo, for example, had their expectations
heightened that these reforms could eventually position the Oromo people
to declare their independence from Ethiopia. Elements of the OLF had long
hoped to establish the independent state of Oromia. However, it was clear
that the EPRDF-led government intended regional autonomy to mean *only
within the context of a unified Ethiopia*—a form of federalism.

Central to moving the country toward a constitution was a sequence of
elections, culminating in the election of a national assembly elected in June
1994 that would make the permanent constitution official. Initially, it had
been hoped that the autonomous regions could be created and regional and
local elections held within three months of the establishment of the TGE,
unless local conditions did not permit. However, these regional and local
elections had to be postponed for a year, and when they did happen they
were fraught with controversy, severely testing the fragile coalition that
had been put in place in 1991. In the early part of 1992, as the date for
regional and local elections approached, a mood of crisis created by ethnic
tensions intensified (National Democratic Institute 1992: 31–32; see also
below).

In preparation for the elections, the council declared that all armed
groups operating in the country—including the EPRDF—would have to be
"encamped." The EPRDF army had been designated by the council to serve
as an interim national army, throughout the country, and to provide police
services where none existed. However, in Oromo areas, tensions arose
between the EPRDF and Oromo cadre, sometimes erupting into armed conflict. The OLF had expanded the ranks of its military wing two- to threefold from its maximum strength of about eight thousand in 1991. This
expansion was made possible in part by the attraction of new recruits in
areas heavily populated by the Oromo, and also in part by the incorporation
of Oromos who had formerly been soldiers in Mengistu's army.

Securing encampment of the armed groups was no easy matter. In
early 1992, at Makele, the EPLF attempted to broker an agreement between
the EPRDF and the OLF. It was not until April that agreement was reached
on an encampment accord, calling for the encampment of the OLF into
eight major camps and sixteen smaller ones. The EPRDF forces were also
to be in four camps in Region 4 (Oromo) and in all but those areas in the

rest of the country where they were needed to maintain law and order. The whole encampment process was monitored by a tripartite commission, made up of 165 teams of three, with representation from the EPLF, the EPRDF, and the OLF.

The final piece in the electoral puzzle was laid down when the National Electoral Commission (NEC) was established in early 1992. The ten-member commission was multiethnic and drawn from the ranks of the Council of Representatives. Eventually, enough political stability was realized to allow for "snap elections" in April 1992, in 450 of Ethiopia's 600 woreda. The objective was to establish temporary local administrations with broad ethnic and political representation. Although these elections were only partly successful, with some results being canceled or disallowed, the TGE forged ahead with plans for regional and local elections in June (National Democratic Institute 1992).

As the elections approached in the spring and early summer of 1992, the NEC worked feverishly to put its infrastructure into operation at all levels. However, it met with only limited success. The failure to ensure that proper electoral institutions and procedures were in place and functioning was given by organizations such as the All-Amhara People's Organization (AAPO), the Ethiopian Democratic Action Group (EDAG), the Gideo People's Democratic Organization (GPDO), and the OLF, in part, as a reason for their eventually withdrawing from the elections with less than a week to go, joining the Islamic Front for the Liberation of Oromia (IFLO) that had withdrawn earlier. As a conciliatory gesture, on the eve of the elections, the NEC recommended that elections be postponed in additional areas of the country. In addition to postponements in Region 2 (Afar); Region 5 (Somali); Harar, and three woreda in Region 7 (Gurage/Hadiya), because of either "civil war conditions" or administrative difficulties (National Democratic Institute 1992: 11) postponements occurred in 37 woreda of Region 4 (Oromo), and in insecure areas of the periphery such as Regions 12 and 11 (Gambela and Kaffa). These actions on both sides called into question just what might be achieved by going forward with elections. The charter and the pact that had created it had been placed in serious jeopardy.

Accurate figures on how many potential voters were represented by the parties that refused to participate in the elections are hard to come by. Most estimates range between 50 and 60 percent of the voting-age population. Despite this, the elections went ahead as planned on June 21, 1992, even as the OLF decamped and broke into smaller units, triggering the resumption of civil war. However, by early 1993, the insurrection was largely contained, even though popular discontent persisted. Some of the opposition was in protest of the TGE's policy on Eritrea; other opposition related to the regime's "ethnic strategy." Some people favor a unitary Ethiopia and others continue to press for ethnically based secession for certain groups.

By the end of 1993, the governing coalition had considerably narrowed. In April of that year the TGE government ousted five political groups (calling themselves the Southern Coalition) from the Council of Representatives for endorsing a resolution adopted at a conference of opposition groups meeting in Paris, calling for a dissolution of the council. Thus the membership of the council was reduced to the representatives of the EPRDF and ethnically based parties it had created. Organized opposition inside the country by this time was generally repressed. Major ethnically based parties were completely shut out of the pact that formed the TGE or were forced out over the first two years of the transition.

In December 1993, the government allowed a "peace and reconciliation conference," organized by internal as well as exiled opposition groups, to take place. But some who returned from abroad to participate were arrested and participants were generally harassed by the government's agents. Moreover, the TGE itself boycotted the conference, demonstrating that there was still a wide chasm between the TGE leadership and opposition groups.

Despite problems, the government of President Meles Zehawi has continued to press ahead with its liberalization policies. It has agreed to a structural adjustment program that has led to a devaluation of the Ethiopian birr, and to various market reforms to stimulate the economy. In October 1992, it formally abolished press censorship; however, there are provisions in the new law that give the government ample opportunity to exercise press censorship as it sees fit (Lycett 1993: 39). Newly formed independent presses proliferate, but journalists are constantly harassed and the TGE clearly attempts informally to censor the media.

In 1993 the TGE made appointments to Ethiopia's first independent judiciary. In addition, with the assistance of the Carter Center of Emory University, plans are under way to introduce human rights education in Ethiopia's schools, despite continued violations of human rights.

Political and economic reforms have been looked upon with great favor by foreign donors. For example, the Paris Club of public creditors canceled $300 million arrears left by Mengistu. On the eve of the 1992 elections, the United States agreed for the first time in twenty years to provide Ethiopia with bilateral assistance ($95 million, out of a total of $800 million to be delivered over several years). In February 1992, the TGE and the World Bank agreed to the terms of a thirty-month, $700 million, multidonor Emergency Recovery and Reconstruction Project (ERRP).

The expectation of the TGE is that this much needed foreign assistance will provide it with the resources needed to address socioeconomic problems and thereby purchase legitimacy from the population. However, ethnic and political tensions continue to run high. In an obvious attempt to demonstrate its commitment to reducing mistrust among ethnic groups, in early 1993 the TGE announced that it was in the process of forming a multiethnic national army. This army has yet to materialize, and it is unknown whether, once it is in place, the EPRDF will allow it to assume a nonpolitical role.

■ Conclusion

In May 1991, the Ethiopian state and its revolutionary regime headed by Mengistu Haile Mariam collapsed under the weight of multidimensional and cumulative pressures emanating from within and without. Although the Mengistu government had tried to introduce a statist development strategy better to enable it to lead development, it had failed. Contradictions relating to Ethiopia's historic poverty and underdevelopment, as well as its inability to resolve the national question, persisted. Like other Ethiopian regimes before it, the TGE was unable to find a solution to the nationalities problem. After two years in power, in a dramatic reversal of policy, rather than try to suppress claims of ethnic self-determination the new government—Tigre-dominated—implemented a policy meant to demonstrate a respect for the language and cultures of historically oppressed nationalities, and a commitment to allowing them a certain amount of regional autonomy based upon their ethnic affinities. This new measure, instead of being a solution, served to heighten tensions and create a "revolution of rising expectations" among several ethnic communities, including the numerically superior Oromo.

The TGE initially orchestrated the creation of a pact among political organizations, most of which were based upon ethnic affinities. It promised to liberalize both politics and the economy. Indeed, it did implement a number of measures in that direction, the intent being to build a sense of trust among various groups and political elites, a trust that would lead naturally to the legitimacy of the new regime and its policies (Keller 1988: 237–239). However, the state had been so severely weakened and its coffers were so bare that the TGE's good intentions were not complemented by an ability effectively to implement its plans and policies. False starts and missteps on the part of the government led to charges of ethnic chauvinism and of veiled attempts to create a new colonialism. By the middle of 1993, the pact had sharply narrowed, being limited mainly to the EPRDF and its affiliated parties, and was unable to broaden again after that.

Constitution-making proceeded, but because of the heightened ethnic tensions, the process slowed considerably. The TGE came to realize that it

would be a grave mistake to advance too swiftly. It continued its liberalization policies, even as it became more and more isolated and autocratic.
Multiparty elections to install a new democratic government were delayed
indefinitely. However, even if these elections take place, they must be kept
in perspective. Pluralistic elections must be accepted for what they are—the
means to a democratic end and not an end in themselves. New democratic
institutions (e.g., independent judiciary, rule of law, free press, a multiethnic national army responsible to civilian authority, and so on) that work on
a regular basis must simultaneously be put into place. There must also be
developed a sense of mutual trust among the various groups and political
elites. Some progress has been made, but the solid reconstruction of the
Ethiopian state and society seems destined to be a long and difficult
process, with re-collapse a dogging possibility.

PART 3
STATES IN DANGER

9

The Collapse of the Socialist State: Angola and the Soviet Union

Leonid L. Fituni

The idea of comparing the collapse of the state in Africa and similar collapse in the Soviet Union may seem artificial and irrelevant to Russia's and Africa's problems. People are usually persuaded that Africa and post-Soviet newly independent states belong to two distant, nonoverlapping worlds, so obviously different that their comparison would be either forced or farfetched. However, as a Russian national who had spent nineteen years studying Angola, I found the last nine years of my own country's transition from socialism to democracy to be an uncanny Africa deja vu.

Rapid "ThirdWorldization" of Russian society showed how feeble is the wall, once so apparently strong, between the rich North and the poor South. The seemingly eternal welfare of a developed industrial society in the USSR turned practically overnight into a chaotic universe of Third World problems: mass poverty, hunger, regional conflicts and ethnic wars, deindustrialization and huge foreign debt, corruption of the elites and governing juntas, bloody coups d'état, outbreaks of long forgotten diseases, refugee problems, environmental degradation, and societal and state collapse. This constellation of problems was but too familiar to me from my Angolan experience. Many of the developments so new to Russians have already taken place (though on a smaller scale) in the rich African country of Angola, where a group of intellectual revolutionaries (or revolutionary intellectuals) attempted to erect a tower of Babel of socialism but failed, bringing suffering and misery to their nation. Recent attempts by their Russian counterparts to move in the opposite direction brought about the same result—the collapse of the state.

My personal experience shows that, no matter what the "scientific" definitions of the term are, a person immediately knows he is in a collapsed state the moment he arrives in one. However, setting broad limits to the term is indispensable. A collapsed state is a state whose economic, political, cultural, and civilizational links have been disrupted to such an extent as to have brought about drastic deterioration of its conditions of existence and subsequent undermining of its capacity to reproduce itself on an extended basis.

The aim of this chapter is to answer the questions: Why did the Angolan and Soviet states collapse? Is there a common pattern in the collapse of the two states? Are there ways to put them back together? What are the chances of collapse for states that are currently stable?

In both cases, the collapse of the state was the consequence of:

1. Attempts to implement reforms that the country was not objectively prepared to undergo
2. Strong foreign pressure and encouragement to plunge into these reforms
3. Heightened expectations of the population combined with populist promises on the part of the elites
4. Overestimation of the importance, volume, and effectiveness of outside support to the cause
5. Corruption of the elites and absence of the rule of law

■ Justification of the Comparative Study

As a first step, it is necessary to give a general idea of the magnitude of the downfall of both countries, and to provide evidence for the legitimacy of the comparison. Comparison is facilitated by the fact that the United Nations recently officially accorded the status of developing nation to all the Central Asian republics of the former USSR, to Georgia, and in late 1993 to the second most developed former Soviet republic, the Ukraine.

The Third World embraces about 150 extremely different countries, ranging from large economies like India and Brazil (or China) and finishing with small, remote, scarcely populated island states in the Pacific. What unites them in the eyes of world community is their predominantly backward state, inherent development problems, and the extremely low standard of living of a large part of their population. In some respects the Soviet Union fell into the category of *developing nation* all through the years of its existence (particularly in terms of the standard of living, but also structurally). In the 1990s, the resemblance is even more pronounced: the economy and society are unprecedentedly close to what is to be found in most developing countries of the Third World. A dichotomy based on income levels, the poor versus the rich countries, defined by the World Bank, unambiguously puts post-Soviet geographic formations (republics) into the ranks of the wealthier poor countries.

In fact, according to the 1993 edition of the World Bank's *World Development Report* (1993b: 326), all former Soviet republics except Russia, Belorussia, and the Baltics are put into the category of the "lower Middle Income" country group. This is the group where one finds Angola and some other African states (Djibouti, Mauritius, Namibia, Swaziland, Cameroon, Cape Verde, Congo, Côte d'Ivoire, Senegal). Russia, Belorussia, and the Baltic republics find themselves in the company of better-off Botswana, Seychelles, Gabon, and South Africa. However, unlike those countries, the newly independent former Soviet states continue their social and economic nosedive, and at least two of them will soon rejoin their sister republics in the lower group. On the other hand, Russia and some of the other former Soviet republics are obviously industrialized countries. However, the type of industrial development, being based mainly on primary commodity production (oil and gas production, mining), and their place in the world trade and international division of labor (i.e., suppliers of raw materials to Western developed economies) also make them similar to Third World countries.

Their joint share in the world GNP is diminishing and there are no visible signs of improvement in the situation. The per capita national income of Russia has fallen to 40 percent of its highest point. The crisis has affected all sectors of the economy. The most important economic proportions have been deformed; and there has been a sharp decline in both investment activity and agricultural production. The monetary system is on the brink of collapse and the situation in the consumer market is critical. There has been mass idleness of enterprises and of whole sectors for lack of materials (including imported ones), numerous instances of failed contract deliveries, and bans imposed by local authorities on the export of particular products outside the region. The share of manufacturing in the GDP is decreasing. The manufacturing sector itself is composed mainly of old industries and outdated imported machinery. Export of raw materials is the main currency earner. With domestic industrial output down to about 30 percent of 1985 output in 1993/94, the Russian economy was thrown back to the post–World War II levels of the mid-1950s. The country is going through its second comprehensive redistribution of wealth in this century. All private citizens were deprived of their savings overnight in 1992, when President Boris Yeltsin freed the prices in the supermonopolized economy. It has become another major Third World country, like India, Brazil, or Argentina.

The comparison may sound unbelievable, but the size of the economy aside, Russia's economy in many ways is now an inflated copy of Angola's. The state continues to exist due to the sale of oil and diamonds. In 1993, about 75 percent of foreign currency exports earning was provided by the fuel commodities sector (oil and gas) and about an additional 7 percent by diamond exports, exactly the composition of Angola's export structure. The only difference is that Angola's third major export commodity is coffee; that of Russia is nonferrous metals and armaments. Here Russia looks more like Brazil. Even the sectors like science, of which Russia was

once legitimately proud, are in ruins. The state budget for 1994 did not
even foresee allocation for the Academy of Sciences, a state-financed organization responsible for over 70 percent of research and development activity and nearly all fundamental studies in the country.

The standard of living for the average person in the former Soviet
Union has dropped to a point very close to that in the least developed
nations. Because of a slump in production and the depressed exchange rate
of the ruble, in 1993 the average annual monetary income of an employed
person in Russia equaled U.S.$350. Social problems like poverty, critically
low standards of health care and education, and astonishing inequality in
income add to the gruesome picture of the ThirdWorldization of the former
Soviet economy. Like the Portuguese once in Angola, many Russians are
now leaving former Soviet republics where their ancestors have lived for
three hundred years and more.

The countries that appeared after the USSR had collapsed are no
longer big brothers to developing nations. They are their rivals, competing
with them for Western aid, food, and investment. In the future they can
either fight each other or band together with the other Third World countries, trying to act on a unified front. The transition is accelerated by the
ineffectiveness of the present economic strategies of the leadership of the
"Newly Impoverished States" (NIS). Their political and educational background—their *life experience*—has trained them to implement theoretically
flawless turnkey schemes, elaborated by their superiors in politburos, rather
than to work out something original that really answers the requirements of
the situation.

On the other hand, it is obvious that nearly all present regimes in
Eastern Europe have a temporary, transitional nature. They were brought to
power in order to destroy the past system, and the old state that represented
it, rather than to construct a sophisticated new economic edifice. In short,
the Soviet experience is that of a rapid collapse of the state. In less than ten
years, Russia slid from the position of a superpower to that of a Third
World country. As a result of Gorbachev-Yeltsin reform policies, the
potential population density has fallen below the current number of inhabitants; current levels of agriculture and industry cannot support the existing
number of people. Russians, as a nation, are dying out. The process is not
compensated for, even given the growing number of Russian immigrants
repatriating to the land of their ancestors from now independent former
Soviet republics.

Angola, on the other hand, never left the ranks of underdeveloped
nations. In the early 1970s, it approached the starting position from which
(provided the situation continued to be favorable) it might have embarked
on the course of rapid, East Asian type development. Had the ideological
factors not intervened, Angola might have been speaking soon about a

newly industrialized oil-rich state, an African dragon with a developed manufacturing industry and highly skilled manpower. However, the contradictions between different factions of the national liberation movement proved to be irreconcilable and the foreign support they enjoyed made reformers believe they could settle their differences by the use of military force.

For more than forty years, Angola has lived in conditions of war. Up to the mid-1970s, the warring sides were, on the one hand, the Portuguese army, and on the other, anticolonial nationalist movements: the People's Movement for the Liberation of Angola (MPLA), the National Front for the Liberation of Angola (FNLA), and later the National Union for the Total Independence of Angola (UNITA). In 1975, Portugal withdrew its forces from Africa, but the national liberation movements continued to fight each other, each seeking to secure control over the entire country. In this war, they extensively relied on outside support in the Cold War conflict.

During the forty years of war, two generations of Angolans have been born and reached maturity. They have never lived in conditions of peace and stability and do not know what peaceful development of the state is about. The country underwent miraculous metamorphoses. The first half of those forty years (between 1953 and 1973) was the time of a dynamic leap in development. In 1973 Angola had the highest average per capita income in sub-Saharan Africa. During the next twenty-odd years, it plunged into the abyss of economic political and cultural crisis, losing its dynamism and all of its previous achievements. Even today—after "free and fair" elections—the production levels of 1973 remain unattainable targets for an absolute majority of Angolan industries (excluding the oil industry). From respectable wealthiness, Angola descended into crying poverty. The downfall was not experienced at an equal level of pain by different segments of the population. More than 300,000 ethnic Portuguese left the country for Portugal. Of the remaining Angolan population, more than 25 percent belong to a traditional subsistence sector. Their standard of living was always low, but even they felt the consequences of collapse. Their limited access to the market was further curtailed.

■ Forces Moving Behind the Collapse

In order to know the real causes of state collapse, it is necessary to clearly see what are the main agents of collapse and what is their nature. In Angola, the prospects for self-sustained development were undermined primarily by the rivalry between the forces of national liberation—anticolonial movements that united in their ranks intellectuals, petite-bourgeoisie, and to a small extent peasants and workers. In Russia, the opposition consisted almost exclusively of intellectuals, who in later stages were joined by part of the government and party nomenclature and the emerging entrepreneurial class. They formed a democratic movement that demanded the dismantling of the old state.

Forerunners of the ruling elites of the 1990s started to appear in both countries in the mid-1950s. An important feature of both new leadership groups was their extroversion. They proclaimed liberation of their countries but ideologically were too dependent on foreign support. This dependency ultimately turned them into worshippers of foreign divinities that were misunderstood and rejected by the masses. This major flaw remained their weakest point, and later it turned into the principal cause of the collapse. However, this foreign orientation and support helped them to gain power, and to hold it up till now.

In Angola, the mid-1950s was the time of unprecedented growth of the national liberation movement. Under the influence of changes in Africa and Europe, the idea of national liberation from Portuguese colonial rule was spreading among Angolan middle-class intellectuals. The seeds fell into good soil and bore a plentiful harvest. In the 1950s, the first contemporary anticolonial movements appeared. FNLA and MPLA were among the earliest, with UNITA soon following them. Though still very distant from what they are now, they nevertheless stated their rejection of the existing (colonial) state and declared the goal of building a new one.

Until 1976, the MPLA was more of a nationalist African movement of the political left than a Marxist party. UNITA openly declared itself to be an adherent of Chinese socialism, though in fact it, too, was a nationalist group, whose leadership, however, was more inclined toward the center of the political spectrum. Under the influence of its pro-Moscow orientation, MPLA's ideology and political line quickly changed to Marxist socialism. In 1978, the popular movement was transformed into a vanguard Marxist-Leninist party. The construction of socialism was named the goal of the development, not only in the party program but also in the new constitution. The institutional structure of the state was cloned from the Soviet one, with the National Assembly in Luanda and provincial assemblies in every provincial capital becoming representative bodies.

In Russia, the 1950s witnessed the first attempts to rid the state of rigid concepts of Stalinism. The USSR was opening vis-à-vis the outer world. Ideological shutters were set slightly ajar. For an ordinary Russian, secret manifestations of discontent no longer equaled inevitable imprisonment. The first dissidents began to appear, usually intellectuals living in big cities with contacts in the West. They, too, demanded an improvement in the state system, and later this evolved into a complete rejection of the Soviet state.

An evolution similar to Angola's took place in Russia. Having started from protection of human rights, the Russian democratic movement, under the influence of close ties with outsiders (in this case, the United States and Europe), became more and more anti-Soviet, singling out the state as the principal target of their struggle and finally selecting market capitalism in Russia as their political aim. The presidential republic mirrored the U.S. system. After the October 1993 coup, a bicameral federal assembly replaced the Congress of People's Deputies.

In the long run, dependence on outside support forces a political movement to adjust its goals to the demands of the main sponsor. In the case of Russia, the main sponsor was undoubtedly interested in the collapse of the Soviet state, which was seen as its main military enemy.

■ Unwillingness to Face Realities

The basic cause of the failure of political elites in Russia and Angola to deliver on their goals and the main reason for the ultimate collapse of their respective states was their narrow social base and their unwillingness to accept the realities of their nations. To some extent the failure was predestined by the social, ethnic, and cultural origins of those movements, and their unawareness of how to cope with practical problems of development and the workings of the economy.

Ethnic nationalism is justly seen as a major force in crises in Angola and the former Soviet Union. The factual side of the problem is well documented and thoroughly studied (Bender 1978). Historical contradictions and rivalry between northern and southern Angolans (represented respectively by the MPLA and UNITA) were regarded as the ultimate reason for the irreconcilable enmity of the two liberation movements. In fact, though rather important, these factors were not decisive in the Angolan tragedy. The personal ambition of Jonas Savimbi, the leader of UNITA, and of Augustinho Neto, the late founder of the MPLA and the first president of Angola, had far greater impact on the collapse of the state.

The same applies in Russia. In the early stages of the collapse of the Soviet state, the Gorbachev-Yeltsin rivalry was a far greater disruptive factor than the ethnic nationalism of the republics. When, later, political leaders tried to capitalize on ethnic ambitions of certain parts of the population, they awoke the dormant monster of nationalism.

In Angola, the MPLA did have the advantage of getting to construct and govern the new polity of Angola from the heart of its own ethnic regional stronghold. The new regime was a product of Luanda-Mbundu society, that 25 percent of the Angolan population most influenced by centuries of Portuguese rule. It was in that "central society" and other urban centers integrated within the colonial economy, as distinguished from the

STATES IN DANGER

more remote but majority "tributary societies" of peasants and herders, that economic and cultural protest first developed into organized anticolonialism in the 1950s and 1960s (Kitchen 1987: 18).

Similarly, the democratic reformist forces in Russia disseminated their influence from the capital and a few heartland industrial centers. These reformers were intellectuals, writers, scientists, journalists—the part of the population most influenced by Western ideas. The non-Russian element was very strong among them and they were more exposed to European and U.S. influences.

Both elites came to power primarily due to circumstances, rather than their own efforts to topple the old governors. As mentioned above, strong international support was crucial for them to stay in power. It is obvious that in those early days the MPLA was unable to contain UNITA's offensive against the capital without Soviet or Cuban aid. Neither would the Yeltsin regime have been able to stay in power without massive support from the West and advisory assistance from Western consultants.

■ Economic Reforms

Attempts to apply foreign civilizational models are most evident in the sphere of the economy. Between 1976 and 1985, Angola was increasingly trying to implement Soviet-style central planning. Massive nationalization brought approximately 65 percent of the GDP under the control of the state. Collective farms (agricultural cooperatives) were mushrooming in rural areas. The bureaucracy was rapidly increasing in numbers. Meanwhile, the economy remained in constant crisis, a situation created by the war and mismanagement. The realities of Angola were not responsive to classical socialist economic therapy.

After it became obvious that the Soviet Union no longer wished (nor was able) to maintain the level of assistance of the 1970s, Angolan leadership tried to adopt a more realistic and pragmatic economic line. In 1987, a policy of economic and financial sanitation was declared by President Eduardo dos Santos. It, too, did not bring long-term positive results. Economic liberalization was Angola's own choice, but to a significant degree it was a local response to Gorbachev's reformist efforts in the USSR; as the last of the Soviet leaders, he undertook an attempt to modernize the Soviet economy through "acceleration"—a fetish word used to denote liberalization, intensification, and increased efficiency of the economy.

In both countries, economic liberalization triggered a rapid spread of corruption. Unlike Gorbachev, President dos Santos had the courage to acknowledge this. Dos Santos even publicly declared that corruption had become the second most important problem of the state after the problem of the war (*El Pais,* June 27, 1990). By contrast, Soviet authorities did their best to play down the significance of the spread of corruption. A continuation of this policy turned reformed Russia into one of the most corrupt states in the world. The collapse was accelerated by the universal disregard for the law and by economic fraud and money laundering.

■ Democratization and the Collapse

When comparing the proposals for the reemergence of the state in the African and post-Soviet environments, one of the core questions is what type of sociopolitical regime proves to be most favorable for national reconstruction. Recent history shows that, under different regimes, the potential for peaceful transformation is not the same. An obvious relationship exists between the type of regime and the internal social and political situation in the country. Strategies of reform, methods of implementation, the tools used to safeguard internal peace as well as those of conflict management—these differ according to the type of regime, making the transformation quicker or slower.

The reformers' efforts to overcome the collapse of the state by changing the structures of institutions are measures intended to slow down, or even reverse, the causes of collapse. In both the Angolan and Russian cases, all previous efforts had been unsuccessful. Both the Soviet and Angolan experiences showed that creation of a multiparty system is neither a panacea nor a guarantee of democracy. Nevertheless, the transition in these countries from an authoritarian to a democratic form of governance is real. Hopefully, this process will end not in an established African-type or Russian-type democracy (as happened often in the past and is likely to happen in Russia) but in a new and genuine democratic system. Marrying democratic principles to the cultural heritage of Russia and Angola might be the optimal way of rapid progress and national recovery; however, the practices of the elites of the 1990s in both countries, and the recipes suggested to them by their foreign consultants, tend to stress that democracy is a set of principles that apply everywhere in the same way. Thus, following the violent confrontations of different durations, internationally monitored elections were held in both Angola and Russia. Their outcomes were very different, but in neither country did the elections change the course of state collapse.

Unlike Russia, where democratization and the new state went hand-in-hand in a zigzag manner, the pattern of democratization in Angola was circular. It can be easily divided into several stages. The milestones were several ceasefires in the civil war, multiparty elections, and the return to civil war. The attempted democratization process in Angola was distinct in a few important ways:

- A ceasefire in 1991 led to a genuine multiparty election in 1992 in which the party in power (MPLA) participated.
- A parliamentary election, judged "free and fair," was won by the incumbent (MPLA), which had been socialist-oriented for a long time.
- The obstacles to the democratization process that emerged after the 1992 election came more from the opposition (UNITA), which rejected the election outcome, than from the MPLA, which by almost all accounts has been cooperative in the process.
- Over two years after the election, efforts were still being made to bring about compromise and understanding between the protagonists in the Angola process. The MPLA declared its willingness to establish a coalition government if it won the elections, and to hold a run-off in the presidential election even though it was only half a percentage point short of a majority and UNITA received only 40 percent. Dissatisfied, it returned to its bloody war. The new truce of November 1994 is unstable.

In Russia, the period of institutional change started with the withdrawal from the Soviet constitution of Article 6, which announced that the Communist Party was the leading and guiding force in society. Other important institutional changes occurred only with Yeltsin's coming to power. Under him, the whole Soviet institutional system was dismantled and a new constitution was adopted. Dozens of new laws, elaborated with the help of U.S. and European advisers, took the place of old Soviet legal documents. As in Angola in the late 1970s, a great number of old laws and regulations continue to exist, often making it difficult for reformers to achieve their goals—but always useful for bureaucrats, some of whom turned the institutional chaos into their main source of enrichment.

■ The Costs of State Revival

Putting together a collapsed state primarily means creating conditions for self-sustained growth and decent living standards for society. Both economic and political logic are important in the process of national reconstruction. To be effective in pushing political and economic reforms, governments must have a comprehensive view of development, must be able to assure the realization of reforms by their civil servants, and must enjoy substantial autonomy from the influence of groups in society who would lose from the restructuring.

A discussion on the topic of economic and political liberalization brings to light different points of view. Some experts state that political liberalization must precede economic liberalization; others insist on the primacy of economic reforms. It is impossible to argue with the view that implementation of structural adjustment reforms in Angola and Russia caused the escalation of political repression. But looked at from another angle this becomes: It is mainly ill-considered government tactics of economic restructuring that provoke social conflicts. When economic grievances are bound up with religious or ideological movements, violence may become self-sustaining. In these conditions, the protection of group interests may outweigh purely economic demands. A coalition of social groups can be organized, fighting against repression and proclaiming political demands, and thus accelerating the process of political liberalization.

A growing middle class may also become the seedbed of political reform. The middle class simply refuses to be governed: instead it demands the right to govern itself. Its members demand their civil liberties, as well as the right to hold and express political opinions. Unfortunately for Russia's bourgeoisie, a clumsy (and confiscatory) price deregulation by the Yeltsin-Gaidar government virtually wiped out the middle class overnight on January 1, 1992. Professionals joined the poorest strata of society.

The success of national reconstruction in Angola and Russia runs into resistance from the different strata of the society, not because the population (taken as a whole) necessarily rejects national revival, but because the vital interests of certain groups are often endangered. The *social* costs of putting the state together may make the program's implementation completely unrealizable. Both the Russian and the Angolan experience show that the recuperative reforms face unprecedented obstacles. Austerity measures and redistribution of income, unavoidable during the implementation of economic reforms, dramatically change living standards on a group-by-group basis. Different groups reject different aspects of reform. Thus, businessmen reject higher taxes and higher prices on infrastructural services; farmers are against elimination of subsidies on agricultural inputs; employees of weaker public enterprises are afraid of the privatization of state property. The protests are expressed in different ways. In Russia, organized labor (e.g., miners in Vorkuta and Kuzbass) go on strike; unorganized and low-income urban groups riot (May 1 skirmishes in Moscow; September–October 1993 uprising). In both Russia and Angola, businessmen have become engaged in the flight of capital, migrant and skilled labor withhold remittances, and the public sector hoards import inputs and overborrows. In an inflationary environment, politically powerful groups (big business, the military, the bureaucracy) tend to guard their level of income through speculation and hoarding.

■   **Weariness in Angola, Anomie in Russia**

The year 1994 in Angola was a time of fierce fighting between the government and UNITA forces, while the peaceful settlement process went on under the auspices of the United Nations. UNITA's tactics at the negotiations were in many ways similar to that of the parties in the Bosnian war: every time some kind of agreement had been reached at the peace talks, UNITA tabled new demands and cited disobedience of field commanders as the cause for the breakdown of ceasefires.

Following the recommendations of intermediaries and trying to allay UNITA's grievances, the MPLA-led government agreed on creation of a government of national unity, offering UNITA four ministerial portfolios, seven vice-ministerial posts, as well as three provincial governor and seven vice-governor posts. UNITA demanded in addition the posts of the governor of Huambo and vice-governor of Malange provinces. These strategically important provinces divide the northern half of Angola in two. UNITA's claims for governing Huambo, an Ovimbundu province when their candidates won elections, seem legitimate, but the opposition's full control over Huambo and strong influence in Malange may strengthen ethnic separatism here and keep MPLA a strategic hostage to UNITA's demands. MPLA suggested that the post of Huambo governor be held by a neutral figure.

In early August 1994 both sides finally signed an agreement on the schedule of the UNITA army's demobilization, gradual withdrawal, and replacement by the newly elected authorities. However, the issues of power decentralization and UNITA's participation in the government of national unity remained under question. The November 1994 ceasefire, following the government's capture of Huambo, resolved these questions temporarily.

The two sides have not exhausted their war potential. To finance the war the government has unlimited oil resources at its disposal, while UNITA controls diamond fields in northeastern Angola. Endless bloody fighting in Angola had reached such intensity that humanitarian organizations stopped delivering relief supplies to internal regions of the country. About two and a half million Angolans have thus lost their only reliable source of subsistence.

It is obvious that there will be no speedy solution to the Angolan crisis. Angola's legitimacy as a unitary state is unquestioned, but the internal contradictions appear irreconcilable precisely because they have been artificially implanted and fostered from outside. In the mid-1990s, with external forces hardly interested in Angola's internal feuds, the confrontation lives on by itself, because the future of each of the warring parties depends on it. Up till now, each side has been more identifiable as an adversary of the other, rather than for any distinct intrinsic features, and surely not as an organizing force behind economic or nation-building achievements. The population in general is weary of continuous confrontation in the society and is divided based on habitual loyalties, rather than the policies and achievements of their leadership.

Here again an interesting parallel can be drawn with Russia. The December 1993 elections had a sobering effect on the Russian president and his immediate entourage. He deftly disposed of radicals in the executive branch, thus regaining a degree of support from the country's political center. Tight monetary policies reduced inflation by 300 percent (from an annual 1,400 percent in 1993) and to some extent stabilized the ruble, bringing commendation from the IMF. The fierceness of internal political confrontation practically disappeared during the two first months of 1994.

In the Russian provinces, nearly all powers, economic as well as political, were in the hands of executive authority. This new quality quaintly reminds one of the competence and powers of regional committees of the Party during communist times. The increased role of provincial governors was a side-effect of Yeltsin's October 1993 decrees aimed at crushing the Soviets, the old, local representative system.

Another pronounced change was the relative independence of the population from the authorities' decisions and of the elites from the population. This may be regarded either as a full collapse of state authority or as an achievement of democracy. The population no longer relies on state authorities for anything, be it security or employment. Nor does it really care what the authorities are doing at the top, and this fact is used by at least some new rulers to consolidate their own economic base. Meanwhile the population at large is engaged in the fight for survival—physical, moral, or economic. The nation is being filtered *naturally* for the strongest to be able to enter the bright capitalist future, much the same way it was *hand*-filtered in the 1930s allowing the "best" to be admitted to socialism. The provisional results are the same: death rates increase to a level nearly twice the birth rate.

From an individual's point of view the most unpleasant component of the current state of Russian society is lack of security in three basic spheres—physical, social, and economic. The present situation in Russia may be defined as a state of anomie, a phrase in social development for when universally accepted values are lost and no socially approved lines of behavior exist. It is a state of disorganization, rootlessness, and lack of purpose, identity, and ethical values (Durkheim 1986; Merton 1951).

What are the reasons for this anomie and the continued drifting apart of the population and the state elites? As in any revolution, Russia's transition to capitalism required the destruction of the old system of social organization, moral values, and human relations. The deformed vision and primitive understanding of capitalism and its ideals ("Money over everything") on the part of the majority of Russians, including the elites, combined with the rigid stance of foreign tutors from international financial institutions ("I am to be obeyed"), brought about total degeneration of the Russian state and society.

During 1992, in complete opposition to their proclaimed goals, the reformists (the rising Russian elite) wiped out an embryo of a middle class that might have become a cementing force of a modern Western-type society, based on the rule of law rather than on latent ties, corruption, and personal loyalties. This twist in Russian state history brought about the demise of its basic social functions. As in the years immediately following the 1917 Bolshevik revolution, the state once again became an instrument of implementation of the ideological (and/or financial) aspirations of a limited number of radicals.

The discrepancy between the proclaimed aims and the real consequences of the reforms has formed a strong belief among the population that the elites fighting for control of the state are only interested in perpetuating their own rule, leading not to a competitive, free market economy or a genuinely strong and independent state, but to a dependent quasi-capitalist Third World–type society run by oligarchies. Due to the limited perspectives of some of the "fathers of reform" and covetous aims of the others, the process of transformation and modernization of what once was a Soviet state resulted in an underdeveloped *comprador capitalism*. The country hardly feeds itself and no longer clothes itself. It is not capable of increasing or updating the means of production to develop itself on an enlarged basis. Its new entrepreneurial class in general does not invest in expanding production, but is satisfied with pocketing what old Soviet investments can still generate. The state is presented in the mass media as the greatest of evils. The decline in open confrontation throughout 1994 was to a great extent explained by growing disbelief in the elites and disappointment in the early ideals of the democratic movement. The nation realized it was practically unable to influence the scramble for power.

The state of anomie will most likely prevail in Russia until the process of wealth redistribution is completed. After that, the newly formed and consolidated elites will be interested in expanding the rule of law and enhancing the institutions of the state. Before that, it will be too early to speak about putting the Russian state together.

10

Zaire: Collapsed Society, Surviving State, Future Polity

Herbert Weiss

Has the Zairean state collapsed? In order to answer this question, one must distinguish between the state as a formal structure, which has in the past attained much of its legitimacy as a result of its relations with other states, and the state as the presumed authoritative manager of society. If one judges the internal functioning of the Zairean state as it exists in 1994, and indeed has existed for quite a few years, one must conclude that it has virtually disappeared. The state's "responsibility" to seek the welfare of its citizens has been almost totally neglected. In fact, little remains of the state's role as a provider of health care, education, justice, the maintenance of the country's infrastructure, and so forth. All of that has indeed collapsed. As Herman J. Cohen, former U.S. assistant secretary of state for Africa stated:

> To say that Zaire has a government today would be a gross exaggeration. A small group of military and civilian associates of President Mobutu, all from the same ethnic group, control the city of Kinshasa by virtue of the loyalty of the 5,000-man Presidential Guard known as the DSP. This same group also controls the Central Bank which provides both the foreign and local currency needed to keep the DSP loyal. While the ruling group has intelligence information about what is going on in the rest of Zaire, there is no real government authority outside the capital city (Cohen 1993).

As noted, there are areas where the state and the Mobutu regime that controls it do exercise power. It controls force and money, those internal levers that are crucial to the regime's—not the society's, not the citizenry's—survival. It can politically manipulate these two levers to weaken the opposition. In addition, externally almost nothing has happened to undermine or withhold international recognition; the regime controls Zaire's mission to the United Nations, and its ambassadors are recognized by virtually all other governments. As will be shown later in this chapter, there are conflicting claims to the leadership of the state, but those opposed to the entrenched regime have not been recognized or legitimated by the international community. Can one therefore avoid concluding that, according to traditional standards of international relations, the Zairean state under the

Mobutu regime exists? It is, in this sense, not comparable to Somalia: a government exists; and it is recognized to exist by other governments. That ceased to be the case in Somalia. In this sense, Zaire cannot be compared with Sudan, either. Although one cannot say that Kinshasa really controls the interior, it cannot be claimed that a substantial part of the state's territory is under the control of another authority. The same conclusion can be made regarding a comparison with Liberia.

The state whose condition is perhaps closest to Zaire's is Haiti. There an established state, brutally controlled by a regime clearly oblivious to the most basic needs of its citizenry, had maintained itself in power through raw force despite a democratic process that placed the authority of government in other hands (President Aristide's). These features closely resemble the situation in Zaire; yet Haiti is significantly different. The international community formally withdrew recognition and support from the Haitian leaders with de facto power; and President Aristide was recognized by the UN as the legitimate head of state. Nothing of the sort has occurred in Zaire.

Formal, traditional standards of international relations are, however, changing. If some of the new tests of legitimacy (human rights; internal conditions that threaten to disturb peace in the region) were to be applied to Zaire, the legitimacy of the Mobutu regime would be very much in doubt. But how would such new standards be applied? Surely, via the will of the governments of other states acting in concert, either through the UN and regional organizations or through ad hoc alliances. Up to the present that will—despite the presence of inviting and easily employable legal arguments and political opportunities—has not been forthcoming.

In the Introduction to this book, Zartman asks: Why do states collapse? and he answers: Because they can no longer perform the functions required for them to pass as states. Formally, the final test of *functions required* has been the judgment of other governments. Has such a judgment against the Mobutu regime been made? The answer has to be, No. The next question Zartman poses is: How do states collapse? Of course, this begs the question as to how collapse will be defined. What is the line between *very badly managed* and *collapsed*? According to Zartman, collapse involves the regime falling and "bring[ing] down with it the power that it has concentrated in its hands," and the consequent creation of a "vacuum."

At least up to the time of writing, these are not conditions that prevail in Zaire. It is a society that is suffering an incredibly great lowering of material standards of living—one in which abuse of power, corruption, and arbitrary application of the law are rampant. It is a society whose leaders have not only ignored the interests of common people; in their avid greed, they have destroyed the goose that laid their golden egg. For instance, the production of copper, at one time the main export commodity, is down to about 20 percent of capacity, as a result of Mobutu's withdrawal of its earnings to such an extent that rolling stock could not be replaced. And yet, the regime has not only not fallen but it continues to oppress Zairean society, and to manipulate political, military, and social forces. Moreover, a power vacuum has not really been created and in my view such a vacuum is not a necessary outcome of the present crisis.

In sum, the following possibilities exist:

1. The Mobutu regime may well survive the crisis that has been created for it by the end of the Cold War and pressures for democratization. For Zaireans this would mean prolonged deepening of current levels of deprivation and oppression. As Cohen stated, "If Mobutu were to run for President in a free and fair election, and if he were to be elected, there would be no hope for Zaire. He and his entourage are totally incapable of change" (Cohen 1993). But without international participation—which up to the present is not even planned—free and fair elections are not very likely to occur. If they do, eventually, become a reality, a Mobutu victory is virtually excluded.

2. A process of democratization started by Mobuto (see below) may in the end prevail, with Mobutu's departure from office and acceptance by the armed forces and the security apparatus of the authority of a new regime. Even with massive levels of foreign aid, under this scenario it would take a very long time to reestablish halfway reasonable levels of goods, services, and peace and security. [In both 1 and 2, the state (as the term has been used here) would have survived.]

3. The obstinate refusal of Mobutu to cede power may yet have the effect of destroying the state. Over time this has become a more real possibility, because in addition to the dictatorial methods he has always employed (terror and the use of state funds to buy support) he has now encouraged interethnic hatred and conflict to such an extent that the specter of secession has reappeared. This is paradoxical, since some observers have credited him with having arrested the secessionist tendencies of the 1960s. It is as if Tito, in the face of pressures to liberalize, had invented ethnic cleansing!

4. There is also the possibility that the departure of Mobutu would occur under circumstances so late and dire that civil war, warlordism, and secession would overwhelm a new, even democratically inclined, government.

■ Recent History

To better understand what is happening in Zaire and what might happen in the future, this chapter analyzes two broad areas of the country's recent history. First, there is a description of the interplay between political forces, both internal and external, that has taken place over the last four years; that is to say, since the Mobutu regime announced its decision to move toward a multiparty system and democratization. Second, elements in Zaire's history and present social, political, and economic makeup are identified with a view to getting clues as to the forces with which a post-Mobutu regime would have to contend in order to maintain the state and establish hope of democratic governance.

The so-called democratization process in Zaire began in January 1990. Mobutu, facing an increasingly desperate internal social and economic crisis and an international constellation that sharply lowered foreign support, decided to organize popular consultations in which the general public would be free to submit memoranda detailing its grievances against the regime (Zaire 1993: 1). Mobutu traveled across the country with the intent of listening. The result must have surprised and perturbed him: thousands of memoranda, many of them extremely critical, were fearlessly submitted. There had been earlier policies with the stated goal of liberalization, all attempts to undermine opposition and appease foreign supporters. The latest example was similarly destined.

The next step was a famous speech by Mobutu on April 24, 1990, in which he announced the end of the single-party state and, in effect, a limited commitment to a process of democratization. Mobutu's tactical retreat speeded up as a result of a particularly vicious attack in May 1990 by some of his security forces on students at the University of Lubumbashi (UN Commission on Human Rights 1991: 57). Foreign reaction, especially in Belgium, was extremely critical, as was that of many Zairois. Indeed, the Lubumbashi Massacre became a milestone in the deteriorating relations between Belgium and Zaire—or, more precisely, between Belgium and Mobutu. The press began to have broad freedom to criticize the government and soon a multitude of new political parties was born (earlier, Mobutu had tried to limit them to three). Eventually there were over two hundred parties but, significantly, many of them were fronts for Mobutu and his allies. In other words, there were early signals that Mobutu intended to manipulate the system rather than allow a genuine democratization process to go forward.

The main center of opposition was a political party and leadership that had defied the dictatorship for many years, the Union for Democracy and Social Progress (UDPS), headed by Etienne Tshisekedi wa Mulumba. Eventually this party became the nucleus of an alliance of opposition movements with the name, Union Sacrée (Sacred Union).

☐ *External Factors*

Two external factors had a great impact on political developments in Zaire during this period. First, Benin and Congo/Brazzaville (just across the river from Kinshasa) had successfully ended their dictatorships by calling national conferences at which a broad representation of the society met in what can perhaps be called a statewide catharsis. In both these early instances, the dictator not only accepted the calling of such a conference but admitted its legitimacy as the society's sovereign expression. In both cases the dictators appeared before the representatives and in a journey to Canossa made their mea culpa. These examples had a most nefarious effect in Zaire, because much of the opposition's efforts went into creating conditions that, it was hoped, would emulate the Benin/Congo examples. This meant getting agreement for the calling of a national conference, negotiating who would be designated as delegates, and gaining acceptance for the notion that the conference would be "sovereign." The more real issue was to be whether in the hard terms of power Mobutu would follow his Benin and Congo colleagues. Events have shown that he was not inclined to do so.

The second external factor was the apparent change in the policies of the major powers with influence in the Zaire arena—Belgium, France, and the United States. Applause for democratization in general and apparent moral encouragement for the opposition gave many of its leaders the impression that Mobutu's foreign supporters were abandoning him and would soon force him to accept real democratization. Since many believed that no opposition could succeed so long as the United States, especially, supported the regime, these signals—or what were perceived as signals— produced a situation that encouraged but ultimately hurt the opposition. First, it led to opposition overconfidence and further strengthened its concentration on legal and constitutional issues. Second, it turned attention away from the necessary but extremely difficult task of local organization and mass mobilization. Opposition leaders were, by and large, personalities who had been active in the independence struggle thirty years earlier. They were ideologically moderate and indeed most of them had at one time or another held high positions in the Mobutu regime. Many of them were well-to-do and, most importantly, had a deep aversion to the use of violence. This latter was due to the heavy cost in lives and property that had been encountered in the unsuccessful revolutionary movement of the early 1960s (the so-called Congo Rebellions) and the Shaba invasions in 1977 and 1978. Thus, the ultimate weapon of any opposition in a dictatorship— meeting force with force—was essentially excluded.

☐ The 1991 Uprising

By the spring of 1991, political jockeying between the regime and the growing opposition had taken on the characteristics of a duel between Mobutu and Tshisekedi. This was often misinterpreted as a "personality conflict." In fact, it had to do with the fact that Tshisekedi was seen, and in fact apparently was, the one person who would not allow himself to be manipulated by Mobutu. As Braeckman pointed out in 1992: "The cause of Tshisekedi's charisma resides in the tenacity which he demonstrated when confronting Mobutu . . . his popularity in Zaire is immense" (Braeckman 1992: 333 and 335). At any rate, during the period of tactical retreats by Mobutu, Tshisekedi was twice appointed prime minister (July 1991 and September 1991); but, when it became apparent that he intended to control government finances and the armed forces, these attempts at "compromise" collapsed, rapidly. Tshisekedi had himself refused the nomination—under pressure from his supporters—the first time; and three weeks after the second appointment he was dismissed by Mobutu (Zaire 1993: 2).

These developments preoccupied the elites of the regime and the opposition as was reflected in the complex tug-of-war over the organization, membership, and power of the imminent national conference. At the same time, a massive decline in the economy was taking place, accompanied by runaway inflation (the zaire—once pegged at $2 for Z1—by midsummer 1991 was at $1 for Z7,500).

In September, dissatisfied soldiers, who had either not been paid or had been paid as little as $4 per month, refused their salaries. When their grievances were not acted upon, they mutinied and started wholesale looting in Kinshasa (Braeckman 1992: 361). The looting was particularly aimed at foreign and Zairean elite stores and homes and the soldiers were soon joined by large segments of the civilian population (the population numbers more than two million). Within days it had spread to other towns and cities: Kisangani, Kikwit, Kolwezi, Likasi (pop. 146,000), and Lubumbashi (590,000) were among the hardest hit. Some estimate that 90 percent of what remained of the "modern" economy was looted and destroyed. Later, army camps became "thieves markets" where looted goods could be purchased. France and Belgium together sent about 2,500 troops into Zaire in order to evacuate their nationals and other foreigners (Reuters newsreport, Paris, October 25, 1991).

Looked at abstractly, the events described above amount to a prerevolutionary situation. Why then did the regime survive? While this uprising will have to be studied more closely before it will be possible to answer with any degree of confidence, a few hypotheses can be suggested. First, the uprising was largely spontaneous and devoid of structured organization. Second, the opposition leadership opted not to attempt any action aimed at directing and/or disciplining this massive upheaval. On the contrary, when some members of the military approached Tshisekedi and suggested he make a radio/TV address under their protection declaring that he had taken over power, he suspected that this was a provocation to discredit the opposition and sent them away, explaining that he did not want to gain control by means other than legal (Braeckman 1992: 363); in other words, there was no leadership for an anti-Mobutu revolution or military coup.

Tshisekedi did ask for foreign military intervention to control the DSP. This demonstrates the great trust that the opposition placed in foreign diplomatic and military intervention. As stated earlier, the key Western powers had encouraged this perception by repeatedly supporting democratization, by withdrawing aid from the regime, by specifically urging Mobutu to relinquish power to a prime minister acceptable to the opposition, and, finally, by sending troops, albeit with the mission of protecting and evacuating foreigners. It is also obvious that, had they wanted to, this was a moment when Belgium, France, and the United States could have ended the regime's tenure of power with relative ease.

For Mobutu, this was probably his weakest moment. He appeared to retain some control over the DSP but virtually nothing else. Under great external pressure—in his own words, "they [France and Belgium] want my head at any price" (Associated Press, Kinshasa, October 27, 1991)—he appointed Tshisekedi to the premiership on September 30, 1991, but when it became apparent that the latter would stop the presidency's unlimited access to the government treasury he was quickly dismissed. It was a revealing act of determination and cunning. The country was in ruins, foreign pressures intense, foreign troops present, the opposition apparently at the height of its popularity, and the armed forces divided and largely undisciplined. Yet, Mobutu would not cede control; neither would he accept an independent prime minister. If nothing earlier was enough to persuade diplomats and observers that he was intent on retaining power, this should have done it.

Yet it also became clear during this period that Belgium, France, and the United States did not quite agree. The U.S. position was that Mobutu should "share power with his political opposition, but stopped short of calling for him to step down" (Reuters, Washington, October 28, 1991). On the other hand, the Belgian prime minister was reported as asking the United States to do more to force Mobutu to surrender power: "If the U.S. changes its position . . . then perhaps there still might be a chance [for Zaire's future]" (Associated Press newsreport, Kinshasa, October 28, 1991). Mobutu was well briefed regarding these differences. Asked what he would do if the three powers were to ask him to leave, he replied: "It was France and Belgium that were expressing that desire. The delegate from the U.S. tapped his fingers on the table. He was not in agreement with the other two" (*Liberation* newsreport, Paris, October 28, 1991). The issue over which of the three powers disagreed was essentially "powersharing" versus "honorable departure—with a helpful push."

☐ Mobutu's Survival

The reason the fall 1991 crisis has been analyzed in some detail is that it constitutes a defining moment in Zaire's current history. There have been

many complex developments since then, but they revolve around the
themes that emerged at that time: (1) How far will the three powers go to
effect a democratic change? The answer was and remains, diplomatic support but no military interference or truly dynamic pressure on Mobutu's
vital interests. (2) How far will the opposition go to effect change? The
answer was and remains, demonstrations, appeals for international support,
and reliance on legal and constitutional principles, but no use of violence or
even disciplined mass mobilization (which is not to suggest that an effort in
the latter direction would have succeeded). (3) How far will Mobutu go to
retain power? The answer was and remains, the sky is the limit.

After it became clear that the September/October 1991 upheaval was
not going to result in Mobutu's withdrawal or his giving up the key elements of state power, Zaire's politics revolved around the deliberations of
the national conference. At the same time Mobutu continued to maneu-
ver—with considerable success—to weaken and split the Union Sacrée.
This was done in several ways. First, leading personalities were induced to
switch sides. Erstwhile members of the opposition leadership who followed
this path included Mungul Diaka, Nguza Karl-i-Bond, Cleophas Kamitatu,
and Faustin Birindwa (three of these four were appointed prime minister by
Mobutu). Second, ethnic antagonism was encouraged, resulting in campaigns of "ethnic cleansing," especially in Shaba, where close to 100,000
people were expelled from their homes because they were Luba (from
Kasai). Third, the fact that Tshisekedi was a Luba (Kasai) and that this ethnic group has aroused considerable antagonism has been used to orchestrate distrust and divisions among opposition ranks. Fourth, with the passage of time and radically worsening economic conditions, and
freewheeling brutality by security forces, support for opposition demonstrations and strikes has declined from the standards set during the opti-
mistic high of 1990 and 1991 (Nzongola 1993a).

Despite these developments, the main focus of Kinshasa politics
remained the national conference. As indicated earlier, it was not destined
to achieve the successes of other African national conferences. The reasons
for this are threefold: Mobutu's absolute intention to retain power; foreign
pressures, far from sufficient to force a change, in part played into
Mobutu's hands; and the fact that the opposition forces did not possess or
develop sufficient power at grassroots level to force the regime to abandon
its control over the state apparatus. They opted for a "non-violent, non-con-
flictual" transition (*Le Monde Diplomatique,* March 1993).

Nevertheless, the Sovereign National Congress (CNS) did make an
impressive contribution to what may eventually be Zaire's democratization.
First, given its size (3,000 delegates), and the many attempts to corrupt its
members and physically to intimidate them, it is to its credit that it elaborated and agreed upon a series of constitutional changes and transitional

arrangements: had they been allowed to develop, these could have opened a hopeful chapter in Zaire's history. Second, the members of the CNS must be credited with the courage of electing Tshisekedi as interim prime minister. This was done despite the certainty that it would arouse Mobutu's ire. The CNS also established a score of commissions. These bodies analyzed the country's plight and sought to shed light on the millions (perhaps billions!) of dollars that had been acquired through corruption and assassination (*Le Monde Diplomatique*, March 1993). The CNS developed a plan to govern the country for a two-year transitional period and a constitution that was to be submitted to a referendum. This involved establishing a High Council of the Republic (HCR) (with legislative powers) and a transitional government (with executive functions headed by a prime minister elected by the CNS; Tshisekedi was chosen by over 70 percent of the votes).

The CNS was responsible for the emergence of a new and powerful political personality: Msgr. Monsengwo, who presided over the conference and then the High Council of the Republic. While he was responsible for achieving many compromises and was highly respected by the foreign governments involved in the process, it is too early to assess his impact. Especially since decisions were often taken by "consensus," his power as presiding officer was very great; and his use of power has been subjected to considerable criticism (Nzongola 1993a).

Perhaps the most controversial decisions taken by the CNS were, first, the extension of Mobutu's mandate as president, albeit with limited and essentially honorific powers; and second, acceptance of a Comprehensive Political Compromise that was to a considerable degree brokered by the United States as a part of its "powersharing" option. By accepting to maintain Mobutu as head of state, the CNS (and more specifically the Union Sacrée) allowed him to retain formal control over the state, which meant that the international community was free to deny the Tshisekedi government effective recognition. Here then was a government, democratically elected (by the CNS), being denied recognition in favor of a dictator who was openly condemned by the very powers doing the denying. And the reason given for this turn of events was that the CNS had, after all, extended Mobutu's term as president—which it had done under considerable pressure from the United States and France! Whether this is seen as ironic or not, the fact is that the Mobutu regime continues to exercise power over the state and the state is given recognition by the world community; whereas Tshisekedi has seen his mandate torn up by the head of state.

Whether this is seen as ironic or not, it led to many months or virtually complete governmental paralysis. Two persons claimed to be prime minister—Tshisekedi and one or another Mobutu appointee—and this situation ultimately produced another "compromise," which was the joining together of the old Mobutu-controlled parliament and the HCR. This body was supposed to resolve the crisis by electing a prime minister agreeable to all sides. For months, however, this body was also unable to agree on a suitable candidate, while Tshisekedi argued that he was the only legitimate one for the position. Conditions on the ground became acutely more critical during this period; pro-Mobutu forces supported an ethnic cleansing campaign in Shaba against the Luba of Kasai (Tshisekedi's ethnic group), severe hyperinflation took hold, soldiers tried to force worthless money on merchants who refused it at the risk of their lives, opposition leaders were increasingly harassed and, given Tshisekedi's inability to produce a change, more and more of them joined those who agreed to find a prime minister acceptable to Mobutu. These pressures finally produced the election of Kengo Wa Dondo, long a close ally of Mobutu, in June 1994; Tshisekedi and the so-called radical opposition refused to recognize the whole process. The international community, more specifically the "troika" made up of Belgium, France, and the United States—tired of the endless Zaire crisis and the thwarted process of democratization and at the same time faced with a far worse crisis in Rwanda—gave the product of this latest "compromise" its blessing. Whether the Kengo government will be able to make a difference in the lives of Zaireans only the future will tell.

In the meantime what is happening to the citizenry, to the society within this state?

> The infrastructure, roads, means of communication have disappeared, the universities are closed, the hospitals have become mortuaries, the campaigns to fight the great epidemics are suspended and one no longer measures the ravages of AIDS (*Le Monde Diplomatique*, March 1993).

This is the portrait of a collapsed society.

■ Future Polity

As will be seen from the above analysis, so long as Mobutu remains president, no reconstruction of Zaire is likely to occur. In the mid-1990s it is difficult to visualize under what circumstances he and/or his close entourage would be ejected from power. It was however possible to look at the current condition of Zairean society and its history since the achievement of independence in order to draw a picture of what conditions might be like in a post-Mobutu Zaire.

□ *Aversion to Violence*

The first aspect to be focused on, especially with the examples of Liberia and Somalia in mind, is the relative aversion to violent struggle felt not only by opposition leaders but also by the masses of Zairois. As noted earlier, this can be linked to the massive revolutionary movement that erupted three years after independence—a revolt that not only failed but that cost about one million people their lives. This traumatic event was, in fact, instrumental in Mobutu's being able to install his dictatorship with such ease in 1965. People welcomed a firm hand, just so long as there was an end to the bloody conflicts that had characterized the period from 1963 to 1965. Soon both economic and political conditions were even worse than they had been in 1963. Revolutionary movements attempting to mobilize the masses did surface, but they never again were able to obtain wide support. This became particularly evident in 1977 when the Front de Liberation National Congolais (FLNC), made up of former Katangese soldiers exiled in Angola, successfully invaded Shaba (formerly Katanga) and routed the Zairean army. Mobutu's popularity was at a low point and his regime was substantially weakened; yet there was no popular uprising. The same thing happened in 1978. Again, the operation was limited to the invaded areas of Shaba, which were recaptured by French and Belgian troops with U.S. logistical support. Again the confrontation bore a heavy price in blood and the long-term effect seems to have been a generalized fear of violent protest in the south Shaba region—an area that had not suffered the traumatic effects of the 1963–1965 uprising. Indeed, apart from isolated instances, one can say that political violence has been the tool of the regime and not that of the various opposition groups that have periodically arisen. This continues to be evident as the regime employs violence against peaceful, church-organized marchers, individual opposition leaders, and, in the case of Shaba, an entire ethnic minority; whereas, the whole Union Sacrée does not even have efficient bodyguards for its top leadership. Thus, one can cautiously predict that, despite endless provocations, the opposition is not likely to employ violent measures in the near future. Even if it decided to adopt such a strategy, it would take a considerable time to launch it.

A related factor is the relative absence of weapons in Zaire. It is of course difficult to know how many and what type of weapons are available, especially since there is virtually an open border with Angola; but it seems that the sort of conditions that produced the Somalia crisis are absent in Zaire. That is not to say that armed robbery, gangs, and especially free-ranging soldiers do not terrorize people. But apart from the regime's activities, violence seems to be on a minimal scale, if one takes into account the economic conditions or compares Zaire with more dramatic African trouble spots.

Another factor worth analyzing is the growing activism among the clergy. This is particularly significant in Zaire because of its long-existing and powerful association with the Roman Catholic Church. Catholic influence is heightened by the fact that, in the interior of the country, the church is often the only national institution still to function. However, in the past the church in Zaire was strictly apolitical; for instance, during the independence struggle priests were by far the largest group with advanced or university-level education, yet they were not allowed to participate in the political and governmental activities of the day. This appears to have changed, as is indicated by declarations criticizing the regime made by the conference of bishops, individual highly placed prelates, and also by the appointment of Archbishop Monsengwo as president of the CNS and the HCR. Perhaps the most significant change is the fact that some priests are now organizing and leading popular protest demonstrations.

□ *The Economy*

Another aspect of Zairean society that will have a major impact on the future is the development of the informal sector of the economy. With the almost total collapse of the modern and large industrial sectors, it is perhaps astonishing how vibrant and dynamic the informal economy has become, Hugues Leclercq, a long-time student of the Zairean economy, has described it as follows:

> This merchant economy functions under quasi-perfect conditions of competition because of the presence of large urban markets [that] constitute the real pillar of the urban economy. [These markets produce] the communications and exchange axis which link this economy to its rural hinterland . . . the modern city and even neighboring countries (CEDAF-ASDOC November 3–4, 1992: 140).

Leclercq contrasts this economy with the high revenue that the Zairean elite depends on. The source of this revenue is not productive activity subject to competition, but rather state funds. Two quite separate economies operate in the same space at the same time. Needless to say, the collapse of the transportation network and such services as health, law and order, and education (formerly supplied by the state) has put severe strains on the informal economy. People have to replace these services as best they can by their own efforts. In addition, the constant adjustments that have to be made because of out-of-control inflation place further burdens on the informal sector. The net result is a constant lowering of the standard of living to a point where many urban dwellers cannot afford to eat more than once a day.

   Yet the dynamism of the informal economy is an important development. In the future it could form the basis of a rebuilt society. Its great advantage is that it is truly indigenous and not dependent on foreign loans or experts.

☐ *The Electoral Situation*

A post-Mobutu Zaire will presumably organize free elections and that will
pose the question of whether and how the citizenry will use this opportunity to empower itself. There have been virtually no truly competitive elections since May 1960, just before independence was achieved. Whether
one can gain useful knowledge of what future electoral behavior might
entail from an analysis of an election over thirty years ago is greatly in
question, yet in at least one respect it is useful to try. Although conditions
have changed drastically, it would be difficult to argue that the Zairean
public, at least in the urban areas, is less politically sophisticated today than
it was in 1960.

At independence, Zaireans were for the first time permitted to participate in national elections, using an electoral system that was almost entirely
adopted from the extraordinarily complicated Belgian model. It employed a
system of proportional representation. Each voter had the option of voting
for a party list or altering the hierarchical order of the candidates on that
list. Since administrative subdivisions were used as electoral districts, each
had a different-sized population, with variable numbers of representatives.
Each party could—and usually did—submit one and a half as many candidates as there were representative seats available, so that alternates would
exist should elected representatives resign their seats to take up government
posts. To the surprise of many, this system not only brought out about 80
percent of the eligible voters but it was used in a wide variety of ways. In
one area, over 85 percent of those voting opted to employ the preferential
voting option, with the result that national leaders were demoted and in
some cases not even elected; while local and provincial leaders rose on the
party lists—and sometimes those designated as alternates were elected.
This behavior cannot but be seen as a high level of sophistication. It also
points the way to enhancing voter empowerment.

In effect, this system, and the manner in which it was used, resulted in
the electorate employing it in order simultaneously to hold a primary as
well as a general election. Since most African constituencies are made up
of ethnically homogeneous populations who tend to vote in a united fashion
for a particular party, empowering the voters means giving them choice as
to who *in their party* will represent them. The lesson for a future Zairean
election is not that this particular system should be reemployed but rather
that, if free elections are organized, one can expect voters to use such an
opportunity to express their self-interest in a reasoned fashion.

☐ *Leadership?*

A post-Mobutu Zaire will have to face a number of additional problems.
First, as has been suggested earlier, political leaders will have to forge a

closer and a more trusting relationship with the masses of deprived, disillusioned citizens. Even in a "democratic" society, the danger will loom that democracy will be limited to the national arena and that at the local level, especially in rural areas, one-party authoritarian rule will prevail. Should this happen, a continuing alienation from government and leadership may result, and a tendency, already present, toward participation in sects of various types may increase. This could easily lead to the masses searching for leaders who offer violent, revolutionary programs to improve the lot of ordinary citizens. For all their current aversion to violence, Zaireans have on several occasions (and especially in 1959–1960 and 1963–1965) risen with revolutionary fervor. One day, the memory of the price and failure of these uprisings will have evaporated from the minds of a very young population.

Finally, a post-Mobutu Zaire will face a question that most postdictatorial regimes tackle only with great difficulty: What to do with the armed forces? How would such a government be able to pay soldiers and induce them to stay in their barracks?

11

Algeria: Reinstating the State or Instating a Civil Society?

Azzedine Layachi

Faced with a deep economic crisis, social, ethnic, and religious conflicts, and potential civil wars, many African countries may have only one hope left for stability, reconstruction, and development: the building of a newly defined and designed state that responds to, and takes into account, the various changes experienced by these countries since independence. Where the state has collapsed, the task is gigantic. In other cases, where the state has experienced a major setback—expressed in the form of diminished legitimacy and authority—the task is enormous, but still feasible if undertaken with extreme urgency and a full consideration of the need to redefine state-society relations. Somalia is a case of the first situation, state collapse; whereas Algeria represents the category of states whose authority and legitimacy have diminished to an alarming extent, that is, to a point of nearing collapse.

■ The State

This chapter looks at Algeria and attempts to explain how the state, long thought to be well established and strong, has lost so much legitimacy and authority that it is on the verge of collapse. The question of whether that state is now reconstituting itself and regaining some of its lost legitimacy and authority will also be addressed. All this will be done in the context of a theoretical and empirical analysis of state-society relations during the process referred to as "democratization." The chapter will tackle these questions from the perspective of both state and society linking both concepts not only in the search of explanations but also in the articulation of normative propositions.

For Hegel, according to Kean (1988: 50) "civil society . . . is conceived not as a natural condition of freedom but as a historically produced sphere of ethical life . . . positioned between the simple world of the patriarchal household and the universal state. It includes the market economy, social classes, corporations, and institutions concerned with the administration of

171

welfare [*polizei*] and civil law." Civil society is thus perceived by Hegel as a set of private individuals, classes, groups and institutions whose actions are independent from the state but are regulated by civil law. There-fore, civil society can exist only with the control of a "supervising strong state."

For de Tocqueville (1835), a civil society that is self-organized and independent from the state is necessary for the consolidation of democracy. Civil society is "the independent eye of society," made of a plurality of self-organized and vigilant civil associations. Without it, those in power can turn into despots.

In *The German Ideology,* Karl Marx (1970: 49, 57) defines civil soci-ety in economic terms when he states that "civil society embraces all the material relations of individuals within a definite stage of the development of productive forces." He further explains that "it embraces the whole com-mercial and industrial life of a given stage and, hence, transcends the state and the nation, though on the other hand again, it must assert itself in its foreign relations as a nationality and inwardly must organize itself as state." Within the Marxist tradition, Antonio Gramsci (1967: 164) found that civil society would be the place where other social groups and classes could undermine the position of the bourgeoisie and prepare for revolution against the capitalist state. Gramsci's view (1967: 171) of civil society has two major aspects: it is a way of "conceptually analyzing existing and emerging empirical relations between social and political forces and their organizational (structural) and ideological (superstructural) manifesta-tions"; and it is also "a 'pragmatic' analysis seeking to formulate a political strategy or action program for the 'progressive' forces in civil society, the 'new historic bloc.'"

Gramsci's work seems to have gained relevance today, especially after the Solidarity challenge to the Polish state throughout the 1980s, where the Gramscian "political strategy" of labor resistance to the domination of the party-state seemed to be at work. Beyond Poland and Eastern Europe, the relatively recent entrance en masse of society in the political arena through-out much of the Third World signals what could be the beginning of the end of the state monopoly over the political sphere and also the start of a process of redefining state-society relations.

In this chapter, civil society is taken as a multifaceted concept and phe-nomenon, as defined in the Introduction to this book. In this dynamic per-spective, it contains a struggle for the political sphere; it constitutes a check on state arbitrariness; it is an independent process of mobilization of vari-ous interests for the promotion of change or the maintenance of the status quo; and it can be understood as a buffer between state power and private spheres.

■ Strengths and Liabilities of the Algerian State

In recent years, especially since the October 1988 riots, the state in Algeria has been facing a major storm, in an atmosphere of great uncertainty about its own fate and that of the country. The authority of the state has danger-ously declined, its legitimacy gravely diminished, and its ability to face off forceful challenges from social groups, especially the Islamists, become uncertain. Since January 1992, following the resignation of President Chadli Bendjedid and beginning with the short presidencies of Mohamed Boudiaf and Ali Kefi over the newly created High State Council (HCE), the state has been trying to rebound, reaffirming its authority and attempting to bring back the law and order that were almost lost.

The collapse or important weakening of the state in Africa and other parts of the world, such as Latin America, was often erroneously attributed to solely economic difficulties or crises. Indeed, in order adequately to comprehend state collapse, one must look first at the state's structures and evolution, its role, and the nature of its leadership. After independence from French colonialism, one of the main priorities of Algeria's leadership was to build a state that would not only complement political independence with economic independence—mostly through nationalization and an autonomous development plan that established an industrial base—but also construct a socialist society, promote national integration, and build a pro-fessional army to protect the national territory. To do all this, a strong and efficient state bureaucracy was needed. As in most African and Arab cases, the rationale for an imposing state was threefold: the desire to attain and protect total economic and political independence; the need to maintain internal stability in the face of potential factional and ethnic divisions and regional threats; and the need to mobilize national resources and to empow-er central institutions with enough authority to use these resources for the purpose of development. Political openness was not encouraged because it was perceived as a source of division rather than unity and efficiency. As a result of a policy that made the public sector the engine of socialist devel-opment, the state bureaucracy and institutions were greatly enlarged in order to reach the stated objectives. State control extended to all natural resources, most economic activities, commerce, investment, foreign exchange, and most of the agricultural activity. The state centralized in its hands the power of distribution and pricing of most products.

□ Boumedienne: Heavy Industry

The first ten years of President Houari Boumedienne's tenure (1965–1975) were thus characterized by an assertive state construction coupled with a strong campaign for economic development by way of mobilizing natural resources, nationalizing foreign assets, centralizing economic planning, and developing a strong public sector whose core was heavy industry. The strategy of building "industrializing industries," which was harshly criticized after the death in office of Boumedienne in 1979, had an overall positive result. Between 1967 and 1978, the national revenue grew by a healthy average of 8.6 percent, the per capita income more than doubled, going from $375 to $830, and employment increased from 1.75 million to 2.83 million (Temmar 1983: 268–271). The per capita gross industrial production increased at an average annual growth of 14.1 percent and the total value of industrial production doubled (Bennoune 1984: 206–207). However, the negative effects of this policy were important enough to justify a policy reversal, and to serve as a springboard for the social upheaval of 1988, later to be captured by the Islamist movement. These effects included a bloated bureaucracy, distribution bottlenecks, rampant inflation, major structural dislocations, and a very poor agricultural performance. In turn, these effects stimulated further urban migrations, food scarcity, and growing inequality in incomes.

The rationale of revolutionary solidarity used by Boumedienne to mobilize the economy was also used to inhibit political dissent and opposition. The state and its leadership asserted hegemony over society on the basis of both historical legitimacy (i.e., the National Liberation Front's [FLN] heroic legacy from the war of independence) and the socioeconomic project outlined above. The Boumedienne era "was characterized by excessive state centralization and control [and a] one-party rule that inhibited political dissent. An authoritarian alliance of party elite, military officers, and bureaucrats, whose legitimacy was based on a mix of revolutionary credentials and technocratic expertise sustained the authoritarian rule" (Layachi and Haireche 1992: 69). Challengers of governmental policies were either jailed or sent into exile; independent civic and professional associations, student organizations, and unions were either disbanded, put under state control via the ruling party, or coopted. The National Assembly was suspended; the media was under strict state control; and, in the cultural sphere, the state controlled the mosques and appointed preachers and used both to promote its societal plan and justify its policy choices.

> Cultural monolithism became an oppressive tool in the hands of the state against cultural rights of minorities—i.e., the Berbers who make up 25 to 35 percent of the population—and, therefore, against their political rights. The state's forced arabization and promotion of a national culture and identity, which reduced minority cultures to folklore, was first resisted through cultural revival and then through political protest (Haireche 1993: 78).

Until the second half of the 1970s, there was no real opposition to the state except a loosely defined religious-liberal group that started gathering around Cheikh Kheireddine, Farhat Abbas, Hocine Lahouel, and Benyoucef Ben Khadda, all former war leaders. As long as the state continued to perform a distributive function, thanks to important oil and natural gas revenues and to heavy external borrowing, such opposition could hardly gather support by attacking the social and economic policies of the regime. Most Algerians benefited from an extensive welfare system that gave them free education, free medical care, subsidized food, and some employment.

□ Reform of the Economy

When a new team took over in 1979, under the presidency of Chadli Bendjedid, Boumedienne's strategy was dismissed through the implementation of a program of "controlled economic liberalization." This reorientation downplayed the role of heavy industry in development and started a frontal attack against the public sector corporations. The latter were viewed as huge bureaucracies in an urgent need of restructuring for efficiency purposes. An overall reform of the economy was gradually introduced by way of a series of measures inspired by International Monetary Fund (IMF) adjustment recommendations—without, however, there being a formal agreement with the IMF. Work ethics, productivity, accountability, and profit became key words in the official discourse. Several industrial projects were put aside, and industrial investment fell 21 percent between 1980 and 1981. Unemployment reached 22 percent of the work force—mostly youth, 70 percent of whom remain unemployed (Daoudi 1991: 26). Some state company managers responded to the calls for competitiveness by simply inflating the price of their products (by 50 to 200 percent) instead of reforming their management and production techniques. Inflation grew unabated at a rate of 42 percent per year, while the population continued to grow at a rate of 3.2 percent. As oil revenues declined by 21 percent in 1985/86, and imports fell by 35 percent, the external debt peaked at $24 billion, and its servicing ratio reached 97 percent of export earnings, which were about $8 billion per year (MERIP 1990). By 1988, with most public companies in deficit (a total of $18.5 billion deficit between 1984 and 1987), industrial output dramatically declined (Charef 1990: 16). On the eve of the October riots, and as the state seemed bankrupt, social inequality increased to a point where 5 percent of the population earned 45 percent of the national income and 50 percent earned less than 22 percent (El-Mondjahid, January 29, 1990). By 1991, this already unequal income distribution worsened: a further 125,000 workers, mostly in the public sector, became unemployed (Daoudi 1991: 26).

□ *The Need for Political Reform*

Between the end of the 1970s and the mid-1980s, various internal and external factors combined to make it hard for the state to continue acting as a development agent and welfare provider. President Chadli Bendjedid introduced economic reforms, but political and institutional reforms remained unaddressed—contrary to what had been hoped after the death of his predecessor. As the Central Committee of the FLN decided in December 1980 to make it mandatory to be member of the party for anyone holding high office (*El-Mondjahid,* December 26–27, 1990), it seemed that an intraelite compromise had been struck. The deal gave the FLN and the army total control of ideological matters; Chadli was to have the upper hand on economic policies. While trying to establish his authority, however, Chadli took the post of secretary-general of the FLN, pushed for political bureau members to be appointed by him, strengthened the Central Committee, and allowed the party to control all national organizations and to supervise parliamentary elections. After 1980, the FLN became more empowered than ever before, making itself the prime target of the grievances violently expressed in October 1988.

■ October 1988: The Political Awakening of Society

Following a series of student and worker strikes—which started back in the 1970s and multiplied after the death of Boumedienne—the social, political, and economic crisis reached an unprecedented level in 1988. Social unrest turned into riots in most cities and towns in the first week of October. The rioters, mostly youths, students, and unemployed people, attacked all symbols of state authority and those of wealth and consumption. The state, which had never before faced such an upheaval, reacted with fierce military repression that left many people dead.

This event marked the beginning of a deep crisis of the authority of the state and of the authoritarian rule in general. From then on, the response of the state was often ad hoc and inconsistent. The authorities were trying to deal with an unprecedented situation that questioned not only the policies pursued and their social and economic consequences, but also the ruling leadership, and more importantly, the state and its preeminence over society. Pressured from different directions, but supported by large segments of the army, President Chadli's reaction included the elimination of those he deemed responsible for the failure of his economic policies—mostly FLN leaders—and a move toward multipartyism through a major revision of the constitution. Political liberalization was pressed on the state leadership just as economic liberalization had been a few years before. Politics had finally caught up with economics. With the help of the army, Chadli eliminated from power the FLN conservative hardliners who opposed his reforms, and he undermined the power of the police, dismissing the head of the secret police, Kasdi Merbah. Doctrinal and institutional reforms, constitutional changes, and new legislation cleared the way for full-fledged political liberalization (for the text of the law on associations, see *Revolution Africaine,* July 21, 1989: 26–27).

An incredible number of political parties, civic, professional, and cultural associations were formed almost overnight, but the only significant players in the political arena were those affiliated with the Islamist movement. In February 1989, the Islamic Salvation Front (FIS) was created and later recognized by the state in spite of a constitutional clause that made it illegal because of its religious basis. FIS suddenly became the main opposition party (other Islamist organizations and parties were also born but never acquired the same popularity). At the first multiparty municipal election, in June 1990, the FIS gained control of most *wilayas* and local collectives, giving a severe blow to the ruling FLN. The electoral appeal of the Islamists was due more to their ideology and challenge to the ruling party than to a clear economic and social program.

The first multiparty parliamentary elections, scheduled for June 1991, were delayed by six months when the FIS took a confrontational attitude. They called for a general strike on May 23 and rejected a new electoral law that seemed to favor districts where the FIS appeared to be the weakest (Lemoine 1991). This first major Islamist challenge prompted the fall of the government of Mouloud Hamrouche and the imposition, on June 5, of a four-month state of emergency by the army. After violent clashes with FIS elements, the army and the police reestablished order. Thousands of people were arrested, including the president and vice-president of the FIS, Abassi Madani and Ali Belhadj, who were later condemned to twelve years in prison for threatening national security. A new government headed by Sid Ahmed Ghozali was formed and a new electoral law, providing for two rounds of elections, was passed by the National Assembly.

The first round of parliamentary elections took place on December 26, 1991 (the second was scheduled for January 16, 1992). To the dismay of not only the FLN, the FIS was the biggest winner, capturing 188 out of 430 parliamentary seats, with 47.28 percent of the votes cast (24.6 percent of eligible voters). The party of Ait Ahmed based in the Berber Kabylia region, the Front of Socialist Forces (FFS), was second, with 26 seats, although with a mere 7.4 percent of votes cast. The FLN, the major loser, obtained only 15 seats, with 23.38 percent of the votes (*Jeune Afrique,* January 9–16, 1992: 20).

Without waiting for the second balloting, which was expected to reaffirm the December results, President Chadli and some FLN members started thinking about cohabitation with the Islamists. In Chadli's plan, he would keep the presidency and the Islamists would control nonstrategic ministries such as education, justice, and religious affairs; technical ministries would be controlled by the FLN. The army, which was left out of the plan, publicly expressed its fear of an FIS-controlled parliament—with the power to change the constitution—and forced the president to resign on January 11; it then started looking for constitutional ways of filling the power vacuum left by the Chadli's "resignation" and the dissolution of parliament (which had taken place a few days earlier). A High State Council, made up of five civilian and military officials, was set up. The council was headed by Mohamed Boudiaf—a hero of the war of independence who was invited to return to Algeria from exile in Morocco—and, after his assassination in July 1992 with suspected official complicity, by Ali Kafi, another wartime leader. Real power rested with the minister of defense, Major General Khaled Nezzar.

The results of the first round of elections and the remaining balloting were canceled and the High State Council gave itself until the end of 1993 to reestablish order and authority and to resume the democratic process (*New York Times,* January 13, 1992). More Islamist leaders were arrested as their movement radicalized further and began using violence against military and police targets. A state of emergency was imposed on February 9 and the FIS was later banned as a political party. Since then, there has been all-out armed confrontation between the state and its major challenger, the FIS. The confrontation has been of a zero-sum nature: the Islamists would not give up the fight until power was handed over to them—a claim based on their electoral victory—and the most powerful elements among the state leadership (the army) refused even to discuss power-sharing with them.

Tactics changed in 1994 as the incumbent leadership split over the way to meet the challenge. Unable to attract even the secular parties to a national conference in January 1994, the army leadership entrusted the government to General Lamine Zeroual, member of a younger generation of officers without ties to the FLN. Zeroual spent the first half of the year consolidating his power and then embarked on the delicate task of trying to talk to the Islamists and bring those among them who would accept dialogue back into the state. The Islamists, in turn, had split into many groups, with the terrorist Islamic Armed Group (GIA) and other uncontrolled groups undercutting the chances of dialogue with the FIS.

As it seeks to reestablish law and order, the state followed a three-track policy in order to regain its badly undermined legitimacy and resolve the crisis without abdicating to the Islamist demands: (1) wage all-out war against radical Islamists; (2) revise the political liberalization rules; (3) pursue economic readjustment. For some observers, the state seems to have rebounded, after a temporary eclipse in the wake of a serious societal challenge to its nature, authority, and legitimacy, while for others, the state is still embroiled in a difficult fight for survival, since the institutional reforms introduced and the policies pursued so far have not really addressed the main issue at stake; i.e., state-society relations in a social, economic, and political context that is extremely different from the one the state was born in, after independence. By the end of 1994, it was hard to claim that the state was secure. The FIS controlled widespread rural areas and, by night, many poorer urban districts. Its armed wings—often not under its control—waged a campaign of terrorist assassinations against intellectuals, civil servants, and police and their families, and high-ranking officials. Law and order, and government services, disintegrated. The state was hobbled, defensive, and ambushed.

■ Causes of the Weakening of the State

Some of the causes of the weakening, or near collapse, of the state in Algeria go back to well before October 1988. They constituted seeds implanted by the very nature of the state itself, its leadership and its relation to society. In Algeria, as in most African countries, and contrary to the Western experience, the state came first as a social institution. This institution's objective was to create a society whose future nature was defined in a blueprint drawn by a revolutionary elite. Politics was to determine the social, cultural, and economic aspect of society, not vice versa. This societal project, which was tacitly adhered to by the impoverished, postindependence masses, was to be carried out almost entirely by the state. The state presented itself as being above society and the guardian of its interest. It became the engine of most developmental activities, besides performing the traditional functions of maintaining law and order. It was responsible for capital accumulation and for distribution.

The implementation of all this required an important expansion and extension of the state apparatus. "The whole process of expanding state involvement in the economy was justified by the need for rapid development and for a more equitable distribution of a rising national income. This provided an important source of legitimation" that increased the authority of the state and diminished the potential for challenge by putting technocrats, scientists, and planners to work on the expansion (Owen 1992: 17). In the ensuing concentration of power in the hand of the state, the political sphere was limited to the state decisionmaking and policy implementation apparatus. Professional, cultural, and student associations were allowed to exist only insofar as they participated in the activities of the state. Even religion, Islam, was "nationalized" and used by the state for the legitimation of policies and for mobilization.

> Control over the educational system and the religious establishment . . .
> the press, radio and television . . . [enabled the state] to establish an ideological hegemony in terms of a statist, universalistic, discourse based on notions of nationalism, socialism and populism (Owen 1992: 41).

With this overwhelming presence of the state, citizens became dependent on the state for all kinds of services and, paradoxically, feared it at the same time.

Structurally, the state was not autonomous from society. Many members of its elite, who had a tremendous amount of power in their hands, used their official positions to dispense patronage and favored public policies that served specific social and economic groups or regions. Later, people's perception of a connection between members of the state elite and particular groups or individuals in society, through patronage relationships, contributed to undermining the image and legitimacy of state authority. A combination of a structural concentration of power with a lack of institutional avenues for expression of grievances and demands made rioting the only means available for many to vent their frustrations. They saw no hope in their future, had watched a minority of people accumulating and exhibiting extraordinary wealth at times of austerity, and had seen many party and state officials using their positions to advance personal and family interests.

The most important turn in the policies pursued took place when Chadli gained power and started undoing Boumedienne's policies. Pressured by both external economic and political constraints, and by the domestic failure of the development strategy, the new regime made several decisions that, together, constituted a sudden retreat, or disengagement, of the state, not only from the economic sphere but also from the political and social control it once held. Faced with opposition on both sides of the ideological spectrum, left and right, within the FLN and the army, Chadli Bendjedid attempted, while guaranteeing a minimum of social and economic benefits to the most impoverished among the masses, to do away with the Boumediennist holdovers in the party. He tried this through structural changes and a tacit encouragement of a growing anti-FLN sentiment among the people—a feeling that was later to be exploited by the FIS. But

> unable to to isolate the opponents to the new strategy . . . Bendjedid was faced with a crisis that festered into a barely concealed struggle inside the FLN—infighting that slowed down the infitah perceptibly and fanned the flames of the struggle between the party and the growing outside opposition (Vandewalle 1993: 25).

These *infitah* policies (economic liberalization and opening to foreign investment) included an overall restructuring, notably through the breakup and decentralization of public companies, as well as calls for their efficiency and profitability; an emphasis on light industry and commerce; a greater role for private initiatives, notably in the agricultural sector; and a greater allocation of oil and gas earnings toward the satisfaction of basic consumer needs. This reform plan may have given positive results if the state's foreign exchange earnings had improved, or at least remained constant. But in 1986, international oil prices fell steeply, from around $32 to $8 a barrel. The combination of big shortfalls in oil and gas export earnings with other aspects of the policies (plus international pressures for economic restructuring) had disastrous effects on the economic conditions of Algeria's least privileged citizens. This greatly undermined the credibility of the state, which was no longer able to deliver on its promises "For a Better Life"— the earliest motto of the Chadli regime.

Perhaps the greatest factor precipitating the demise of the Algerian state was the sudden institutional retreat at a time when civil society was not organized enough and balanced enough to take over the areas left vacant. Most of that vacancy was filled by the Islamist movement, which effectively mobilized hundreds of thousands of disaffected youths against the system.

From the early 1980s onward, a process of deinstitutionalization was brought about; first by the *logic of liberalization,* which called for a lesser state intervention in the economy; and second by the *logic of power struggle* at the top, which pitted those for liberal reforms against the holdovers from the old regime. This period lasted for twelve years. During these years, the state seemed to retreat from most areas, even law and order. At the height of the struggle for influence between President Chadli and conservative factions in the ruling party, illegal activities flourished: crime and corruption jumped to levels previously unknown in Algeria. There was a thriving black market (referred to as *trabendo*) making up for the empty shelves caused by failure of the state distribution system; graft and appropriation of state funds by state officials multiplied. Both high- and low-ranking officials were involved. And political and social challenges by Islamist militia remained unchecked. In addition to this institutional retreat, an ideological vacuum developed, resulting directly from the replacement of the socialist project by what seemed to be nothing more than a series of ad hoc, ill-articulated, ill-coordinated, and rhetorical pleas for liberalization. These could best be understood as part of the fierce power struggle that was taking place among the fragmented state elite.

The state was no longer providing adequate services or needed subsidies. The decline of the state presence in social services provided the Islamists with a tremendous opportunity to make headway: they challenged the state in territory that had become one of the main pillars of its legitima-cy. As political disputes, strikes, and inefficiency caused ever greater hard-ship for the people, numerous Islamic networks grew to match, surpass, and even replace state action. In 1989, for example, when an earthquake hit Tipaza, west of Algiers, they performed the disaster relief work. Islamists also opened "Islamic Souks" (markets), where prices were well below those of the regular distribution circuits. They also established popular courts, settling disputes with more justice, speed, and efficiency than did the state system; established neighborhood militia groups; and directed traffic at times when no policeman was in sight. Islamists visited the poor and the sick and gave them food and symbolic monetary stipends; and on the street, they set, and imposed, often by force, dress codes and behavioral norms for both men and women. By June 1991, radical Islamist groups such as the "Afghans" (Algerians who had returned from volunteer service with the Mujahedeen against the Communist regime in Afghanistan) had started bold, armed attacks against police and military personnel and posts, killing as many as twenty people.

In sum, the state appeared to be on the verge of collapse. From June 1991, when the army was called in, a core of the elite, with the defense minister, General Nezzar, at the center, undertook the mission of reinstat-ing the state. But even after the first big, violent clash in June, the steps taken were in essence conciliatory—notwithstanding the arrest and intern-ment in camps of FIS leaders and thousands of militants. Chadli accepted the possibility of sharing power with the new popular movement. Working with the Islamists seemed to be the only way for him to defeat his ideologi-cal rivals and to reduce the growing popular discontent. But the army, which had declared itself the guardian of democracy and modernity—incompatible values in the situation—moved directly and forcefully into the political arena, removing Chadli in January 1992 and working behind a civilian facade to restore the presence, authority, and legitimacy of the state.

■ The International Conjuncture

From the late 1970s into the 1990s the international environment has been full of events and developments that have had a tremendous impact on Algeria's economic, political, and cultural evolution. In fact, they con-tributed both to the crisis of the economy and to that of the state. Starting with the Iranian revolution and continuing through the Gulf War and the collapse of the socialist states of the USSR and Eastern Europe, and through the international economic recession and oil glut, this period of more than a decade showed that Algeria was not as shielded from outside influences as might have been thought.

The Iranian Islamic revolution provided an early impetus for the Algerian Islamist movement that started first as a challenge only of the cultural and religious policies of the state. Iran represented for the Algerian Islamists a successful challenge to secularism that could be duplicated. The fomenting demise of the Soviet and Eastern European states in the second half of the 1980s further encouraged challenges to the state in Algeria. The war in Afghanistan constituted a training ground for many Algerians who later returned with skills in guerrilla warfare that could be used against the state. In 1991, the Gulf War unleashed the mobilizational potential of the Islamists, as it widened the gap between a pro-Iraqi popular movement and the state leadership. The Algerian regime took a neutral stand, not condemning the actions of the U.S.-led international coalition. The Islamists' popular stance was an important stimulus for recruitment, especially after a relative lapse in their popularity due to poor management of the municipalities they inherited after winning the June 1990 elections. Furthermore, Western calls for democratization, as the USRR was on its knees, encouraged the rebellion of society against the authoritarian state.

On the economic front, both the rise of the Islamist challenge in Algeria and other Arab countries and the Gulf War contributed to the deepening of the crisis. Many Western states and private international investors and moneylenders expressed reservations about investing and extending financial aid to Algeria. It was feared that an Islamist takeover of the secular state was imminent. Hence, given the sharp drop in oil prices of 1986 combined with diminished foreign aid and investment, state resources declined dangerously. It became extremely difficult to satisfy the most basic needs of the people. The state was on its knees in the face of the growing Islamist societal challenge.

■ Reinstating the State

The process of restoring the state by the secular military and civilian regime has involved the difficult task of undertaking, simultaneously, several urgent actions in three main directions: restoring order, rebuilding state legitimacy, and restructuring the economy. For various reasons, a lesser priority has been given to the reconstruction or revival of some important institutions, mainly the legislative body.

□ Rebuilding Legitimacy

The first concern of the army when it intervened in January 1992 seemed to be that of acting with as much constitutional legitimacy as possible. The army insisted on the constitutionality of its actions—the "voluntary" resignation of Chadli and the establishment of a temporary security council headed by Abdlemalek Benhabiles, president of the Constitutional Council. When the latter resigned, the army, out of concern for legitimacy, invited the heroic leader Mohamed Boudiaf to preside over a newly created High State Council. Boudiaf, who incarnated the revolutionary legitimacy, made it a personal priority to reestablish state authority and legitimacy. Before he was assassinated, six months later, Boudiaf attempted to do that by cracking down on radical Islamists, restoring the policing function of the state, and by trying to forge national consensus around a new state-society understanding, not to say social contract. As a big part of his effort to rebuild confidence in the state, he started a well-publicized, large-scale campaign against corruption among current and former members of the state and army elite. This was a direct response to popular calls for justice and accountability. A Patriotic Movement started gathering momentum around Boudiaf, its initiator, symbolizing a growing trust in a man who had been previously unknown to young people. He was perceived by many as a trustworthy person taking on two major forces: both the "politicofinancial mafia" and radical Islamists. His death—in circumstances that are still a mystery—drastically retarded the legitimation process.

Ali Kafi, another figure unknown to the majority of Algerians, replaced Boudiaf as head of the High State Council, but he was not as effective as his predecessor.

Moreover, the bulk of the work in this area remained to be done: there is more to it than restoring security and holding court trials of corrupt officials. The legitimation effort must encompass a wide variety of areas that are intimately interconnected and mutually supportive. These areas include (1) guaranteeing a minimum of security for citizens, protecting them against both violent social elements and state arbitrariness; (2) delivering on democratization promises (i.e., free elections, freedoms of association and political and economic competition, freedom of the press, accountability of state authority holders); (3) efficient management of the economy, without necessarily going back to the statism of the past; (4) building a new state ethos that inculcates values of rationality and instills fear of sanctions for wrongdoings while encouraging performance and efficiency.

☐ *Internal Security*

In the matter of restoring order and as part of the process of bringing the state back into the picture after its relative eclipse from 1988 to 1990, police, military, and paramilitary actions have multiplied as fast as have Islamic violence. Specially trained forces were established to take on the often sophisticated hit-and-run tactics of radical Islamists. As violence escalated, many forces (including private hit squads) joined in trying to isolate and eliminate armed Islamists. The Islamist terrorists, reported to belong to at least twelve major armed groups, conducted sporadic attacks, not only against army and police but also against civilian services, industrial installations, and intellectuals, which spread to many parts of the country, multiplied, and became bolder. A state of emergency was imposed in February 1992, with a night curfew later being added. New antiterrorist measures reserved very harsh punishment for violent activities against the state. Hundreds of people have been arrested and accused of terrorism. More than 10,000 people (including 250 in the security forces) were killed in the first three years of the state of emergency.

To make sure that the police and military response to the Islamists' violent challenge does not undermine ongoing efforts to reestablish state legitimacy, a system is needed limiting the response to prevention and reaction. All legal requirements for judging the accused must be observed, otherwise, security actions may turn into power abuse. This would further alienate those who are caught in the middle of the strife, between a rebellious religious movement and a state seeking to restore its authority at all costs.

There have been moves in this direction; for example, the newly state-created National Observatory for Human Rights (NOHR) has been "given the green light to disclose to the public opinion the existence of grave police misbehavior." The NOHR has reported several cases of the use of torture by the police against detainees (Messoudi 1993: 1). The Algerian Human Rights League (an independent organization headed by a lawyer, Abdenour Ali-Yahia) has also handled many such cases.

□ *Economic Restructuring*

The task of economic restructuring may be the most important one for rebuilding public confidence in the state. But it remains a very difficult endeavor, given the limited financial means available to the state, the precarious state of the economy, the international pressures that impose austerity measures and diminish the freedom of action of decisionmakers, and the growing climate of insecurity. The economic area is where most of the popular grievances originated—the arena of inequality and failure of the state to deliver on its promises. The infitah policies initiated by Chadli highlighted the existing contradictions and then dashed expectations, stimulating popular upheaval. It is, thus, in this area that the strongest elements of legitimation reside.

In Algeria, as in other African countries, "there has been a growing concern with economic rationality, stimulated by international economic considerations and a simultaneous attempt to ignore political rationality—or at least an attempt to disconnect the two" (Vandewalle 1993: 33). But this attempt to ignore political rationality has carried great risk for the state.

It was almost fatal. To be effective, economic restructuring must respond simultaneously and adequately to pressures from a difficult international economic environment *and* to domestic demands whose satisfaction is often limited by internal structural inadequacies and international constraints. While remaining committed to disengaging itself from direct management of economic activities, the state should remain the engine of capital accumulation and development. Even if the public sector is expected to be the most important sector of the economy, the private sector must be further encouraged; but it must also be asked to abide by clear, strict rules of behavior to integrate it into the development plan. Foreign investment must continue to be invited, but with a constant concern, albeit relaxed, with economic and political sovereignty. The current economic revival efforts should continue to emphasize the revival of the agricultural sector. Ideally, there will be food self-sufficiency and a lowering of the import bill.

As the state regains its place as the accepted authority with responsibility for maintaining security and regulating social and economic activities (although to a much lesser extent than before) and as a new consensus builds around the state about the future, foreign confidence is likely to grow. This will lead to assistance and new opportunities for the economy in process of revival. This scenario already has started to unfold. There was a recent wave of government-to-government assistance (French, Turkish, Portuguese, and Chinese loans and development contracts); foreign investors are probing the Algerian market; and international organizations have expressed a renewed, if limited, confidence in Algeria's restructuring policies, extending symbolic financial assistance. If foreign governments, international institutions, and business are to contribute to the reinstatement of the Algerian state, it will be in the form of financial and technical assistance and cooperation.

■ Instating a Civil Society

It is impossible to think of the reinstatement of the state without the growth of a civil society that would not only extend legitimacy to state institutions and processes but would also exercise a constant check on their power, offering competing policy options, demanding accountability, questioning policies, and aggregating and articulating demands from different social, economic, and cultural actors. Paradoxically, to carry out the three major tasks outlined above (order, legitimacy, and economic revival) in difficult domestic and international environments requires a relatively strong state— a state that is able to mobilize resources, to command respect of legal norms, and to guarantee the implementation of decisions. A *strong state* means not only a state with the coercive capabilities needed to make and implement authoritative decisions; it means also a state that is autonomous enough from society, and enjoying enough support from it, that it is possible for it to make decisions that respond, not to specific interests in society, but to the aggregated requirements of an efficient management of economic, social, and cultural preferences. These emanate from a developed civil society and from differentiated state institutions. Citing Goran Hyden (1991), René Lemarchand (1992: 190) avers that "governance, we are told, involves trust in state-society relations, legitimacy in the exercise of power, structures of accountability, and 'reciprocal relationships' . . . based on an underlying normative consensus."

The important assumption underlying this dynamic, normative scheme is that the state elite and civil society must not be too fragmented, as is the case today in Algeria. Such fragmentation inhibits any state effort to reestablish legitimacy and undertake consistent and long-term policies of institutionalization and economic revival; it also makes society unable effectively to articulate its demands in an aggregate fashion, in the form of a new consensus on the future. If, instead of a new institutionalized and balanced state-society interaction, such fragmentation persists, Algeria is likely then to continue experiencing sporadic and violent expressions of demands from ill-defined groups attempting to claim hegemonic leadership over the entire social plan (e.g., the FIS today).

By Western standards, civil society in Algeria is not yet established. It is slowly trying to assert itself next to a state that, because of recent signs of vulnerability and incoherence, seems not only to be receptive to it but is also trying to use it as a major tool for reestablishing its tarnished legitimacy. The spring of 1993 could be rightly called the "spring of civil society" because it witnessed relatively intense interaction between elements of this nascent civil society and the state. The High State Council met with the most active elements among the various associations and parties that had come to occupy the social and professional landscape of Algeria since 1988. These included the leaders of the moderate Islamic party, Hamas, the Islamic Supreme Council, the National Association of Imams, the National Association of Zaouias, the National Union of Public Entreprises, the Federation of the Management Associations of Local Public Entreprises, the Association of the Friends of Algiers, Protection of the Casbah, the Culture and Progress Circle, the National Syndicate of Algerian Jurists, the Lawyers National Order, and the Rally for Culture and Democracy (*Le Matin,* March 31, April 4, 6, 1993).

This receptivity of the state constitutes a great opportunity for civil society to make headway in institutionalizing itself in the political sphere of Algeria. Civil society is not only a set of associations and parties aggregating and articulating interests, it is also a strategy for political change. Depending on other surrounding factors, the birth and development of this civil society may be inhibited if the state coopts its most active, moderate elements and eliminates its most challenging ones. Evidence that the state is flirting with this risk is to be noted in the creation by the state of a consultative council—an advisory body, that somehow makes up for a suspended parliament—and the recruitment in it of sixty members from the professions and other areas of activity, and in the continuing armed battle against radical Islamists who have resorted to violence to impose their demands.

In Algeria, the concept of civil society remains unclear; and there is even more doubt about its impact, as an instrument of democratic change and democratic life, on the current precarious situation in that country. Now that the state has managed to make headway in reestablishing itself, will it be able to coexist with a civil society that is more and more active, demanding, and critical? It needs to be remembered that behind the abstract notion of *state* there are individuals whose interests are best served by state hegemony over society, despite the heritage of illegitimacy that it has built out of its past record.

■ Conclusion

To lift Algeria out of its current, multidimensional crisis, only a politically brokered and lasting understanding between society and the state can help. This understanding would set a peaceful and coherent course to follow; it would institutionalize newly defined rules of interaction between a governing and accountable state and a civil society entrusted—and empowered—with looking after most of the affairs of its members.

Several factors mitigate against a meaningful dialogue on this future understanding or social contract. Predominant are:

- The absence of a constitutional president
- The suspended legislature
- The appointment of municipal officials in place of dismissed elected FIS officials
- The recurring substitution of military courts for civilian ones
- Police work being done more and more by the army (a dangerous politicization of the only institution that can protect the state and hold the country together)
- The absence of any leading party in the political arena—the FLN having been discredited and the FIS banned
- An ideological vacuum
- A media that is restrained in the name of national security
- A fragmented legal opposition

These factors are important obstacles to recovery from the current growth crisis. They need to be addressed by both the state and civil society if the former is to be reinstated and the latter to be instated in the context of a peaceful transition to democracy.

12

South Africa: State Transition and the Management of Collapse

Sipho Shezi

The factors that make weak states are embedded in the nature of the state itself, in the manner in which it evolves, and in the interests it represents. In the case of South Africa, the state never enjoyed any legitimacy to exercise political authority. The immorality of its ideological framework always put into question its legitimacy as the supreme institution of political authority over the inhabitants of its political terrain. Therefore its replacement was an inevitable reality; just a matter of time. The more important question is whether the end of the apartheid state can be achieved without the collapse of the state in general, i.e., authority, law and order, in South Africa or whether it will present insurmountable difficulties for the successor state. What are its implications for the future evolution of South African society?

This is what makes the South African case unique compared to other African states in collapse. Other countries enjoyed at least a degree of political legitimacy during the early stages of their independence, whereas the South African state's survival and legitimacy were a matter of controversy and political contest between the white minority and the black majority. While the white minority ferociously tried to maintain the state as a vehicle for entrenching its supremacy and prosperity, the black majority fought to dismantle the state as the instrument directly responsible for their oppression and total denial of basic human rights. Now, when for the first time it can also construct a new one to replace the old, it is obliged to build a new legitimacy in cooperation with the heirs of the old.

■ **1970–1990: Context for Collapse of the State**

After 1970, the collapse of the South African state was a gradual process and it generated its own momentum (Ohlson and Stedman 1994).[1] This momentum assumed new proportions during the 1980s when it became clear that any degree of voluntary control and obedience that the state could claim was becoming elusive. The economy plummeted into deep crisis because of the flight of capital, domestic economic pressure, international isolation, economic and diplomatic sanctions and arms embargo, increasing foreign debts, and loss of international creditworthiness.[2] The war in Angola and Namibia and destabilization activities in the region further aggravated the economic crisis of the state. Politically, a similar process assumed new proportions during the 1980s. The intensification of mass struggles, boycotts, and stayaways, the increasing level of political mobilization, particularly among young urban black South Africans, the ungovernability of the townships, and increasing challenge to the homeland system by its inhabitants were factors indicative of the extent to which the impending collapse of the South African state was creating its own political momentum.[3]

Any soberminded political and economic supporter of the status quo in the mid-1980s had to come to terms with this painful reality. For example, the attempt to impose mechanisms of political control and authority of the black majority through the establishment of the black local authorities, intensification of repression through the imposition of the state of emergency, mass detention and political trials, and assassination of political activists failed to achieve the intended political objective.[4] Equally, the failure of the homeland system, as well as the tricameral system of 1983, which included the participation of the Indians and so-called Coloured communities in Parliament to the exclusion of the black majority, proved beyond any reasonable doubt the inability of the government to orchestrate some form of legitimacy for the South African state.[5]

The failure of these initiatives further eroded even that very limited level of legitimacy that the state claimed as a justification for its continued survival. Most particularly, contradictions and tensions developed not only within the white constituency in general, but also between owners of capital and the holders of political power. These internal contradictions and tensions between the ruling elite and its constituency were reflections of the broader crisis of legitimacy facing the state and its surrogate forces. The manifestations of this crisis were diverse, but they laid the basis for the subsequent developments of the 1990s.

These manifestations could be broadly divided into two types. The first relates to the general acknowledgment on the part of the wide range of sectors that comprise the traditional constituency of the state that the South African state in its then form was obsolete. Some mechanism for changing the nature and the form of the state had to be developed. It was no longer possible to rely on the intensification of repression as the means for the survival of the state. Because this acknowledgment was neither voluntary nor unanimous, the period of the 1980s was marked by divisions, tensions, and contradictions in white politics. The sudden resignation of Frederick van

Zyl Slabbert from the parliamentary opposition Progressive Federal Party; increasing backlash from the white right and a conservative trend in the 1987 elections; increasing protestations from the South African white business sector; the dramatic resignation and departure for London of former Barclays Bank director Chris Ball because of the immorality of the apartheid system; and the flight of expertise and drain of brainpower—all these are examples of the extent to which the changing political and economic dynamics within the ruling minority were beginning to contribute to the immediate demise of the state. The most striking sign came through Dr. Piet Koornhof, then minister of cooperation and development, who infuriated his colleagues in the cabinet by his publicly stated opinion that South Africa would ultimately be led by a black president (*Sunday Tribune*, July 8, 1984).

Feeling the loss of political initiative and control, the state resorted to the intensification of repression. Increasingly, the control of the state shifted to the securocrats—a tightly knit security bureaucratic infrastructure led by the top echelons of the South African Defence Force, South African Police, and the National Intelligence Service, who assumed a significant political role of the state, especially under P. W. Botha in the 1980s (Johnson and Martin 1989; Grundy 1986). The consolidation of the state in this manner proved to contain an internal paralysis of its own. In return, the resilience of the democratic movement combined with the international pressure of sanctions and arms embargo exacerbated the legitimacy crisis.

The second dimension in which the crisis manifested itself relates to the search by members of the ruling elite for some means to facilitate a relatively smooth political transition, given the imminent collapse of the state. It is in this perspective that a series of preliminary negotiations began between a wide range of sectors and the antiapartheid movement in the period 1984 to 1989. In the Eastern Cape and Natal, there was an increasing effort by the business community—notably the chamber of commerce and industry—to reach out to the trade union movement, the United Democratic Front (UDF), civic associations, and youth organizations to resolve issues such as consumer boycotts through negotiations. Contacts were made with the ANC to find ways to resolve the political impasse through trips to Lusaka by prominent business leaders, academics, church figures, and the Broederbond leaders, most of them formerly strong supporters of the status quo. The visit to Robben Island by President P. W. Botha and Minister of Justice Kobie Cootzee for a meeting with Nelson Mandela, imprisoned for life because of his leadership role in the ANC's struggle for the creation of a nonracial, democratic state, was a turning point in these events, even though the offer of release—originally to exile—in exchange for nonviolence was not accepted (Zartman 1995).

■ From Repression to Transition

All these factors laid the framework for the dramatic events that have unfolded since President F. W. de Klerk announced the liberation of Mandela and the unbanning of the ANC on February 2, 1990. The repeal of the various laws that have underpinned the existence of the racist and undemocratic state in South Africa convinced most political players that the collapse of the old state and its replacement by a democratic one was irreversible.

These political events included the unconditional release of anti-apartheid leaders like Mandela, the unbanning of the liberation movements, and repeal of the Group Areas Acts of 1950 and the Population Registration Act of 1950. These were all monumental developments in the demise of the apartheid system and they gave rise to a political environment conducive to negotiations between the National Party government and major anti-apartheid organizations led by the ANC and its allies, culminating in the ANC's April 1994 election victory.

After 1991, multiparty talks involving more than nineteen South African political players, originally termed the Congress for a Democratic South Africa (CODESA), and then the multiparty conference, aimed at promoting dialogue among South Africans of various political persuasions. These were accompanied by a series of bilateral talks between the government and representatives of the major political players. While the political dialogue between these different political players did not proceed without problems, and at times breakdowns and political posturing, it nonetheless generated an element of rapport, a degree of understanding between a wide range of political actors across the political divide. The ANC in 1992 and the Pan-African Congress (PAC) in 1994 unilaterally suspended armed struggle, in contrast to their initial position requiring mutual cessation of hostilities. On its side, the government finally honored its undertaking unconditionally to release all political prisoners, including those sentenced to death.

In particular, these multiparty and bilateral talks were instrumental in bringing the major protagonists much closer in their perception of the need to dismantle the apartheid system. Most relevant to the management of collapse was the development of consensus between the National Party government and the ANC about the need to facilitate a smooth transition from the apartheid state to a nonracial democratic state. Even though the years after 1991 were characterized by acrimonious debate between the ANC and the government pertaining to the nature of the future democratic state, there was throughout broad agreement on fundamental principles. Both parties agreed on the need for a universal suffrage, nonracial democratic elections, proportional representation, a bill of rights, and an interim government/

transitional authority and a constituent assembly, to be followed by the formation of the government of national reconciliation/unity (now in place).
The devil was in the details.

The common agreement about the need to ensure a smooth political
transition from apartheid almost led to the total derailment of the entire
process over the form of the transition. While the government insisted on
retaining the present state in all its forms for the sake of ensuring an element of continuity in various sectors of society, to minimize the political
and economic disruptions characteristic of political transition, the ANC
argued the opposite. Premised on the argument that the National Party government could not be a player in the negotiation process and a referee at the
same time, the ANC insisted on the formation of an interim government,
representing all political players with significant support. The liberation
movement also argued for a constituent assembly as the only elective body
that could be charged with the responsibility for drafting and approving a
constitution for a new democratic state.[6]

It was the fundamental common perception with regard to the management of the collapse of the apartheid state that provided the basis for the
dramatic compromises and concessions that brought about the demise of
the apartheid state. The culmination of these compromises and concessions
was the common agreement about the formation of a Transitional
Executive Council in September 1993, under whose authority were placed
several administrative councils charged with the responsibility of facilitating joint management of the various important spheres of political life such
as the judiciary, army and police, and the South African Broadcasting
Corporation and other forms of mainstream media. The Transitional
Executive Council, installed in September 1993, also ensured the election
of delegates to the constituent assembly and the formation of the government of national unity.[7]

Beyond merely leveling the political field for a fair and equitable political settlement, the formation of the Transitional Executive Council sent a
signal to the multilateral institutions, developed countries, and development agencies to support the political transition (*Star*, September 15,
1992). There was consensus that an unmanaged collapse of the apartheid
state could result in the loss of confidence on the part of these international
institutions and governments about South Africa as a potential source for
investment. Maintaining a degree of political and economic stability in
order to attract desperately needed foreign capital, investment, and development aid was a major preoccupation during the transition.

The establishment of the Transitional Executive Council also gave
courage and inspiration to the internal participants shaping the new state.
An agreement at the same time provided for an interim constitution, a set of
basic principles, and an elected legislative and constituent assembly operat-

ing under an executive in which the leading elected parties would share power. The constitutional principles, the two-stage constitution process, and the powersharing arrangements, which were to govern the executive exercise of power for a five-year period, were all measures to manage the collapse of the apartheid state and prepare the formation of the state of all South Africans under majority rule.

South Africa's first free and fair elections for all occurred on April 26–29, 1994, and gave an overwhelming majority—nearly two-thirds of the vote—to the ANC. Despite a late start in the development of its political infrastructure, the ANC showed its immense popularity and extensive support, overcoming the attempt of the political violence that rose right up to the time of the elections to deny it its position of leadership. The installation of Nelson Mandela as South African president on May 10 marked the end of the managed collapse but only the beginning of the new period of reconstruction, during which the establishment of the new state needs to be assured against the remaining attacks from the remnants of the old system and during which the tremendous pent-up demands of the victims of the old system need to be addressed.

■ **The Legacy of the Apartheid System:
   A Liability to the Transition Process**

These developments were paralleled by other events that made the course of the transition process unpredictable. There were several reasons for this. On the surface these reasons may appear superficial and distinct from each other, but in actual fact they were real and mutually reinforcing. At worst they constitute an internal paralysis of the political and economic consensus and produce an improperly managed state collapse—a feature common in the contemporary initiatives to create a new state in the majority of African and other cases.

The launching of the democratic state in South Africa out of its collapsing predecessor does not take place in a political vacuum. It is being constantly shaped by the historical and material conditions existing on the ground. The history of South Africa has not been the best in the continent. In fact, throughout the contemporary international system, very few societies have had to undertake the dismantling and creation of a new state under political conditions such as those that existed in South Africa. The legacy of apartheid created conditions in which conflict and confrontation were turned into a culture, not only leading to the collapse of the state but also providing the political and economic context bound to shape the future of the emerging democratic state.

In spite of the amazingly peaceful election period in April 1994, political violence and the culture of confrontation, defiance of authority, mass boycotts, political intolerance, deep-seated distrust, and racial hatred have become deeply enmeshed in the evolving South African political culture. At once products of the apartheid state and instruments of its demise, they threaten to survive beyond the collapse of the apartheid system and pose serious challenges for the democratic state. The disappearance of the collapsing state is unlikely to be followed by a radical change in the conditions created by decades of political oppression and economic deprivation. The reality experienced by millions of young South Africans under extreme conditions of militarization, political intolerance, mass detention and security legislation, disobedience and defiance of political authority, denial of national identity and responsibility, racial injustice, hatred, and suspicion, lingers to haunt they new political order.

This reality can be seen from the intensification of political violence that engulfed the country after 1987, and assumed new proportions during the first four years of the 1990s, increasing as the election approached. Between 1987 and 1990, more than 5,000 lives were lost as a result of violence; between 1990 and 1993, more than 9,000 lives were lost nationally due to political violence (Human Rights Commission 1992); in the first four months of 1994, 4,000 more people died. Many explanations for this phenomenon have been advanced, including the role of the South African Security establishment commonly referred to as the "Third Force elements," the so-called ideological rivalry between the ANC and the Inkatha Freedom Party (IFP), and the competition between different sections of the deprived communities for limited resources and infrastructure (NDL 1992; Goldstone 1992; Mare 1992). In reality, at different moments of South African life, these factors in one way or another fueled the intensification of political violence. Besides the damage to human life, political violence has become so deeply embedded into the South African polity that it constitutes one of the crucial threats to the emergence of a strong, viable democratic state. It will require a deliberate effort to maintain a conducive environment in which the victims of apartheid will be able to associate the values of democratic practices with the amelioration of their social and economic condition.

From the midst of the transition, between collapse and reconstruction, it remains difficult to be sure how the democratic state will address the damage that has been done to the social fabric by political violence. The breakdown in social ethics and morality manifested in a variety of ways. Since 1987 an escalating number of crooks, gangsters, and hoodlums received more publicity than any attempt to demonstrate leadership, consensus, and cooperation among political players. This trend has increased over 1994 since the elections, surpassing the declining political violence. Instances of rape and various forms of abuse of women increased throughout the first half of the 1990s. In Natal, where violence was more concentrated than in any other part of the country, instances of rape followed by killing of the victims (including women sixty to seventy years of age) have become commonplace.

Apart from the sociological effects of the apartheid system, which has always been held responsible for the high rate of crime in black communities, the intensification of political violence generated its own momentum in the area of crime. Communities were coerced, without the authority of any political leadership, to pay "protection fees" for defense against attacks by alleged political rivalries. This increased burden on the impoverished communities was coupled with an increasing rate of theft of furniture and other valuable personal belongings.

The failure of the apartheid police and legal system to intervene effectively in such instances further exacerbated these conditions. In particular, the fact that police, agents of the state, were seen to collaborate in the perpetuation of violence in these communities made communities lose the little confidence they had in the South African legal system. Because of the racial and political situation, the majority of the local criminals were deliberately not apprehended, and as a result communities generally adopted a cynical attitude toward reporting most crimes and thefts. Communities were told by police officials that they would not intervene because the criminals were supporters of an organization like the ANC, which—at that time—was still very much perceived as an enemy of the South African legal and security establishment. Evidence to this effect came from a wide range of instances, including the deliberate release of some of the most feared common-law criminals before the completion of their prison sentences. In places like Pietermaritzburg and Kwa-Mashu in Durban, these criminals have gone back to the communities and formed gangs that committed the most gruesome atrocities—the murder of families, theft of cars and property, and looting of shops, supermarkets, and delivery trucks. Rape, particularly of girls between the ages of seven and fifteen years, was common.

In the beginning of 1992, stunning and dramatic revelations were made about a deliberate effort to use common-law criminals in the perpetuation of violence and general destabilization of communities in Natal (*Natal Witness,* March 7, 1992). Police and prison warders began to develop "arms factories" inside prison workshops, manufacturing spears and pangas for use in township violence. There were several reported instances where the police collaborated with released criminals in targeting and assassinating certain people, particularly the local leadership of organizations like the ANC and allied organizations. In such cases the acts superficially appear like ordinary crimes, when in fact they were politically motivated and were explicitly or implicitly sanctioned by police authorities themselves. In the new era, marked by the installation of the ANC-dominated, powersharing government, the scars of these events remain. Managed collapse means that the new state will have to restore faith in its functions.

■ Redefining the Role of the Political Player

The tragic dimension of the violence was that most of the acts were committed under the pretext of political activism or rivalry between the ANC and the Inkatha Freedom Party (IFP). Most of the culprits involved in these activities wore the T-shirts of particular organizations and claimed to be their members and supporters. The problem posed is greatest for the ANC. Its popularity, with two-thirds of the vote, means that the support and membership of the organization cannot be strictly confined to its card-carrying militants. There is a general tendency for the majority of young South Africans, particularly the product of mass mobilization of the 1980s, to associate themselves with it as a liberation movement. This dimension has posed a serious challenge to the ANC, not only as a political player in South African politics but as a central and indispensable actor in the future democratic state.

The implications for the political transition and beyond are far-reaching. All the efforts to minimize the political and economic dislocation from the collapse of the apartheid state need to be buttressed by a strong political organization and leadership. In a situation like South Africa's where the level of expectations has been raised beyond reasonable proportions, and the level of political consciousness and mass mobilization is equally high, the ability to absorb these features into organizational forms becomes crucial, both for purposes of effective management of the collapse of the state, and for the viability of the emerging democratic state.

As the ANC makes serious concessions and compromises to ensure a relatively peaceful transition to a future democratic state, the need for a well-developed infrastructure and communication has become crucial. The peaceful resolution of the South African conflict and the reconstruction of the state not only depends on the removal of the statutory features of the apartheid system, but also on the ability of the ANC to sell its compromises and concessions to its constituency. In other words, a peaceful transition from the collapsed apartheid state to a democratic political order lies not only in allaying the fears of white people, but most crucially, in linking the compromises made to achieve this objective with relief for the social and economic deprivations that the majority of black people have always hoped will be immediately removed by a nonracial democratic state.

It is one thing for the ANC to talk about a shift in emphasis from nationalization to a mixed economy and the need to guarantee pensions and employment of the white workers in the present local government and security structures; and it is completely a different thing to explain the logic of these concessions and compromises to the majority of its supporters who have suffered the legacy of the apartheid system (ANC 1993). They have fought all their lives to dismantle the apartheid state and all its remnants, and therefore it requires intensive political education and explanation to make logic of the fact that a peaceful resolution of the South African conflict may not necessarily meet these expectations overnight. In the context of South African politics and the damage that has been inflicted by the collapsing state on the lives of millions of South Africans, the connection between a peaceful political transition and the survival of a strong democratic state in the future can never be taken as a given.

Similar violence is done to the culture of human rights. The struggle against apartheid was primarily motivated by the need to protect the most fundamental basic human rights of life and dignity. The extent to which the effects of political violence undermined this culture can be seen from the manner in which innocent lives were lost. The repercussions were compounded; communities in mass meetings would take decisions to resolve a problem by resorting to the harshest measures of punishment, possibly involving a decision to kill. These are direct and indirect manifestations of the effects of political violence that accompany the impending collapse of the state.

The culture of conflict and confrontation, which was highly instrumental in bringing about the collapse of the apartheid state, continues to assert itself in a manner that may ultimately prove to be detrimental to the postapartheid era. As the political transition unfolds at an accelerated rate, its momentum threatens to usurp the high degree of political control that the liberation movement and its allies had always prided themselves in exercising over a large portion of its constituency. This is an angry and volatile constituency whose expectations have been raised both by the legacy of the apartheid system and the mass mobilization of the 1980s. The popularity of the ANC's Freedom Charter during that period encouraged the political and economic expectations of the majority of South Africans. Young and old people expect that the demise of the apartheid system would immediately open the doors to social and economic improvement in their standard of living. The collapse of basic infrastructure, housing, and normalcy as a result of political violence exacerbated these expectations.

In the context of South Africa, the majority of whose people have inherited extreme levels of poverty, malnutrition, and political, social, and economic deprivations, democracy means much more than the right to vote in a multiparty system. It means the ability of the new government to satisfy the basic educational, social, and economic needs of the victims of oppression in a manner that will significantly narrow the gap between white affluence and mass poverty. The problems in implementing the National Peace Accords that were designed to end political violence in black communities should convey the practical lesson that the democratization of South Africa has its own unique requirements. Communities supporting the major players in the ongoing conflict in Natal repeatedly stated that there would be no end to the fighting as long as they lack shelter and educational institutions for their children. These were either completely destroyed during the fighting or were unavailable to certain sections of the communities because of their political affiliation. More than 60 percent of young black employable people were unemployed in 1993 and the figure was rising as a result of an increasing school dropout rate produced by the unchanging conditions in black education and the intensification of political violence.

There is no magic by which the new democratic state can redress the social and economic underdevelopment of the black communities in the short run. The only practical remedy is to implement the process of infusing a new sense of realism and pragmatism to the majority of people who have been denied these opportunities. All measures that will be undertaken to redistribute the wealth, as the popularity of the Freedom Charter made the majority of people believe, will indeed be undertaken by the government in which the ANC is the major player, but the economic and social benefits for these redistributive measures will not be felt overnight. Expectations were raised through the political process; therefore any attempt to mediate the adverse effects of these expectations has to take place through a political process, and on more or less the same scale on which the mass mobilization and organization against the apartheid system took place. Only the ANC and its allied organizations are in a position to translate the political rhetoric of the past and convert the energy of the majority into a political vehicle that can sustain multiparty democracy. Failure to undertake this imperative task will raise serious questions not only about the viability of a peaceful political transition, but equally, with regard to the prospects for a political and economic stability of a future democratic state.

■ Conclusion

Administrative and racial integration are major tasks facing the post-apartheid state. It is one thing to talk and preach nonracialism, it is another to implement the concept. Former President F. W. de Klerk continued, into the 1990s, to deceive the white people that a postapartheid South Africa would not alter anything with regard to their living conditions. Perhaps this may be true for the near future, but definitely not for the long-term future.

Before the election, this was the ticket on which he received his mandate to continue with the reform process, and on which he won his March 1992 referendum. In the 1994 election, he won his votes as the person (and party) that could best defend that way of life under the new conditions. It was a false mandate, based on the fact that, after 1990, he consistently built his vision for the white constituency on the concessions and compromises made by the ANC. Obviously it will not be long before reality strikes, with destabilizing consequences for the new state. Signs to this effect could be seen in the preelection proliferation of the private armies of the white right. It was estimated in 1993 that there were more than 30,000 members of "Boere Kommando units" dispersed throughout the country. Their defeat in Bophutatswana in February 1994 showed their weakness at a crucial moment before the elections. Even though their impact was not as great as feared, they nevertheless constitute a rogue element for concern in the future stability of the country.

Reflecting on all the issues that have been raised by the collapse of the apartheid state and the transition to a democratic one is a roller-coaster experience. One morning one wakes up full of hope and the following morning one feels that the prospects for the future are fascinating but unfeasible. This is what constitutes a dilemma between thriving on the collapse of the apartheid state on the one hand, while avoiding the effects of collapse that threaten to throw society into chaos and political turmoil on the other hand. The mind never reaches an answer to questions such as: What are the chances that South Africa will not drown in the quagmire of continuous unrest and confrontation? What is the potential for professional people emigrating in the thousands? With how much certainty can we claim that institutions—the basic foundation of a sound society—will not collapse under the weight of exaggerated demands? Given the present political and economic flux, to what extent will hope for the future—the source of energy and courage—not evaporate?

The most positive thing is that South Africans across the political spectrum have realized the intensity of the challenge. Well-meaning members of society are constantly attempting to evolve possible solutions to these issues. It is this vigor and determination that will ensure that the collapse of the apartheid state does not precipitate the deterioration of South Africa into an anarchical society. Development and reconstruction have become an overriding preoccupation. Communities are being encouraged to initiate development and reconstruction projects according to their own sense of priorities. Institutions such as the Independent Development Trust Fund, the Development Bank of Southern Africa, and the Development Resources Institute are some of the development entities that are focusing resources toward this end. Most importantly, the international business community through increased and returning investment and other nations of the world through development agencies are also increasing their involvement in the initiatives aimed at redressing the underdevelopment of black communities.

The collapse of the old and birth of a new state that requires a redefinition of every layer of what has defined it in the past is not an easy task. It requires a lot of patience, determination, and perseverance. This becomes even more difficult when dealing with a society whose majority of the population says "We have waited for too long." The fact that the state collapsed bears testimony to the fact that South Africans have proved their ability to destroy. The challenge for the immediate future is to demonstrate a similar level of ability to rebuild. For the major political players and their constituencies, this is what constitutes the test for their ability to maintain a balance between the need to accelerate the demise of the apartheid state on the one hand, and create a conducive environment for the emergence of a nonracial, nonsexist democratic South Africa on the other hand. From afar, the historical moment triggers a sense of pessimism, but as one gets closer to the reality, one draws an incredible strength of optimism and hope from the fact that political actors, institutions, and a variety of community-based networks are engaging with the process. The task is certainly not going to be easy, but it shall be done.

■ Notes

1. The post-1970 period is important as it marked the first indices (following the banning of political organizations and imprisonment of their leaders in 1960) to the effect that the state was once again susceptible to political and economic pressure. For purposes of economic growth, the state could no longer afford disruptions by black workers in demand for the recognition of their trade union rights. Black trade unions received recognition for the first time in the history of South Africa. Equally, growth in manufacturing significantly increased reliance on external debt to finance economic growth.

2. Also see the IMF discussion paper on the South African economy, January 1992.

3. The growth of the mass democratic movement during this period delivered impeccable political blows to the South African government. In every part of the country, there was development of strong grassroots organizations, the majority of whom identified themselves with the African National Congress. This political tide resulted in the formation of the United Democratic Front in August 1983. It was also accompanied by the growth of the strong trade union movement, resulting in the formation of Cosatu in 1985.

4. For example, the imposition of the black authorities through the introduction of the Black Authorities Act of 1983 further ignited antiapartheid protest. The imposed government became even more discredited. Although the imposition of the State of Emergency in 1985 and 1986 restricted political activity, it failed to decapitate the growth of the mass democratic movement. The ANC's armed struggle intensified during this period.

5. The tricameral system was introduced through the Parliaments Act of 1983. According to this act, Indians, Coloureds, and Whites were to be represented in Parliament. Black South Africans were denied this opportunity and the Black Local Authorities Act of 1983 was passed as a measure that would accommodate those black people who lived in urban areas and could not be classified as falling under any of the homeland governments. These black local authorities were appointed by the Department of Co-operation and Development.

6. For more information on this, see *Report on the Deliberations in CODESA I and II*, African National Congress. See also *Negotiations Bulletin*.

7. See Report of the ANC on the multiparty conference held on April 3, 1993.

PART 4

POTENTIAL AGENTS
OF RECONSTRUCTION

13

State Collapse: The Humanitarian Challenge to the United Nations

Francis Mading Deng

In most cases, the collapse of the state is associated with humanitarian tragedies resulting from armed conflict, communal violence, and gross violations of human rights that culminate in the massive outflow of refugees and internal displacement of the civilian populations. It is the lack or loss of capacity to cope with the crisis that leads to the collapse of the state and necessitates the intervention of the international community through the United Nations. Yesterday Somalia and Rwanda, and outside of Africa, Bosnia and Haiti, tomorrow Zaire and Sudan come to mind as example. As the Introduction to this book notes, states collapse "because they can no longer perform the functions required for them to pass as states." The crisis is particularly acute in Africa where 15 million of the 25 million internally displaced persons worldwide are found. Africa also leads the world in its refugee population.

When the breakdown of civil society or the outbreak of unmanageable civil violence necessitates a humanitarian intervention from the international community, a further crisis situation arises with respect to the precise objectives and conduct of the operations involved. Usually, the immediate purpose of delivering urgently needed relief supplies becomes compelling and overwhelming. Little attention is paid to the conditions leading to the crisis or the longer-term perspective of reconstruction and normalization of a self-sustaining order; in other words, putting the collapsed state back together. Understanding the causes leading to the collapse of the system is critical to developing workable, long-term solutions. But the issue is not only one of managing short-term crises or embarking on the longer-term solutions. The spectrum is even larger: it should begin with the question of whether or not the deterioration of a particular situation merits international intervention, how such intervention is to be conducted, and what precise objectives it should aim at attaining.

■ The Quest for a Global Strategy

The strategy for international response to internal conflicts and communal violence leading to the breakdown of civil order and the actual or potential collapse of the state should aim at addressing the challenges comprehensively through a three-phase strategy that would involve monitoring the developments to draw early attention to impending crises, interceding in time to avert the crisis through diplomatic initiatives, and mobilizing international action when necessary. A comprehensive strategy of intervention in three phases would require arresting the immediate crisis, appraising the situation with reference to the root causes, and designing a plan of action for the reconstruction of the society and the state, as the case may be.

The quest for a system of international response to conflict and attendant humanitarian tragedies was articulated by Secretary-General Boutros Boutros-Ghali (1992) in *An Agenda for Peace,* referring to the end of the Cold War and the surging demands on the United Nations Security Council as the central instrument for the prevention and resolution of conflicts and the preservation of peace:

> Our aims must be: To seek to identify at the earliest possible stage situations that could produce conflict, and to try through diplomacy to remove the sources of danger before violence results;
>
> Where conflict erupts, to engage in peacemaking aimed at resolving the issues that have led to conflict;
>
> Through peace-keeping, to work to preserve peace, however fragile, where fighting has been halted and to assist in implementing agreements achieved by the peacemakers;
>
> To stand ready to assist in peace-building in its differing contexts: rebuilding the institutions and infrastructures of nations torn by civil war and strife; and building bonds of peaceful mutual benefit among nations formerly at war;
>
> And in the largest sense, to address the deepest causes of conflict: economic despair, social injustice and political oppression. It is possible to discern an increasingly common moral perception that spans the world's nations and peoples, and which is finding expression in international laws, many owing their genesis to the work of this Organization.

These aims address "the global law-and-order deficit" that has been described by the former U.S. assistant secretary of state for African affairs, Chester Crocker (1992). In an effort, first, to understand why the wave of state collapse in Somalia and elsewhere is flourishing, and its effect on U.S. national interests, he wrote:

> Historic changes since 1989 have profoundly destabilized the previously existing order without replacing it with any recognizable or legitimate system. New vacuums are setting off new conflicts. Old problems are being solved, begetting new ones. The result of this process is a global

law-and-order deficit that is straining the capacity of existing and emerging security institutions.

A new load of demands is now being placed on the United Nations to deploy peacekeepers, ceasefire observers, election monitors, and even civilian administrators. In addition to the requirements of peace accords that create new challenges, these demands stem from the disintegration of governments, states, or empires that no longer enjoy the legitimacy and domestic or external support to survive. Crocker writes:

> We preach to the rest of the world the post–Cold War litany of U.S. goals and hopes: democracy and human rights, free markets and peaceful settlement of disputes. This sermon is fine as far as it goes, but it is a hopelessly inadequate answer to our era of change. Democracy and free markets are not capable of being "exported" by Voice of America broadcasts or "taught" through exchanges of scholars. They cannot be imposed by isolation and sanctions.

Crocker proceeds to outline some principles for meeting the challenges of the law-and-order deficit he diagnoses:

> We do need to address the mounting lack of consensus on basic norms of global political life combined with the shortage of legitimate institutions for handling the resulting security problems. We also need to remedy the scarcity of means for "enforcing" whatever solutions may be agreed upon. Not since the Napoleonic upheavals (if not the Peace of Westphalia in 1648) have the rights of states, people and governments been so unclear.
>
> Under what circumstances are territorial borders to be considered sacrosanct and who shall determine the answer? When do "identity groups" (peoples or ethnic fragments) have the right of secession, autonomy or independence? What "sovereign" rights, if any, do governments have to prevent outsiders from telling them how to treat their people, their economies and their environment? And what about the rights of outsiders to come to the aid of peoples victimized by the actions or inactions of local governments—or to create the functional equivalent of government where, as in Somalia, none exists?
>
> The law-and-order deficit cannot be eliminated by relying solely on ad hoc, unilateral U.S. actions, no matter how forceful the decisions or masterful the execution. We urgently need some internationally agreed-upon rules and criteria as well as dedicated mechanisms for planning and conducting the internationally sanctioned uses of force.

From an institutional or organizational perspective, problems should be addressed and solved within their own framework, with international involvement necessitated only by the failure of the internal efforts.[1] This means that conflict prevention, management, or resolution progressively moves from the domestic domain to the regional and ultimately the global levels of concern and action. Conflicts in which the state is an effective arbiter do not present particular difficulties since they are manageable within the national framework. The problem arises when the existence of the state itself is the subject of the conflict. Under those conditions, external involvement becomes unavoidable.

In the African context, it is generally agreed that the next best level of involvement should be the Organization of African Unity (OAU). There are, however, constraints on the role of the OAU. One has to do with the limitation of resources, both material and human. But perhaps even more debilitating is the lack of political will, since in the intimate context of the region, governments feel vulnerable to the generation of conflicts resulting from the problematic conditions of state formation and nationbuilding and are therefore prone to resist any form of external scrutiny. Since the judge of today may well be the accused of tomorrow, there is a temptation to avoid confronting the problems. The result is evasiveness and neglect.

Beyond the OAU, the United Nations is the next and ultimate level of recourse, representing, as it does, the international community in its global context. But the UN suffers from the same constraints as those that affect the OAU, though to a lesser degree. It has the problem of resources and the reciprocal protectiveness of vulnerable governments.

As recent events have demonstrated, the role of the major Western powers acting unilaterally, multilaterally, or within the framework of the United Nations, though often susceptible to accusations of strategic motivation, has become increasingly pivotal. Indeed, although their motives continue to be questioned, the problem is more one of their unwillingness to become involved or lack of adequate preparedness for such involvement.

Perhaps the most important impetus for the involvement of Western industrial democracies in the breakdown of order abroad is found in the gravity of the humanitarian tragedies involved. While this motive guarantees their involvement in arresting the tragedy, it limits their involvement in its prevention at an earlier stage. This is what brought the United States and the United Nations into Somalia and Rwanda, and also with less fanfare into South Africa, Angola, and Mozambique, and would provide the strongest rationale for intervention into Zaire. Even with respect to humanitarian intervention, however, lack of preparedness for an appropriate timely response is generally acknowledged as a major limitation. Rather than fostering preparation, practices that drive the international system—loose sanctions, military detachment, and uncontrollable arms flows—inadvertently reinforce violent disintegration. Nevertheless, there is a strong presumption that the interests of the Western industrial democracies are powerfully engaged and will eventually be used to uphold and promote humanitarian intervention in crisis conditions of state collapse. Industrial democracies cannot operate without defending standards of human rights and political procedures that are being egregiously violated. Indeed, they cannot themselves prosper in an irreversibly international economy if large contiguous populations descend into endemic violence and economic disorder.

The combination of these compelling reasons and lack of preparedness for well-planned response makes the United States and Western European countries become particularly prone to crisis-induced reactions that are relatively easy to execute and are more symbolic than effective in addressing the major substantive issues involved. Principles are needed to justify effective international intervention, focusing on the objective of establishing basic civil order under conditions where it has fundamentally broken down and is unlikely to be regenerated within a reasonable time or at tolerable cost in human and material terms. As intervention is a major intrusion from outside, and despite the obvious fact that there will always be elements in the country who will welcome such intervention, especially among the disadvantaged groups to whom it promises tangible benefits, resistance on the grounds of national sovereignty or pride is also a predictable certainty, as discussed by Gambari in the next chapter. For that reason, the justification for intervention must be reliably persuasive, if not beyond reproach. "The difference between an intervention that succeeds and one that is destroyed by immune reaction would depend on the degree of spontaneous acceptance or rejection by the local population" (Steinbruner 1992).

To avoid or minimize this immune reaction, such intervention would have to be broadly international in character. The principles used and the objectives toward which it is targeted must transcend political and cultural boundaries or traditions and concomitant nationalist sentiments. In other words, it must enjoy an effective degree of global legitimacy.

> The rationale that could conceivably carry such a burden presumably involves human rights so fundamental that they are not derived from any particular political or economic ideology. . . . Any government that fails to provide the most fundamental rights for major segments of its population can be said to have forefeited sovereignty and the international community can be said to have a duty in those instances to reestablish it. If the absence of functional sovereignty is declared in any situation, assertive measures to recreate it would be allowed (Steinbruner 1992).

The three-phase strategy to meet this need would involve monitoring the developments to draw early attention to impending crises, interceding in time to avert the crisis through diplomatic initiatives, and mobilizing international action when necessary.[2] The first step would aim at detecting and identifying the problem through mechanisms for information collection, evaluation, and reporting. The strategy for preventive or corrective involvement in conflict should comprise gathering and analyzing information and otherwise monitoring situations with the view to establishing an early warning system through which the international community could be alerted to act. If sufficient basis for concern is established, the appropriate mechanism should be invoked for the taking of preventive diplomatic measures to avert the crisis. Initially, such initiatives might be taken within the framework of regional arrangements; for example, the OAU, the Conference on Security and Cooperation in Europe (CSCE), the Organization of American States (OAS). In the context of the United Nations such preventive initiatives would naturally fall on the Secretary-General, acting either personally or through special representatives. If diplomatic initiatives do not succeed, and depending on the level of human suffering involved, the Secretary-General may decide to mobilize an international response, ranging from further diplomatic measures to forced humanitarian intervention, not only to provide emergency relief, but also to facilitate the search for an enduring solution, addressing the causes of the breakdown of internal order. A strategy aimed at this broader objective would require a close understanding of the causal link with the conditions and developments leading to the outbreak of the crisis.

The main objective is that efforts, whether by internal or external actors, should enhance the prospects for providing effective protection and assistance for the needy. Since they fall within domestic jurisdiction, this can best be done through dialogue and cooperation with the government, when one is present. Such cooperation with governments should be predicated on the assumption that sovereignty carries with it responsibility for ensuring protection and assistance for the citizens. Where there is a failure to discharge that responsibility, and masses of people fall victim in consequence, it should be established whether there are objective reasons that may have to do with lack of capacity or resources. In such cases, international cooperation in providing the required protection and assistance can be expected to be invited, or at least welcomed. However, where the need is apparent and masses of the population are affected, and the government is incapable or unwilling to provide protection and assistance, whether by itself or in cooperation with foreign donors, or the state has simply collapsed, then some form of international action becomes imperative.

As Secretary-General Boutros Boutros-Ghali (1992) observed, "The time of absolute and exclusive sovereignty . . . has passed" and it is the task of leaders of states today "to find a balance between the needs of good internal governance and the requirements of an ever more interdependent world." The Secretary-General went even further: "One requirement for solutions to these problems lies in commitment to human rights with a special sensitivity to those of minorities, whether ethnic, religious, social or linguistic."

On the need for balance between the unity of larger entities and respect for sovereignty, autonomy, and diversity of various identities, the Secretary-General noted:

> The healthy globalization of contemporary life requires in the first instance solid identities and fundamental freedoms. The sovereignty, territorial integrity and independence of states within the established international system, and the principle of self-determination for peoples, both of great value and importance, must not be permitted to work against each other in the period ahead. Respect for democratic principles at all levels of social existence is crucial: in communities, within states and within the community of states. Our constant duty should be to maintain the integrity of each while finding a balanced design for all.

While the Secretary-General underscores respect for the sovereignty and integrity of the state as crucial to the existing international system, the logic of the transcendent importance of human rights as a legitimate area of concern for the international community, especially where order has broken down or the state is incapable or unwilling to act responsibly to protect the masses of citizens, would tend to make international inaction indefensible. Even in less extreme cases of internal conflict, the perspectives of the pivotal actors on such issues as the national or public interest are bound to be sharply divided both internally and in their relationship to the outside world. After all, internal conflicts often entail a contest of the national arena of power and therefore sovereignty. Every political intervention from outside has its internal recipients, hosts, and beneficiaries. Under those circumstances, there can hardly be said to be an indivisible quantum of national sovereignty behind which the nation stands united.

Furthermore, it is not always easy to determine the degree to which the state in a country devastated by civil war can be said to be truly in control; it is often the case that sizable portions of the territory are controlled by rebel or other forces. Often, while a government may exercise effective control of the capital and the main garrisons, its writ over much of the countryside in the war zone will have practically collapsed. How would such partial, but significant, collapse be factored into determining the degree to which civil order in the country has broken down?

A historical perspective on the significance of sovereignty should also reveal that the concept cannot be a value-free property of whomever claims to represent the country. Initially, sovereignty was the prerogative of the crown: the crown was supreme and above the law. The evolution of democratic values and institutions gradually devolved sovereign will and authority to the people. It is through the will of the people, democratically invested in elected leaders or symbolically claimed even by nondemocratic governments, that entitles national authorities to invoke and uphold the sovereignty of the state. Where governments fail to meet their fundamental obligations to the whole or significant parts of the population, the latter are justifiably entitled to withdraw explicitly or implicitly the trust they have placed upon them to be the symbolic custodians of their sovereignty. No government that will allow thousands, or maybe millions, to starve to death when food can be made available to them, to be exposed to deadly elements when they could be provided with shelter, to be indiscriminately tortured, brutalized, and murdered by opposing forces contesting the very sovereignty that is supposed to ensure their security, or otherwise to suffer in a vacuum of moral leadership, can still have a clear face to keep the outside world from stepping in to offer protection and assistance in the name of sovereignty.

As the crises of nation-building that have been building up over an extended period of time, covering significant historical phases, begin to explode into internecine conflicts, creating ethnic or religious cleavages in which large numbers of innocent civilian populations find themselves dispossessed by their own governments and abandoned without protection and assistance, the international community is called upon to step in and fill the vacuum of moral responsibility created by such neglect.

A high-level group convened by the InterAction Council of Former Heads of State and Government (January 21–23, 1993) on the theme, "Bring Africa Back into the Mainstream of the International System," observed:

> During the cold war period, these humanitarian tragedies were not subjected to international scrutiny, partly because they were obscured from external observation and partly because the needs involved were relatively met through the cooperation of members of the ideological camp concerned. The contemporary scene is now marked by a combination of accessibility of media information about internal conditions and lack of ideologically or strategically based support systems. This has created a situation where the pressures of international public opinion, combined with a growing global consciousness resulting from the removal of cold war barriers, inhibitions and constraints are increasingly prompting the international community to demand humanitarian action. On both moral and political grounds, this pressure can no longer be ignored or resisted.

The same questions emerged as the key to the normative framework that the international community is called upon to address: What degree of humanitarian suffering under what conditions should justify what form of international action, by whom, through what operational mechanisms, and with what precise objectives?

> This means clarifying the principles, the organizational framework, the operational doctrine, and the precise goals of such intervention. The clarification of the principles would provide guidelines or standards on what

would trigger and justify intervention. The organizational framework raises questions as to who would initiate the decision making process for intervention, and once approved, who would conduct the operations. The issue of operations itself raises questions on the military or civilian forces to be used and their preparedness or training for the task. The issue of objectives raises the question of whether the operations should stop at meeting the short-term emergency needs or extend to addressing the causes of the crisis in order to reconstitute a self-sustaining system of public or civil order.

These considerations make it even more important to monitor developments in order to determine the appropriate stage for intervention; how to conduct the process in a particular context; what resources—material, human, and cultural—there are to work with; and what outcome of the intervention should be postulated. In its continued examination of the Secretary-General's *Agenda for Peace,* the Security Council considered the questions of humanitarian assistance, peacemaking, peacekeeping, and peace-building, finding that under certain circumstances "there may be a close relationship between acute needs for humanitarian assistance and threats to international peace and security" (UNSC 1993). The council indeed "[noted] with concern the incidents of humanitarian crises, including mass displacements of population becoming or aggravating threats to international peace and security"; it expressed the belief "that humanitarian assistance should help establish the basis for enhanced stability through rehabilitation and development" and "noted the importance of adequate planning in the provision of humanitarian assistance in order to improve prospects for rapid improvement of the humanitarian situation." This naturally requires planning for the phase beyond the call of emergency.

■ Beyond the Call of Emergency

A dilemma in the international rescue operation lies in the fact that it is often triggered at an advanced stage of deterioration, with law and order broken down, large numbers of people victimized, state authority and legitimacy in collapse, and any protection and assistance by definition only a partial salvation for the survivors. It would be preferable to have in place a preventive strategy to apply before the crisis of collapse: monitoring the developments closely, detecting those trends that threaten disaster, and authorizing timely action to avert the crisis. Even when UN-coordinated intervention can only be mobilized by crisis, a similar strategy for restoring the collapsed state is needed, one that entails keeping basic order in the aftermath of a pacification campaign as an essential aspect of an even broader objective of reconstruction and reconstitution of a functioning and self-regenerating system of legitimacy and authority.

A strategy aimed at this broader objective would require a close understanding of the causal link with the conditions and developments that led to the outbreak of the crisis. It is in this context that the historical evolution of the crisis of governance in the affected countries, and the manner in which the policies and responses of the various actors, from local to global, have interplayed to generate the chain of actions and reactions, becomes a useful guide for designing the action necessary to provide appropriate remedies. An international action triggered by an intolerable degree of deterioration in the situation thus becomes both the end of the three-phase strategy aimed at arresting the crisis and the beginning of a more ambitious process, with the objective of reconstructing and consolidating peace, security, and stability.

As the postulated strategy of international response to the crisis of collapse involves three phases, so does the process of restoring and invigorating a self-sustaining system in the country concerned, putting a collapsed state back together. The first phase in this process is one of gathering and processing information about the context to determine how the past explains the present. Then comes the second phase of designing the appropriate measures to be taken in the light of the findings. The third phase would be to put into operation the strategies developed on the basis of a comprehensive analysis of the available information. Just as the three phases of the strategy of response to the crisis are closely intertwined, so would be the phases of the strategy of repair. Indeed, since the pressures of actual involvement are usually considerable, these three phases may have to be conducted in an intense process of simultaneous gathering and processing of information, designing appropriate measures, and applying them with a degree of flexibility that will continue to respond to new information, findings, and policy adjustments as they come.

Much of what is required in this conceptual framework of understanding the various aspects of the problem, in its underlying causes, dimensions of manifestations, and appropriate manner of response, is appropriate policy analysis of conditions and design of strategies. Even with the minimum level of international and operational innovations, the strategies outlined for international response would require the United Nations and the international community to make available resources adequate to the work being effective in providing what it promises. But, at least at the intellectual level, a great deal may depend on the manner in which the potential concern of the international community is tapped and utilized. Since what is needed far exceeds what can be generated through the established state institutions, universities, research institutions, and the NGO community constitute a potential resource that is as vitally important as it is needed.

Among the wide range of tasks that could be independently undertaken would be developing criteria for determining the degree of human rights violations or the scale of human suffering or the degree of breakdown in internal order that would move the international community to intervene. Such a clear setting of standards, even if not formally endorsed by governments and rendered a legally enforceable instrument, if well disseminated, could provide a useful guide and a deterrent to governments and other pertinent actors. Once prepared, its finalization and formal adoption as an official yardstick would in itself be a significant part of diplomatic initiatives in and outside the United Nations system. Such a standard-setting exercise could have a broad policy dimension whose authority would rest more in the moral value-oriented framework than in its legal enforceability. The goal, ultimately, would be for the legal and the moral dimensions to converge in an international instrument setting new standards by which governments would be held accountable. Again, while the final outcome would bear the official seal of governments, the process of preparation could be broad-based, involving individuals and groups, universities and research institutions, lawyers and policy analysts, scholars and activists—a wide network that would benefit from coordination and cooperation.

■ Seizing the Global Opportunity

The prevailing situation in the world today indicates that the international system is going through a significant transformation in two major respects. One is the emergence of human rights as a legitimate area of concern for the international community and a basis for scrutinizing the performance of governments and other domestic actors. Another is the related humanitarian concern of the international community with state collapse and other causes of domestic violence that inflict hardship and suffering on masses of people. Together, these two areas reveal early signs of a new world order in which human dignity for all people at all levels will become a matter of cooperative security for the international community (cf. Zartman and Kremenyuk 1994). This offers a global opportunity that must be seized.

What makes this change particularly significant is that, until fairly recently, the human rights field was considered so sensitive that it was either ignored or treated gingerly as a subject of confidential communications with the governments concerned. Complaints were received by the appropriate United Nations bodies and, if found to be admissible, were transmitted to the governments involved for comments. It was hoped that bringing the complaints to the attention of governments and asking them to respond would raise their level of awareness and motivate them to remedy the situation in question. The actual behavior of the government was not monitored to ensure that the desired result was achieved.

The altered circumstances of the post–Cold War era have now opened doors onto internal conflict and enabled the international community to have a closer and more sympathetic look at the internal conditions and the needs of the large masses of the world population. Along with the increased exposure of internal dynamics to the outside world, a better understanding of these conditions has developed in the international community; and, with it, a concomitant rise in the level of international concern about the conditions of the masses of people trapped and victimized by internal wars and the gross violations of human rights that often follow as a consequence.

Of course, the removal of the centralized controls of the old order has in certain parts of the world resulted in upheavals that have created new problems for both peace and respect for human rights. Conditions in both the former Soviet Union and former Yugoslavia illustrate quite dramatically the consequences of the breakup of the centralized controls of authoritarian regimes and the transformation of the Cold War international order. The "ripple effects" of this breakup have not by any means run their course and it is not yet clear what their consequences might be in terms of alternative arrangements. However, even these upheavals signify a process of liberation from repression. The challenge to the international community is to assist in the reconstruction of durable arrangements based on respect for fundamental rights. With no major strategic or ideological interests creating obstacles to international cooperation, the international community, and more specifically the United Nations, now can play a more assertive and constructive role in promoting peace and respect for human rights.

What all this means is that a new momentum in a global moral imperative is gathering and that world leaders are called upon to transcend national boundaries to meet their moral obligation toward humanity in a world that now claims a higher degree of sensitivity to the ideals of the Universal Declaration of Human Rights than ever before in its history. And if this call is directed to all those who see themselves in an international leadership role because of the global power and authority that they wield, it should obviously be associated with the role of the United Nations. As this role is redefined to meet the emerging global imperatives and challenges, the United Nations itself will need to be reinvigorated structurally and operationally to meet the challenge.

In nearly all the countries where internal conflicts are a major cause of massive human suffering, there is much that the international community, and more specifically the United Nations, can do, not only to provide needed assistance and protection to the affected population, but also to help bring durable peace to the beleaguered countries. It should always be remembered that even an impending collapse of a state is an acute manifestation of a generalized crisis that, unless arrested and resolved at the roots, threatens not only the peace and security of the country, but often also of the neighboring countries, and ultimately international order itself. For that reason, the international community cannot afford to wait too often until conditions have reached the level of a Somalia, Rwanda, Liberia, or Yugoslavia in order to act decisively. Much by way of preventive action could be taken. Such action could make international involvement far more cost-effective than the massive intervention that developed crises require to put a collapsed state back together.

■ Notes

1. The lack of normative principles and enforcement mechanisms for international response to the humanitarian challenges of civil disorder has also been a matter of concern among scholars in the Brookings Institution's Foreign Policy Studies program. See John Steinbruner, "Civil Violence as an International Security Problem," a memorandum dated November 23, 1992, addressed to the Foreign Policy Studies program staff. Much of the line of argument in the following pages is based on this memorandum.

2. For a more elaborate discussion of these phases as applied to the crisis of the internally displaced, see the UN study in document E/CN.4/1993/35 and the revised version of that study in Deng (1993). The study was considered by the Commission on Human Rights at its forty-ninth session, its findings and recommendations endorsed, and the mandate of the Special Representative of the Secretary-General extended for two years to continue to work on the various aspects of the problem as presented in the study.

14

The Role of Foreign Intervention in African Reconstruction

Ibrahim A. Gambari

In considering the role played by external forces, both African and non-African, in reviving collapsed states on the African continent, four main themes emerge. First, although the phenomenon of state collapse is not unique to Africa, its consequences tend to be particularly drastic for the socioeconomic fabric of the fragile states and civil societies there. Second, the incidences of state collapse in Africa appear to have increased in the period since the high point of the Cold War, continuing into the aftermath of superpower confrontation. Africa's growing marginalization in the post–Cold War period may, in fact, have accelerated the process of state collapse. Third, the domestic effort essential for putting back together the collapsed states in Africa has to be substantially supplemented by subregional, regional, and international support. Indeed, it may well be that the more complete the collapse of a state, the greater will be the role of foreign intervention in its reconstruction. Finally, foreign interventions are not "neutral," neither in motivation nor in impact; they may be part of the solution to state collapse, or part of the problem, or both.

Domestic collapse and foreign intervention are related to the nature of the state. It is a matter of some controversy among scholars when the state, as distinct from society, originated. Sabine (1962) argues that *State* was first used as a generic term for a body politic by the medieval political philosopher Nicolo Machiavelli; but historical evidence indicates that the first studies of organized political societies were in fact made in Greece by Plato and Aristotle in the fourth century B.C. The word they used was *polis* (city-state). The term was later adapted by the Romans and applied to larger territorial areas, resulting in the coining of the term, *status rei publicae;* i.e., a state of public affairs—a concept that appears closest to its contemporary meaning.

As defined in the Introduction to this book, states have basic characteristics. The state must have a population, territory, governmental apparatus with a monopoly of force for the preservation of peace and order, and "a plenitude of authority, independent of external control except that of international law" (Freid 1968: 144). Freid complements this with his assertion that

221

> At one extreme of argument the State is identified with one or more high-
> ly specific features, such as organized police powers, defined spatial
> boundaries or a formal judiciary. At the other end of the definitional spec-
> trum the State is regarded simply as the institutional aspect of political
> interaction, no concrete structures are specified, and the State, being
> coterminous with society, vanishes in universality.

Within this spectrum, foreign intervention means that state functions are
being performed—whether as assistance or as interference—by another
state or groups of states.

The modern African state, though sharing in many of these attributes,
is special in several ways. It emerged from the ashes of colonialism, a
regime of alien rule that sought to forge political entities out of diverse
nations and peoples. African state boundaries, being colonially inherited,
are permeable and ill-defined. They contain nations and peoples who strad-
dle the lines—peoples who never really accepted the white man's boundaries, although the independent governments of the new states have tried to
enforce them, often with great difficulty. One of the problems faced by
states with colonially inherited boundaries, according to Nzongola-Ntalaja
(1987: 79), is that "the dogma of the preservation of colonially inherited
boundaries" became a license that governments used to oppress minorities
and hide their incompetencies and indifference to the suffering of the peoples.

Even in the best of times in Africa, the maintenance of law and order
as an attribute of statehood has existed only tenuously, because the instruments of the state, such as the judiciary, the police, and the army, have
never really been sufficient to cope with the full demands of governance.
As noted by Ekwe-Ekwe (1990: 155), the African state is still essentially
the trading post created by European imperialism. Hence, for its peoples,
particularly its national minorities, it has no organic essence, and its structure and polity are inherently weak. It is a "nonnational state" and it hardly
makes any difference whether the prevailing political economy of a given
state is capitalist (for example, Nigeria) or postcapitalist (for example,
Ethiopia).

■ Intervention Defined

Intervention in international politics is an old concept. Sometimes it has
been defined by international legal publicists to mean "dictatorial or coercive interference by an outside party or parties in the sphere of jurisdiction
of an independent political community" (Bull 1984: 1; cf. Oppenheim
1985). However, not all the examples discussed below will be dictatorial,
coercive, or interfering. Interventions can take the forms of forcible or non-

forcible interference. In the former sense, intervention is open and direct, made often by the use of military force; in the latter, intervention takes the form of coercive economic measures, such as economic embargoes or sanctions; as, for example, U.S. economic sanctions against Cuba or UN economic sanctions against South Africa or Iraq. Intervention can also take the form of proxy interference, through the use of a third party (state or organization). Many wars fought in the Third World during the Cold War were proxy wars, undertaken essentially at the behest of the superpowers, albeit with local collaboration.

Interventions in whatever form they manifest themselves are perceived as directives against the intrinsic sovereign rights of states as political entities. This subversive attribute of intervention reinforces criticism of, and objections to, intervention as a mode of international political behavior. Yet some interventions—as shown in the following cases—take place at the invitation of the state in question, introducing another distinction and ambiguity in the types of intervention.

Foreign interventions in Africa have been both frequent and varied, with both constructive and negative consequences. While on the one hand foreign interventions complicated nation-building processes in Mozambique and Angola soon after these states attained independence from Portugal, intervention also helped to salvage from total collapse Liberia, Chad, and Somalia (discussed in the case studies in this book). The United States–led Operation Restore Hope of December 1992 and the United Nations peacekeeping operation in Somalia have been crucial in helping to restore the collapsed Somali state. The same can be said of the Nigeria-led ECOMOG that (together with UNOMIL, the United Nations Military Observer Mission) is helping to reconstruct wartorn Liberia.

The lessons of modern peacekeeping operations in Africa indicate that it is simply not sufficient to pump resources into states to keep the peace in the short-term: efforts must be extended to include long-term assistance for sustainable political and economic development, to protect against regression and relapse.

Scholars and practitioners debate whether preventive intervention can be separated from reconstructive intervention. For example, can a distinction be drawn between preventive interventions in Shaba (Zaire) and Macedonia and reconstructive interventions in Liberia, Chad, and Somalia? The former are actions whose purpose was seen to have been served as soon as the crisis or threat to the existence or survival of the state was removed; whereas in the latter cases, the purposes of the intervener go beyond restoring peace to include rebuilding political and economic structures, the conducting of elections, and distribution of humanitarian and relief services. These elements may, of course, be preventive as well.

Recently, preventive diplomacy has acquired added importance in efforts to preempt crises from developing out of otherwise minor incidents (Lund 1994). There is now some careful deployment of early-warning systems (Gurr and Harf 1994). If further developed, preventive diplomacy can be combined with preventive intervention to achieve peace and development. As donors grow weary of incurring additional financial expenditure for peacekeeping, preventive diplomacy may appear better and cheaper than reconstructive diplomacy or direct involvement in the restitution of collapsed states.

■ Objectives of Foreign Interventions

External intervention in Africa's internal affairs did not begin in the post–World War II era of independent states. It was in fact such intervention that led to colonial wars during the European scramble for Africa in the nineteenth century. The Berlin African Conference, held at the behest of European powers in 1884–1885, during which African territories were partitioned, was international intervention par excellence (Uhomoibhi 1991: 98, 144, 187, 197).

Foreign interventions in contemporary African polities for the purpose of assisting collapsed states have definite objectives. In some cases, a foreign power may intervene for the purpose of protecting the life and property of its own citizens in an African country. This was the reason adduced by France and Belgium for intervening in the Congo/Zaire crises in 1964, 1977, 1978, and 1993. In other cases, foreign states intervene primarily to profit from the spoils of the African states—out of what some critics have called "crass opportunism" (Davidson 1990: 175). Some interventions are undertaken in furtherance of specific geostrategic and political interest, as in the Cold War. Unilateral foreign intervention originates in the national interest or foreign policy objectives of the intervening states. The French and Libyan intervention in the protracted conflict in Chad, Cuba's decision to send troops to Angola, and, also in Angola, covert U.S. support for UNITA were all linked to the national interest of the intervening states.

In cases of multinational interventions, especially those undertaken through multilateral institutions, the objectives, motivations, and interests tend to be diffused and multifaceted. The OAU intervention in Chad from 1981 to 1983 and the ECOWAS intervention in Liberia after 1990 were motivated by a set of objectives that do not readily fit into the standard categories of national interests. In both cases, member-states (of the OAU and ECOWAS respectively) acted collectively in the interests of both regional and subregional political and economic development.

Another form of African intervention that addresses collective interests is intervention within the intervenor's subregion. In this case, subregional and contiguous states intervene unilaterally either to uphold the tenets of extant bilateral agreements or in pursuit of national interests in a subregional context. An example in this case was Tanzanian unilateral action against Uganda in October 1978, resulting in the overthrow of President Idi Amin. In this case, one scholar has aptly argued that "the ultimate determination of which sector of the interventionist forces emerges hegemonic in a given conflict does depend on the complex interplay of the interest and roles of regional powers" (Ekwe-Ekwe 1990: 134f).

Thus it can be seen that another way of categorizing foreign intervention in African state collapse is into African and extra-African interventions. This will be the focus of the next two sections.

■ Non-African Intervention

These interventions take place either at the express invitation of the collapsing state or at the invitation of a rebel faction seeking to effect regime change. From the intervenor's side, some actions take place purely to satisfy the intervening state's national interest and some for more collective or humanitarian purposes. The most prominent among such extra-African powers that have intervened in Africa's conflicts are:

- France, mainly on behalf of its former colonial dependencies
- The United States and the former Soviet Union, primarily in pursuit of their strategic global and ideological interests
- To a lesser extent, Belgium and Cuba

Interventions can take many forms. The most visible is military, but other forms of economic and political relations between strong and weak states have interventionist aspects that are hard to separate from normal interactions.

□ France's Intervention in Chad and Zaire

The legal basis of France's intervention in the affairs of its former colonies has been the series of bilateral defense agreements entered into with these African states on the eve of their independence, entitling France to deploy troops to the countries when asked to do so (Kouassi 1993). It was on this basis, for example, that French troops were deployed to Chad and Zaire when those states felt that their security was imperiled.

France's first intervention in Chad took place in 1969, when several military operations were launched against the National Liberation Front of Chad (Frolinat). France stationed a garrison of troops in Ndjamena. French soldiers halted the advance of Frolinat in 1979.

Between 1980 and 1982, when the state system in Chad was in collapse, the French intervened on behalf of their protégé, Hissein Habré. When Libya became involved in Chadian affairs, to the extent of bombing parts of Chad on the side of one of the parties to the Chadian crisis, France protested foreign intervention and canvassed for an OAU intervening force to be sent to Chad. France gave logistic support to the abortive OAU peace-keeping force in Chad when the force was eventually established (McNamara 1989; Chipman, 1989; Zartman 1986).

In 1983, France again sent troops to Chad—a third time—to repel Libyan-supported rebel attacks under an operation codenamed Operation Manta. On this occasion, French troops numbered 2,800 and enforced an "interdiction line" on behalf of the Chad government to prevent the rebel and Libyan forces from pushing south. Though the French did little more than enforce the interdiction line, an uneasy peace prevailed in Chad between Libya, its local allies, and the government. In this way, French intervention helped to sustain Chad from another total collapse.

In Zaire in 1977 and again in 1978, France's support was motivated partly by the desire to protect its growing investment in the country as well as a response to a U.S. appeal for Western intervention to protect the central African state from falling prey to what was perceived to be Cuban and Communist encroachment (Ekwe-Ekwe 1990: 120–170; Zartman 1989: Chap. 4). French assistance included the airlifting of Moroccan troops and equipment to Shaba, when the rebels had invaded the first time, in 1977. It also included the deployment of paratroops, army engineers, and technicians who directly engaged the insurgents in Shaba and subsequently forced their retreat from Kolwezi into Angola the second time, in 1978 (Zartman 1989).

Military assistance and/or economic assistance from one state to another may not constitute intervention per se. It is what follows such assistance on the part of the giver that determines intervention. What are the motives of the state giving the military and/or economic assistance? What is the reaction of contending groups within the receiving state to such assistance? In the case of Zaire, France's intervention went beyond military assistance: it included urging fellow Western creditors and donors to offer increased financial help to the Mobutu government. France and its Western allies believed that increased Western financial and credit support to Mobutu's Zaire would strengthen the government's hand in dealing with insurgencies and the dangers of Communist encroachment. Accordingly, two conferences were held in May and June of 1978, specifically on ways to restructure the Zairean economy and enhance an Africa/Zaire security network.

More recently, while French intervention in Zaire continued to take the form of supporting the Zairean government against rebel attack (e.g., the deployment of French troops to suppress the violence of September 2, 1991), changes began to crystallize in France's attitude. France joined the United States and Belgium in pressing for democratic reforms in Zaire, although there are significant differences when it comes to pressing President Mobutu to relinquish power (see Chapter 10).

☐ *Belgian Intervention in Zaire*

Belgium's King Leopold II entered Europe's race for colonies rather late and the only Belgian colony in Africa was the Congo (Belgium's presence in Rwanda and Burundi was as an international trust: the territory had been put under its administration first under the League of Nations mandate and subsequently under the UN trusteeship system). It is in Zaire that Belgium's influence in postindependent Africa has been most widely felt.

Belgium's intervention in the Congo (now named Zaire) was aimed at protecting investments that, at independence, amounted to about $1 billion (Hull 1979: 225), as well as Belgian nationals resident in the country. In all its intervention in Zaire, Belgium consistently supported the African government with troops and equipment to ward off rebel attacks. For instance, in early 1965, Belgian troops assisted in quelling the rebellion against the government in southern Kivu and northern Katanga Provinces. When the second Shaba war erupted in 1978, Belgium sent 1,700 troops, not only for direct combat purposes but specifically to police industrial sites in the troubled region so as to forestall sabotage of production sites.

More recently, Belgium joined pressure groups in Zaire calling for democratization and reform, denouncing Mobutu's authoritarianism. Following the killings of students and university professors in the Lumumbashi riots, Belgium froze all official and bilateral assistance to Zaire, but has been reluctant to press Mobutu to withdraw.

☐ *U.S. Interventions*

U.S. interventions in Africa have ranged from the geostrategic to the humanitarian. In the earlier phase, the United States considered African conflicts from the perspective of the Cold War and felt a need to forestall Soviet expansionism in Africa. The United States adopted counterinsurgency measures to deal with conflicts it perceived as inspired by left-wing, pro-Soviet parties and organizations. Humanitarian intervention increased after the end of the Cold War. The United States sent food and medical supplies to crises spots, aimed at alleviating the hardships of people suffering in collapsed and collapsing states.

In the early 1980s, while the United States recognized France's overarching influence in Chad, it intervened nonetheless to neutralize Libya's expansionist tendencies, beginning with covert support for Habré in 1981. The United States also contributed military and financial support to the post–civil war reconstruction efforts of the OAU peacekeeping force. In 1983, following the collapse of the OAU peacekeeping efforts and the renewal of civil conflicts in Chad, the United States signed a new agreement with the government and delivered military hardware to underscore its support. In 1985, U.S. military supplies were given in support of France's Operation Epervier, aimed at warding off Libya's attack on Chad.

In Zaire, U.S. actions have been two-pronged—aimed at both ensuring the survival of the government and protecting Western capitalist interests in resource-endowed Central Africa. The United States was disposed to supply military hardware to the Zairean government to fight rebel invasions. During Shaba 1 and 2 in 1977 and 1978, the United States supplied C-141 transport aircraft to aid the French and Belgian interventionist force. The United States has also supported economic assistance to Zaire through the Bretton Woods institutions. The United States has consistently contended that Zaire should be kept afloat financially, considering it to be of crucial significance as a Western raw-materials resource enclave.

In late 1992 in Somalia, the United States led a coalition of states in Operation Restore Hope, an unprecedented mission of mercy. The U.S. contingents to Somalia comprised 36,000 servicemen and women—the largest peacekeeping and humanitarian force ever mounted. In the complex war zone of Somalia, they were charged with making the country safe for humanitarian relief. They were also later involved in controlling Somalia's warring factions and maintaining peace until the United Nations could resume its peacekeeping role there.

Subsequently, the United States–led operation was replaced by the United Nations Operations Mission in Somalia (UNOSOM 2), established under UN Security Council Resolution 814 of March 26, 1993. The resolution mandated a UN presence of about 30,000 personnel; the United States agreed in principle to provide a tactical quick reaction force in support of the force commander of UNOSOM 2.

On October 3, 1993, an incident occurred in Somalia when a group of some U.S. soldiers on a mission to capture a number of Somali factional leaders suspected of complicity in the previous attacks on UN personnel and facilities suffered severe casualties. Eighteen U.S. soldiers lost their lives and 75 were wounded. The bodies of the U.S. soldiers were subjected to humiliating treatment.

This even turned out to be a turning point for U.S. involvement in peacekeeping operations in Somalia, with implications for U.S. policy elsewhere. Meanwhile, the United States reinforced its quick reaction force in Somalia and at the same time announced its intention to withdraw its forces from Somalia by March 31, 1994.

■ African Interventions

Military interventions in Africa by African states have taken place in two forms: intervention by regional or subregional African organizations, such as the Organization of African Unity (OAU) and the Economic Community of West African States (ECOWAS); and intervention by individual, and usually contiguous, states, acting either unilaterally or in conjunction with other African states. In the first category, three cases can be cited; namely, the OAU Inter-African Force in Chad (1981); the ECOWAS Observer Monitoring Group (ECOMOG) intervention in Liberia, since 1990; and the OAU's Neutral Military Observer Group (NMOG) in Rwanda (1992 to 1994) and in Burundi (1994).

□ *OAU Intervention in Chad*

The OAU intervention in Chad was a novel experience in the history of African peacekeeping operations, for the charter of the organization originally contained no provisions for such action. The only charter reference to conflict management invoked the OAU Conciliation and Mediation Commission and resort to ad hoc institutions in the settlement of disputes.

The decision to establish an OAU force in Chad was taken in Nairobi at the organization's summit in June 1981. The force, commanded by a Nigerian officer, comprised 4,800 troops from Nigeria, Zaire, and Senegal. The OAU force failed to achieve any concrete solution to the Chadian problem and within months was compelled to withdraw. The reasons for the failure—the subject of many scholarly works (Pittman 1984; Zartman and Amoo 1992; Amate 1986)—were inadequate financial and material support combined with logistical, mission, and communication difficulties. A big disappointment was that out of the seventeen states listed to contribute troops, only three mustered the political will and resources to do so. So paltry was the assistance from other African states that Nigeria incurred a debt of $80 million as a result of the exercise, a debt that was never repaid and had to be written off by the Nigerian government. In the end, Habré pushed the inter-African force aside and went to Ndjamena to restore the state himself, as described by Foltz in chapter 2.

☐ ECOMOG in Liberia

Though the Economic Community of West African States was established in 1975 to foster economic cooperation and development within the West African subregion, the heads of state of the organization, at their meeting in Banjul, Gambia, in May 1990, felt compelled to intervene in Liberia as mediators, creating a standing committee. In August they intervened militarily to try to halt the country's slide into anarchy via civil war, as Lowenkopf discusses in Chapter 6.

From the outset, a number of difficulties impeded the full operation of ECOMOG. First, the force lacked universality of membership. Only five countries contributed troops and four of these were Anglophone countries (these four "locals" were joined in 1994 by Uganda and Tanzania). The Francophone states of the subregion accused ECOMOG of being a force with a purpose only to foster the hegemonic interest of particular states, although Guinea, and later Senegal, joined the operation (Gambari 1991: 117–125).

Secondly, it was argued by some member-states of ECOWAS that the creation of ECOMOG had no basis in the instrument establishing ECOWAS, notwithstanding ECOWAS protocols on nonaggression and defense (Vogt 1993).

Thirdly, the mandate of ECOMOG, at least at first, was ambiguous. Neither the diplomats nor the soldiers charged with implementing it knew what to make of it. They did not know whether they were a peacekeeping or a peace-enforcing body; whether they were policing or imposing a ceasefire. Consequently, "complications, dissensions and dissonance" were rife in their interpretation of the ECOMOG mandate (Gambari 1991: 132).

Finally, ECOMOG faced enormous financial and logistical difficulties. Only a few ECOWAS member-states contributed to the fund for ECOMOG. Nigeria bore the brunt of the financial expenses.

In spite of these difficulties, the ECOWAS initiative produced positive results. First, it stopped the carnage and bloodshed that had been rampant in Monrovia prior to the inception of ECOMOG. Secondly, by establishing an interim government in Monrovia, it prevented the continuation of anarchy in the country and averted a disaster that would have equaled that in Somalia. Thirdly, through subsequent diplomatic initiatives, ECOWAS meetings in Côte d'Ivoire produced the Yamoussoukro and Catonou peace accords, which spelled out plans for peace in Liberia, including the encampment and disarmament of the warring factions.

☐ OAU in Rwanda

The OAU intervened in Rwanda in October 1990 following the outbreak of a civil war in which an estimated force of 10,000 guerrillas, representing the exiled Tutsi-dominated Rwandan Patriotic Front (FPR), attacked northeastern Rwanda and occupied several towns. Though the Rwandan government succeeded for a while in repelling the attack, civil unrest continued in parts of the country, making the intervention of an OAU force necessary.

The primary objective of the OAU in Rwanda was to monitor a ceasefire brokered in July 1992, in Tanzania, between the Rwandan factions. Unlike the OAU force in Chad, the peacekeeping force had a structured chain of command. The OAU secretary-general was the political boss. Furthermore, it collaborated with a joint political military commission, to which it reported violations of the terms of ceasefire. The commission comprised representatives from Burundi, Tanzania, Uganda, Zaire, Belgium, France, and the United States. The commission's mandate included implementation of both the ceasefire agreement and the peace agreement at the conclusion of the political negotiations. The role of the OAU peacekeeping force was expanded in February 1993 to include not only monitoring of the ceasefire but also ensuring resettlement in demilitarized zones of people displaced as a result of the war. In August a peace agreement was finally concluded at Arusha, under the auspices of the OAU and with Tanzanian mediation, providing for a 2,500-person UN Assistance Mission (UNAMIR) to replace the OAU peacekeepers.

Next door, in Burundi, assassination of the elected president in October 1993 and genocidal warfare between the Tutsi army and the Hutus in the population led to the intervention, six months later, of a small OAU force of 50 officers, down from a proposed group of 200 troops from Mali, Burkina Faso, Cameroon, Niger, and Tunisia.

The situation was complicated, however, in April 1994 when an aircraft carrying the presidents of Rwanda and Burundi crashed at the Kigali airport in Rwanda, under circumstances yet to be clarified. Following this incident and the resulting death of the two presidents, the eight-month-old peace in Rwanda was shattered. Ethnic hostilities resulted in up to 500,000 death, mainly Tutsis killed by the government soldiers, who were mainly of the Hutu ethnic group.

The OAU has again been active in the efforts of the international community to stabilize and resolve the situation in Rwanda. It is at the forefront of the efforts to raise an envisaged African force of 5,500 to constitute the expanded UNAMIR established by the UN Security Council under Security Council Resolution 918 of May 17, 1994.

However, in Rwanda as in other places, the OAU remains incapacitated by the lack of resources among its member states to carry through their political decisions. This is clearly illustrated by the continuing difficulties it faces in giving concrete expression to its political will to help find a solution to the problems of Rwanda and, to a similar extent, Burundi.

■ Intervention and Reconstruction: Conclusion

In almost all the cases of foreign interventions in Africa, the evidence suggests that they do not generally provide early or full solutions to the perennial problems of political instability and state cohesion. On the contrary, some unilateral interventions, be it from Africa or elsewhere, have exacerbated and prolonged the crises, introducing extraneous ideological and political dimensions to what were essentially local conflicts. It can be argued that foreign countries intervening in conflict situations in Africa have had little or no interest in the preservation of the state structure as such. Their concerns have almost always been the political complexion of those in control of the state.

Multinational interventions appear to have greater relative merits than unilateral interventions, for two main reasons: First, such interventions diffuse the specific interests that the foreign powers are seeking to project or protect. This may lead to relative impartiality. This has been particularly so with regard to extra-African multinational forces such as (1) the UN peace-keeping forces (ONUC) in Congo that put an end to Katangan secession in the early 1960s; (2) the United Nations Forces (UNAVEM 1 and 2) that monitored elections in Angola in 1992; and (3) the Commonwealth intervention to put down the army mutiny in Tanganyika in 1962. The longer multinational intervention forces stay in a collapsed or collapsing state the greater the danger of a loss of impartiality and/or effectiveness in carrying out their mandate. Proximity (of countries contributing troops to the intervening force) also contributes to loss of impartiality. Moreover, on the issue of mandate, it is important that the terms be clear and achievable. An imprecise mandate can become a recipe for confusion and worsening of the crisis.

Secondly, few countries are able to intervene in conflict situations entirely on their own. The financial and political costs are prohibitive, unless vital national interests are involved. In the era of superpower rivalries, the risks were considered to be worth taking, but in the post–Cold War era, with socioeconomic difficulties facing most states, the prospects for a single power to save a collapsing state have diminished considerably. Even though Liberia had close historical and economic ties with the United States, it was little surprise when that situation was simply ignored by the big powers, at least until the multinational ECOWAS force went to the rescue. And in Somalia the great powers did little for a very long time until the United Nations Secretary-General accused them of having a double standard.

It can be further argued that the multidimensional nature of peacekeeping in collapsed or collapsing states *requires* multilateral intervention. Before actual peacekeeping can begin, the external powers must first try to stop the fighting between the warring factions. They must then try to monitor or impose a ceasefire and this requires considerable experience in peacekeeping and peace-enforcement. Second, efforts must be made to promote political reconciliation among the contending parties and this requires the involvement of countries or multilateral organizations with experience and clout. Third, the countries or organizations involved must be able and willing to provide financial and other resources. It can be seen that the responsibilities involved and the resources needed are too great for unilateral interventions. The topic continues to be the subject of intense discussions and negotiations at the United Nations and the OAU.

UN Secretary-General Boutros Boutros-Ghali (1992) has highlighted aspects of multilateral peacekeeping problems in his report to the organization entitled *An Agenda for Peace;* and Dr. Ahmed Salim has nudged the OAU toward the adoption of new conflict resolution mechanisms. Specifically, Salim's proposals include the setting up of early-warning systems, the training of international peacekeepers and peacemakers, and the establishment of a pool of international mediators and standby national forces for peacekeeping duties in Africa.

Foreign interventions play a strong role in putting together collapsed or collapsing states, but in conclusion it should be stressed that the domestic dimensions of the requirements of state reconstruction are critical. State reconstruction goes beyond the imposition of a foreign-inspired "solution"; rather it involves a complex process of political, social, and economic engineering that must affect positively the internal dynamics of powers and resource distribution in African states. This requires the development of new attitudes by both the political leadership and the citizenry. The adoption of a particular form of democracy is far less important that the practice of political participation from the grassroots up. The institutions underpinning civil society must be carefully rebuilt in collapsed or collapsing states and the rights of both minority groups and individuals must be protected. The rule of law must gradually prevail.

The issue of prudent resource distribution and management by the state is of fundamental importance in this process and prospect. With Africa these days seemingly marginalized, Africans must realize that the days of passing the buck are over. Africa must mobilize its human, physical, and other resources for the good of all its people. Africans must truly become the masters of their own destiny, no longer objects of international relations.

15

Democratization in Collapsed States

Marina Ottaway

The collapse, or threatened collapse, of many African states at the present time has its ultimate cause in the mismanagement, pillage of resources, and abuses by authoritarian regimes that left the majority of the population without a stake in the existing system. As long as the authoritarian regime, no matter how perverse, maintained control, however, the state was held together. Indeed, the proximate cause of state collapse in Africa has invariably been the failure of an authoritarian regime to continue imposing its control.

Looking ahead at what could prevent the collapse of now threatened states, or reintegrate those where authority and order have already broken down, two major solutions appear possible. Collapse can be avoided or reversed by the rise to power of a new and more successful authoritarian regime—discussed in Ng'ethe's chapter in this book (Chapter 16) as the "strongman" solution. Or the problem can be solved by the development of more democratic political institutions that give a much larger segment of the population a stake in the system. This chapter discusses this democratic solution.

The authoritarian solution—perhaps more promising in the short run— in the long run is very likely to lead to a new cycle of discontent and collapse. The democratic solution is certainly the most desirable and probably the only viable one in the long run, but it is unfortunately the most difficult to implement in the short run. Democracy by definition cannot be imposed by force. Rather, it is based on largely voluntary compliance with a set of rules of the political game. Unfortunately, in a collapsing state, agreement on anything is by definition in short supply. Furthermore, democratization, by which I mean the transition from authoritarianism to a stable democracy, is a highly disruptive process in itself: it encourages the conflicts that exist in a collapsing state to manifest themselves freely, but without the restraint of the checks and balances, and of agreement on the basic rules, that regulate conflict and make it manageable in a well-established democratic system. Democracy as a stable state is highly desirable, but democratization, or the process of getting to such stable democracy, can trigger highly undesirable side effects. Therein lies the conundrum of democratization in collapsing states.

■ Pitfalls of Democratization

The beginning of a democratization process in Africa has given rise to hopes for change from the cycle of instability and disintegration that has lately become the lot of a number of countries. But democratization so far has had mixed results at best, particularly in the countries with which we are concerned here—as Chapter 1 indicates, those where "structure, authority (legitimate power), law, and political order have fallen apart and must be reconstituted." The Sudan in the mid-1980s and Angola in 1993 provide unfortunate examples of countries where attempted democratization accelerated the process of disintegration, making state collapse more imminent and the long-term prospects for democracy dimmer.

A change of regime always entails increased conflict. As Bratton and van de Walle (1992: 27–56) have pointed out, a sustainable change of regime can only take place if the elite fragments. Transition to democracy, however, requires the elite to remain permanently divided, rather than to reconsolidate, as happens, immediately, in the transition to a new authoritarian regime. It also requires an agreement on the rules by which the fragments will compete; and by which conflict will be managed in a nondestructive fashion. But an elite can fragment in different ways, and not all lead to democracy and conflict management.

A country's political elite can break up into groups competing in the same political arena. In other words, the elite fragments, but the political arena does not. This leads to pluralism and democracy: different segments of the elite form political parties that vie with each other for the support of the same pool of voters. The parties that lose an election will have another chance at a later date, because voters can choose any party and change their preference. This pluralistic fragmentation does not lead to the collapse of the state.

□ Somalia

Another form of elite fragmentation, however, is threatening to both democracy and the state. If the new segments refuse to compete with each other, but try to establish monopolistic positions in separate areas, not only is democracy impossible, but the collapse of the state becomes much more likely. Competition becomes turf war among political organizations trying to keep each other out. A tragic example is offered by Somalia, where the fragmentation of the elite after the demise of Mohamed Siyad Barre led to the emergence of warlords fighting with each other for exclusive control over territory. The fragmentation of the elite was accompanied by the fragmentation of the country, resulting in the most extreme example of state collapse in Africa yet.

☐ *South Africa*

An example of incipient monopolistic fragmentation is offered by South Africa, a state that has certainly not collapsed but could easily do so in the future. The existence of a large number of black and white political organizations initially suggests that the managed collapse of the apartheid state and emergence of a democratic state is likely to succeed. Closer analysis, however, shows that many political organizations do not want to compete with each other to attract individual future voters, but seek instead to consolidate monopolies over areas or populations. This may mean physical control over a township or squatter-camp—much of the black-on-black violence is related to these attempts, with or without the meddling of the security forces—or claim to exclusive right to represent certain groups—Chief Mangosuthu Buthelezi likes representing himself as the leader of seven million Zulus. ANC comrades seek to keep Inkatha supporters out of certain townships, but in turn they are not allowed to operate in KwaZulu or Bophuthatswana.

These, it could be argued, are simply somewhat extreme forms of the dirty politics common in many formally democratic countries at times—the New York City of Tammany Hall was not exactly welcoming to Republican Party workers. If this was the only manifestation of monopolistic fragmentation in South Africa, it could probably be dismissed as an inevitable phase in the consolidation of a democratic system. But the refusal to compete goes beyond this level. What augurs poorly for the future of both democracy and state survival are the appeals to ethnic nationalism used by an increasing number of leaders to bolster their position. Buthelezi in KwaZulu, Lucas Mangope in Bophuthatswana, Oupa Gqozo in the Ciskei, a variety of militant Afrikaners and even supposedly ANC-aligned Bantu Holomisa of the Transkei promoted nationalistic visions of the postapartheid system that include as a minimum a high degree of autonomy for largely ethnic regions, and their legacy remains to be worked out in the final constitution, due before 1999.[1] Monopolistic fragmentation is thus manifesting itself in a continuum of positions, beginning with the dirty politics aiming at reducing competition, and culminating in appeals to ethnic nationalism that could create protected turfs where no competition is allowed. Such a continuum could easily turn into the slippery slope to state collapse.

☐ *Ethiopia*

Democratization requires not only a pluralistic rather than monopolistic fragmentation of the elite, but also a redefinition of the relationship between the state—in countries where institutions are weak this means the political elite—and civil society. Crucial to this transformation is the emerging of the concept of self-determination, or the right of the population to control its own political destiny. But the concept of self-determination is open to different interpretations. It can mean the right of *individuals* to determine their political destiny by choosing their own government from among competing political parties—the democratic, pluralistic interpretation—or it can mean the right of *groups* to determine their own destiny by having their own state (Cutler 1992: xi–xii). The latter is a nondemocratic, monopolistic interpretation of self-determination, because it gives greater importance to the creation of a separate, exclusive state than to the question of how such a state will be governed: invariably, a focus on group self-determination supersedes the idea of individual choice.

An example of a country where self-determination came to be defined as rights for groups rather than for individuals is Ethiopia. The result is that since 1974 the country has not moved closer to democracy and has instead started disintegrating, with Eritrea now an independent country and many ethnic liberation movements still pushing forward their revindications.

Since the fall of the Mengistu regime in May 1991, the Tigrean People's Liberation Front (TPLF), the dominant party in the governing coalition, has tried to reconcile the two concepts of self-determination, acknowledging the strength of the ethnic nationalism of which it was a product, while trying to accommodate external pressure for democratization (discussed by Keller in Chapter 8). First, it organized a transitional government, giving representation to all the major and many minor ethnic movements (Lyons 1991). Then it proceeded to divide Ethiopia into strangely shaped ethnic regions, the equivalent of the South African homelands. The plan was to build the political system on these regions, starting with elections for district and regional assemblies and culminating in the election of a national assembly.

But the TPLF tried to combine recognition of ethnicity in politics with the determination to maintain firm control over the reins of power. This control was threatened by the independent ethnic movements. The TPLF thus attempted to organize new ethnic movements in each region, in opposition to the preexisting ones.

Ethiopia's first multiparty elections for the district and regional councils in June 1992 were contested by ethnic parties. Essentially, each ethnic group was represented by two political parties, one aligned with the TPLF, the second, independent. Unwilling to risk the victory of the independent ethnic parties, TPLF officials kept them from registering their candidates, turning the election into a single-party exercise. In almost all electoral districts, only the names of the three candidates from the progovernment party appeared on the ballot, for three positions (National Democratic Institute 1992).[2]

The elections, in the end, did nothing to move the country toward democracy, because they were not competitive and voters were not able to exercise a choice. Neither did they do anything to assuage ethnic conflict. The most important opposition group, the Oromo Liberation Front (OLF), and some smaller independent ethnic movements pulled out of the election in protest. The OLF also pulled its militias out of the camps, where they had been confined, in an attempt to demilitarize the country before the vote. Soon thereafter, it also withdrew from the government. Fighting resumed. Ethiopia had taken one more step in the direction of collapse, rather than moving back from the brink. The attempt to reconcile the two concepts of self-determination had failed.

Democratization is thus no panacea for a collapsing state. It can lead toward democracy, but it can also hasten state collapse. Conflict becomes more overt. There is initially no agreement on rules. And not all political forces that emerge in a society in transition to democracy are democratic in nature. There may be genuine prodemocracy forces, but the majority of the groups entering the fray are bound to be deeply antidemocratic, because opposition groups in nondemocratic systems tend to be quite undemocratic themselves, and they will be the first to compete in a transition. The liberation movements that emerged in opposition to undemocratic colonial regimes were undemocratic—for example, seeking self-determination for the group but disregarding the rights of individuals. The parties that competed in Ethiopia's so-called democratic elections in June 1992 were the undemocratic ethnic liberation movements that had succeeded in overthrowing the regime of Mengistu Haile Mariam. In the Sudan, democratic elections have invariably enhanced the importance of the Islamic brotherhoods, intensifying the conflict between the north and the south. In the Mozambican elections of October 1994, the main contenders were FreLiMo, which ruled Mozambique as a single party for almost twenty years, and ReNaMo, an organization better known for its brutality than for its political program.

The problem of nondemocratic tendencies does not reside only with the elites and with the political organizations directly vying for power, but also with what is usually called civil society. Academic writers and practitioners in organizations seeking to promote democratization agree that civil society must be strengthened in order to promote democracy (Chazan 1988; Goulbourne 1987; Landell-Mills 1992). On the abstract level, the argument is unassailable—all the more so because it is essentially tautological. In practice, in specific countries at a specific time the strengthening of civil society may put an end to, rather than strengthen, the democratization process and it may even hasten state collapse.

□ *Sudan*

Sudan offers a particularly vivid example of this. The religious brotherhoods are part and parcel of northern Sudanese civil society. This means that whenever the Sudanese political system enters a democratic cycle, as it has done periodically since independence, these organizations become prominent political players, making it more difficult to find a solution for the conflict between the Muslim north and the non-Muslim south. The urban intelligentsia's efforts to promote democracy lead in the end to the transfer of power to political parties identified with the major religious brotherhoods. But the stronger the Islamic identity of the north becomes, the stronger grows the nationalism of the south; and the more irreconcilable become the differences that promote civil war.

For this reason, it took a military government not beholden to organizations of civil society to bring the first civil war to an end. Jafaar Nimeiri negotiated the Addis Ababa agreement in 1972, and this led to ten years of peace under an authoritarian regime. State collapse was avoided most successfully when democracy was at its lowest. A second attempt at democratization following the overthrow of Nimeiri in 1985 again brought the religious organizations to the fore, exacerbating the civil war that had resumed in the south, and eventually dashing all attempts at reconciliation and compromise. The democratic elections of 1986 halted the liberalization that had been possible for a year under a provisional military government and brought the dialogue with the southern parties to an end. The forces of civil society proved inimical to long-term democracy and hastened the collapse of the state (Niblock 1991; Salih 1991; Ottaway 1987).

□ *Democracy and Identity*

The example of Sudan is extreme, but it is not unique. In other countries, too, it is not just political elites but also the organizations of civil society that make democratization a threat not only to the regime but to the state as well. It is true that, as Nelson Kasfir (1986: 88) put it, "ethnic identity is both fluid and intermittent," and so, I will add, is religious identity. It is also true that communal identities and conflicts are often deliberately promoted by political elites for their own purposes. Nevertheless, these conflicts become a very real part of the dynamics of civil society, and thus, of the democratic process.

An example of this is offered by South Africa. Narrow, ethnic identities were deliberately promoted by whites and they eventually became the basis for the organization of the apartheid state. Historians have argued convincingly that Zulu nationalism was deliberately fostered by the South African government in the twentieth century, and thus that it has little to do with primordial sentiments or the historical legacy of Shaka's empire (Marks 1989). Other ethnic nationalisms are even more artificial (Anonymous 1989). But while they were resisted by blacks in the days of apartheid, these narrow, ethnic identities are being brought to life by democratization. The difference was that, under apartheid, ethnicity was a tool of white domination. In the transition period, it turned into a tool of survival for black organizations afraid of faring poorly in a competitive election and, increasingly, for common people caught in communal strife. In the final analysis, the fact that ethnic identities are artificial and not primordial is largely irrelevant to the dynamics of democratization and state disintegration.

Prodemocratic forces tend to be particularly weak where the process of democratization, instead of being triggered by domestic events, is a derivative process stimulated by the example of other countries or by the pressure of foreign-aid donors (Gurr, Jaggers, and Moore 1990). The fall of socialist regimes in Europe and the Soviet Union signaled to many governments that political change had become an imperative. In the following years, democratization was deliberately promoted by Western governments (particularly the United States), linking the delivery of economic assistance to the holding of multiparty elections. As a result, elections were held in most countries, including many without a genuine prodemocracy movement.

Among the political forces that most seriously threaten democratization in collapsing African states, ethnic nationalism and less frequently religious fundamentalism have emerged as particularly important, as the above examples indicate. Once before, at the time of independence, democracy was suppressed in Africa in the name of nationalism—although at the time the nationalism was of the independence struggle for a nation-state, rather than the ethnic nationalism of a particular group (Ottaway 1992). The argument that multiparty systems would threaten fragile national unity by encouraging the rise of political parties with a narrow, ethnic base was regularly set forth by African leaders and generally accepted by the international community. The reaction against the ensuing authoritarian regimes eventually took several forms: competition by other equally authoritarian, often military, elites; ethnic nationalist movements seeking a degree of autonomy or even independence; and, more recently, uncertain movements for democracy. After gathering new strength in the early 1990s, many of the latter movements are threatened by a resurgence of nationalism, this time narrow, ethnic nationalism rather than the broader nationalism of the 1960s. This increases rather than decreases the probability of state collapse.

The transition toward democracy is thus a path fraught with perils for states already threatened with disintegration. And yet, democracy can be a powerful integrating factor, and has proven so historically in other parts of the world. The next section will set forth some hypotheses concerning the factors that make democracy an integrating or a disintegrating force.

■ Democracy and State Integration

The expectation that democracy will act as an integrating force capable of consolidating collapsing states or of creating viable new ones is largely based on the experience of nineteenth-century Europe. That period saw the crumbling of the Austro-Hungarian empire but also the merger of small principalities and city-states into large entities. Both processes led to the emergence of viable new states. The nationalist movements that led to the collapse of the empire and the disappearance of smaller states were also democratic movements (Greenfeld 1992).

The demand for self-determination that characterized the period took two forms: self-determination as the right of nation-states to become independent; but also self-determination as the right of citizens to elect their government. The nation-state was also broadly rather than narrowly defined, encompassing populations much more divided in terms of language, culture, and historical experience than the advocates of the new states cared to admit. As a result, nationalism was not just a force of disintegration, but also one of integration. The outcome—admittedly arrived at after considerable conflict—was viable states, capable of resisting splintering, and much more democratic than what they had replaced. The new states proved remarkably successful in handling internal tensions and divisions through a "contractualization of state-society relationships" (Young and Kante 1992). The road to democracy was not a smooth one, but states survived and democratic systems eventually consolidated.

The relationship between democracy and nationalism is not proving so benign at present, and not only in Africa. In parts of Eastern Europe and the former Soviet Union, an initial movement toward democracy triggered a nationalist reaction that, in turn, undermined democratization. Nationalism, furthermore, became increasingly narrow-based, threatening the viability of the existing states. In the most extreme cases, such as that of Yugoslavia, it became impossible to devise territorial arrangements that could both satisfy nationalist demands and create coherent states. Nationalism became so narrow that it destroyed not only the old states, but the new ones as well. It also put an end to the process of democratization.

The example of Eastern Europe is important because it points to the weakness of the cultural arguments that are often used to explain the failure of democracy in Africa. It is true that democracy—at least, Western-style democracy—is not part of the African tradition. But then it was not part of the European tradition, either, before it became the dominant system. We need to look beyond culture for an explanation of why democratization succeeded and had an integrating effect in some countries, while so far it has failed and contributed to disintegration in others.

One characteristic shared by both Eastern European and African countries under the old regimes was the primacy of what Kwame Nkrumah called the political kingdom. The economy was not a separate sphere where people could wheel, deal, and enrich themselves even if they had no control on the levers of power. As a result, there is little to be fought over in many of these countries except political power. In Africa as in Eastern Europe, democratization started in countries whose economies were badly battered by years of economic mismanagement. While in theory the economic reforms that are being universally adopted—with or without democratization—will open up great economic opportunities for emerging entrepreneurs and create an economic kingdom independent of the political one, in reality the transformation is proving extremely difficult everywhere. In the countries most threatened with collapse, economies are even weaker, and the primacy of politics even sharper.

The elites have few economic interests that could best be safeguarded by the continued existence of a unified state providing access to a more important market. And politically, a unified, democratic state offers few political rewards to its elites: power positions are few, tenure is insecure, and the future for an out-of-office politician is bleak—there are no lucrative private sector jobs awaiting those who step out of the political fray. For the political elites of a state that is collapsing economically as well as politically, nationalism has greater rewards—it can create new, protected ponds for the fish in danger of being eaten in the larger one.

It is the political elites, it should be remembered, not the mass of the population, that initially define the nationalist agenda. As many studies have shown, in Africa the emotional allegiance of most people is not directed originally to the group that politicians choose to define as the nation, or the tribe (Chazan, Mortimer, Ravenhill, and Rothchild 1992: 101–104). The Oromo Liberation Front in Ethiopia does not build on a primordial sense of affinity among all Oromos. It is leaders, not a primordial attachment, that define the boundaries of Oromia. Popular sentiment is usually created by the political agenda of the leaders, not vice versa, but once it is unleashed, it becomes very real.

The economic vacuum within which democratization is taking place in Africa, even more sharply than in Eastern Europe or the former Soviet Union, encourages the interpretation of self-determination not as the right of individuals to elect their government and to hold it accountable, but as the right of groups to their own state. The ensuing explosion of ethnic nationalisms in turn hurts the economy, and further hampers the emergence of business groups with a vested interest in political solutions that preserve markets and do not destroy the economy. The outcome of the process, seen all too clearly from Yugoslavia to Ethiopia, is more nationalism and the demise of democratic trends.

Other factors are making it difficult for democratization to become a force for state integration in Africa. The steps toward democracy—usually the holding of an election—have been taken very suddenly, indeed before a strong prodemocracy movement had been formed. The driving force of democratization was simply opposition to the existing regime—in the Senegalese elections, for example, the main slogan was simply, *Change* (Young and Kante 1992: 65). Change, of course, is not synonymous with democracy.

Where elections led to a regime change, as in Zambia, it was because of the weakness of the old regime more than of the strength or coherence of the supposedly democratic opposition. Some of the ideas Samuel Huntington (1968: 266) used to analyze revolutions are relevant here. The demise of the old regime, the mobilization of new groups into politics, and the creation of new political institutions are part of all processes of regime change, not just revolution: what differs is the speed and thoroughness of the process, and the kind of institutions eventually created. The sequence of these changes is important, not only for revolution but also for democratization. When the old regime falls easily, before new groups are mobilized into politics or new institutions created, a lengthy period of conflict can follow. It is not just a sudden revolutionary takeover, but also sudden democratization that leads easily to state collapse.

■ Rethinking Democratization

Democracy, we have argued, is the political system that can best accommodate the conflicts of a divided society in the long run, preventing the collapse of the state. But democracy cannot be confused with democratization. And the process of moving from an authoritarian to a stable democratic system is an extremely dangerous one for a divided country and it can accelerate rather than prevent the collapse of an already weakened state. The old political organizations and the new ones that come into existence as the elite fragments must find a place in the system, either by competing or by creating a monopoly. Competition eventually leads to democracy; monopoly is likely to lead to state collapse.

Awareness of the destabilizing impact of democratization contributed in the past to the widespread acceptance of the argument set forth by African leaders, namely that democracy did not suit the conditions of their countries. Single-party regimes, they argued, were much more apt to contribute to stability and nation-building. The argument was undoubtedly self-serving, but it contained enough truth to acquire a measure of credibility. Furthermore, in the Cold War period, all that really mattered to the outside world was the foreign alignment of African states, not their domestic politics.

In the present climate, the international community is encouraging democratization, and occasionally forcing it on reluctant governments by withholding aid. Democratization, however, has been interpreted very narrowly as the holding of elections, and the sooner the better. But elections, or the prospect of elections, are highly destabilizing in countries threatened with collapse. The question thus is whether democracy should again be written off as a political system that does not fit African conditions, or whether a different approach to democratization would lead to a different outcome in states threatened with disintegration. The following section offers tentative ideas on this issue.

Elections appear to be the wrong place whence to start a process of democratization in a collapsing, conflict-ridden state. In recent years, African elections have been typically organized in a hurry, in some cases before parties had time to consolidate or armed movements had agreed to disarm; and invariably before political parties formulated a political platform and presented it to the voters. As a result, losers have found it easy to reject election results, and voters had little choice but to vote on the basis of ethnic or religious identity, or at best of a desire for change. Elections held under the wrong conditions can be a real setback for democratization (the example of Angola is the most dramatic to date). Such elections should not be encouraged, much less supported with funds and observers' missions, even when opposition parties ask for them.

Simply waiting until conditions are right for democracy is not an answer, however, for conditions may never become right, or at least not soon enough to prevent the collapse of the existing state. The obstacles to democratization need to be addressed directly. In the early part of this chapter, I singled out three issues as pivotal to the success of democratization: whether the fragmentation of the elite is pluralistic or monopolistic; whether self-determination is defined in terms of individual rights to control the government or of group rights to a separate state; and whether economic interest groups with an interest in a broad market exist and can counterbalance the political elite's attempts to carve out areas of monopolistic control. These issues are extremely complex; they cannot be ignored.

☐ *The Policy Connection*

The tendency to monopolistic fragmentation, particularly on the basis of ethnic or religious appeal, can probably not be addressed directly—there would be little point to preach to Inkatha to abandon its appeals to Zulu nationalism or to the Umma Party to stop identifying with the Ansar. But even ethnic or religious organizations can be encouraged or helped to discuss policy and to develop programs. There are some precedents for this in South Africa, where many foreign organizations are working with the ANC to help it develop policies on the major issues confronting the country. Policy debates will not change the ethnic or religious identity of political parties, nor eliminate their desire for monopolistic control over specific groups of the population. They could, however, begin to inject other elements in the political process, show the parties that they may have common concerns and that there is scope for compromise, and eventually provide the voters with a basis on which to make a choice other than ethnic or religious identity.

A possible avenue for injecting consideration of policy in the political debate might be a broadening of the "national conferences" that are becoming a standard feature of political transitions in Africa. Beginning with Benin in February 1990, at least a dozen countries have held national conferences, mostly in Francophone Africa, but also in Ethiopia, Somalia (in Addis Ababa), South Africa, and Namibia (Lancaster 1991). These conferences have dealt with politics and not policy. They have focused on how to engineer a political transition and how to structure a new political system; in other words, on how to determine who shall exercise power. What has been largely absent from these conferences is a discussion of what should be done with power, what reforms should be introduced, and what policies enacted.

Promoting a definition of self-determination based on individual rather than group rights is extremely difficult to do under any circumstances, and probably impossible in situations of heightened ethnic conflict. It is difficult to conceive of anything the international community could have done during the 1980s to convince Eritreans that self-determination did not have to mean the right to a separate state, but could be the right to hold the government accountable, no matter where the boundaries of the state lay. This might have been possible in the 1960s, however, before Eritrean nationalism was so fully developed. In the same vein, it is difficult to imagine what could be done now to convince Serbs that the form of government practiced in Serbia is more important than how much of Bosnia is controlled by Serbia. The prospects for changing a concept of self-determination based on group rights once ethnic nationalism has become salient appear to be quite poor.

☐ *Economic Considerations*

Creating economic groups with a greater interest in political stability and access to a broad market than in raw political power is possible, but not in the short run. The structural adjustment policies supported by the multilateral and bilateral donor agencies in Africa are supposed to create such economic interest groups. One problem is that, even under the most favorable circumstances, these policies are bound to produce slow results, especially initially. The World Bank keeps revising upward its estimates of the length of time required before structural adjustment programs succeed in relaunching growth (*Africa Confidential* 34, June 11, 1993, 12:2). Furthermore, serious questions are also being raised concerning the impact of democratization on the implementation of structural adjustment programs. Drawing on the experience of the new industrial countries of Asia, some writers have argued that the governments most capable of implementing consistent economic policies leading to rapid economic growth are technocratic ones not accountable to an electorate or beholden to special interests. Democratic governments that need to maintain popular support, on the other hand, would find it very difficult to implement the unpopular and socially costly adjustment policies that economists deem to be necessary to relaunch the development process in troubled African economies (Callaghy 1990: esp. 262ff).

The debate on whether democratization is an obstacle to economic adjustment has remained largely abstract, because there are not enough African countries that have been sufficiently democratic for a long enough period to allow the question to be answered on the basis of firm empirical evidence. But it is clear that the relationship of politics and economics in collapsing African states at the present time is perverse, with political instability worsening economic performance and a weak economy failing to provide an autonomous economic kingdom to counteract the primacy of the political one. Democratization may dim the prospect for economic restructuring, and even under the most favorable circumstances, economic reform is not going to change swiftly the constellation of political forces existing in African countries. The political kingdom is bound to remain paramount in the foreseeable future.

In the short run, democracy—in the sense of a political system in which individuals freely choose their government, and in which elites accept pluralistic competition and have interests that go beyond the immediate grabbing of power—is thus probably not possible in the collapsing states. But collapsing states do not have the luxury to wait for the long run. Short-term solutions cannot be democratic yet, but do not need to be inimical to democracy. Measures that promote the spirit of democracy by enhancing participation, compromise, and hopefully a debate of policy issues may be helpful first steps, even if they do not yet amount to full-fledged democracy.

☐ *Powersharing—with Reservations*

One solution proposed with increasing frequency in the wake of failed elections is powersharing. The debacle in Angola in particular has led many to conclude that divided societies need powersharing, not winner-takes-all elections—a disturbing characterization of democratic, competitive elections, it should be pointed out. But powersharing is a broad and vague concept, and unless carefully defined it can turn into a meaningless magic formula (Lijphart 1985).

A few points need to be stressed at the outset. First, powersharing is not the only political system that can work in ethnically plural societies. Democracy, with its attendant winner-takes-all elections, has worked reasonably well in an ethnically plural society like the United States. Secondly, powersharing is not a democratic system. The building of a grand coalition of all major political parties deprives the voters of the possibility of ousting the incumbent government, and a government that cannot be voted out of office is not accountable, thus not democratic. Indeed, permanent powersharing arrangements recreate a de facto single-party system, a coalition of elites that will inevitably turn corrupt and unresponsive because it cannot be removed. The present experience of Italy and Japan, trying to come to grips with the legacy of nonaccountability and corruption resulting from over forty years of rule by the same party or coalition of parties, is a good reminder of what happens in systems where the incumbent government stays in power for a very long time.

But in conflict-ridden countries on the verge of collapse, a powersharing pact, and without early elections, may be the only attainable short-term goal compatible with long-term democratization. Powersharing would amount to the creation of a continuing negotiating forum in which conflicting groups would be forced to work toward a long-term agreement. What may be needed is some sort of long-term national conference. It should aim not at rushing the country into elections—this has not worked in most cases—but at facilitating a long period of negotiations and pactmaking before competitive elections for a majoritarian system, the ultimate hallmark of a democratic system, can be held. And while such negotiations continue, the country must be governed somehow: this is where powersharing becomes a necessity, with the modalities for sharing differing, depending on the country's problems.

There is no guarantee that powersharing, as part of a long-term negotiating and pactmaking process, will succeed in moving collapsed states toward democracy. State collapse is simply not a good starting place for democracy. In his book *In My Father's House,* Kwame Anthony Appiah (1992: 26) tells the story of the peasant who, asked by a passing motorist how to get to the capital, answers, "If I were you, I wouldn't start from here." Unfortunately, like Appiah's motorist, collapsed states can only start from where they are.

■ Notes

1. Buthelezi and the Afrikaner right have been particularly vehement on regional autonomy and group self-determination. See, for example, *Southern Africa Report,* vol. 10, 48, December 4, 1992, and vol. 11, 19, May 14, 1993.

2. The discussion is also based on personal observations by the author, who monitored the elections in Dire Dawa and Awassa.

16

Strongmen, State Formation, Collapse, and Reconstruction in Africa

Njuguna Ng'ethe

For many African scholars who have gone through the last few years of political turmoil, the subject of *strongmen* is not the kind to inspire poetry. Many of us would rather discuss such issues as whether the new political rebirth currently sweeping the continent will inspire and be inspired by a new political theory; whether the academy will rise from the ashes and once again function as the source of inspiration to society; or whether society has finally tamed the African leviathan.

I therefore may be forgiven if it becomes all too obvious that I am perhaps oversensitive to any suggestion, no matter how delicately put, that rule through "strength"—other than strength derived from democratic legitimacy—could be of some function to those genuinely seeking African reconstruction. Feelings are conditioned by experience: in my case, the experience of living through the nightmare of fear of state power concentrated in too few hands.

We had Rick—one of those "few hands" in the system we called "Total Man," a somewhat humorous reference to his constant public boasting of his immense powers in all spheres of state and society, his constant assertion that this was for the good of the public and the state, his even more assertive statements to the effect that he owed his powers to no one but the president, "who is always right." What this individual did not say was that a great deal of the "total powers" was for his personal welfare. He was corrupt enough, wealthy enough, and fearsome enough to get away with murder (of his own cabinet colleague), all in the name of the state and the perceived challenge to "state security" and state survival.

Still, as social scientists, we have the responsibility to confront social reality, no matter how unpalatable; to try to make some sense of it. In this case, the reality is the strongman.

In this chapter, I argue that (1) confronting the reality of the strongmen poses several challenges; (2) one of the challenges is the very fuzzy nature of the concepts; (3) the dominant theoretical literature on postcolonial state

251

formation, while rich in useful suggestions, is thin on the relationship between leadership styles and state formation; (4) strongmen have been as much responsible for state collapse as any other factors; and (5) what is needed is a theoretically much tighter conceptualization of strongmen and the historical process through which such persons are likely to enter and exit. The latter has major implications for constitutional and institutional arrangements and therefore for the viability or nonviability of the state.

■ Strongman: Splitting Hairs

Under normal circumstances, the term *strongman* is used in a fairly loose, journalistic fashion to refer to styles of leadership in political settings that could be as divergent as the styles of leadership themselves. At one time or another, leaders such as Sukarno, his successor Suharto, Mao Tse-tung and his successors, Nasser (but not his successors), Tunku Abdul Rahman, Muamar Qadhafi, and Fidel Castro, among others, have all been referred to as strongmen. Even Saddam Hussein of Iraq has on occasion enjoyed that reference. In sub-Saharan Africa, one has heard of Jaafer Numeiri of Sudan, Muhamed Siyad Barre of Somalia, Kamuzu Banda of Malawi, Felix Houphouet-Boigny of Côte d'Ivoire, Mobutu Sese Seko of Zaire, Mengistu Haile Mariam of Ethiopia, to name just a few, all referred to as strongman in a given time and place.

Strongman, therefore, is a rogue concept that refuses to march with its better-known cousins such as authoritarian leadership, dictatorial leadership, and even, under certain conditions, charismatic leadership. Perhaps the most important question to raise then is: On what does one predicate the notion, *strong?* More specifically, should it be based on leadership styles and personal attributes such as one would normally discuss under charismatic leadership or sometimes patrimonial leadership? Should it be attached to an institutional setting so as to indicate the power relationship between the strongman and other bodies? When we talk of a strongman, are we referring to an individual or should we also include situations where power is shared by a small group, albeit with one spokesman?

If *strongman* refers to styles of leadership and personal attributes then is it any different from related notions such as strong leadership? But then one senses that the term means more than this, otherwise there would be no need to coin another term to describe such a straightforward phenomenon as strong leadership. Ronald Reagan was a strong president. Margaret Thatcher was a strong prime minister. Both had plenty of charisma. Neither was a strongman/woman.

It seems that *strongman* is meant to refer to institutional power relationships in which power distribution is skewed in favor of the person(s) *who claims* to head the state/regime at that particular time. Whether such a person is actually *perceived* as having the power, and *accepted* as having acquired it *legitimately,* is a matter of very serious consequences on what he does with that power. The issue of how the strongman comes about his strong status should therefore not be assumed away. The temptation is to assume that once the state has collapsed, a total power vacuum develops. In the Hobbesian statelessness that ensues, whoever can muster some support from whatever sources thereby becomes a good candidate for strongman. It might not be that simple.

Although, following the collapse of the state, a power vacuum might indeed occur, it is also possible that a state could collapse without necessarily entailing leadership collapse (Zaire is perhaps a case in point). In that case, the organization, and institutional focus of power to replace the non-collapsed leadership, becomes the most urgent matter. This simply complicates the situation of ascendancy to the status of strongman, if indeed the situation requires or allows the emergence of a strongman. The dynamics of becoming a strongman could therefore contribute to our understanding of the term.

Equally important are our own images of what it means. It would appear that the term is more evocative than descriptive. First, the term evokes a style of leadership closer to patrimonialism than populism. Whether it is benevolent or not is another matter. Second, the term evokes the image of authoritarian leadership and powers. On occasion these powers could verge on the dictatorial, though in conventional usage the term *dictator* seems to have been reserved for those whose activities are highly disapproved, especially by the liberal minded. In this sense then, reference to the leadership as *strongman* seems to be ideologically loaded; while it might convey some sort of disapproval, the rebuke is less than total. One is therefore not surprised that at one time Mobutu was a strongman to the media, but is currently a dictator. His style of leadership and his powers have not changed for years, but the international political environment has; hence, the change of terminology from mild rebuke to a term suggesting total disapproval.

Strongman evokes the theoretical image of power that might be too concentrated for the comfort of the liberal minded but that could conceivably be rationalized, if not be made to appear quasilegitimate, given the use to which it is being put, in this case reconstructive of the collapsed state. The logic here seems to be that ontologically the state comes before considerations of power distribution and legitimacy. Its construction therefore takes precedence over these other considerations of political life. This is essentially a Hobbesian argument that raises the question: Assuming one wants to go the Hobbesian route, then what happens after the Leviathan has been erected? On a less theoretical level, a supplementary question would be: What if the strongman was responsible for the collapse of the state in the first place because, again to use Hobbesian terminology, he violated the most essential elements of the contract; namely, security of the individual and his property? Can we then, as rational contractors, entrust the reconstruction of the state to the same leadership genre? Not unless we assume that the new strongman is an extremely farsighted and, at the same time, highly enlightened and selfless leader who is almost above society—though at the same time part of it—and who will somehow embody the aspirations of both state and society (a deliberate echo of Hegel).

■ State Formation in Africa: In Search of Insights

At the beginning of the current (third) wave of African state collapse, it is correctly noted that in the past we have tended to assume that the African state has significant common characteristics. These include (1) its postcolonial status, with all the implications that has for the evolution of civil society; (2) its a priori problematic relationship as regards its territorial jurisdiction; (3) its heavy involvement in a restricted resource base (usually primarily agriculture); (4) its still relatively undifferentiated yet ethnically heterogeneous social infrastructure; (5) its salient processes of centralization and consolidation of power by new ruling classes; and (6) its pervasive external dependency (Doornbos 1990: 180).

While it might be safe to assume that each of the above characteristics has somehow affected the general phenomenon, if not the actual pattern, of state formation in Africa, we are on less secure ground when pressed to show *how* each of the characteristics has affected the process of state formation in a specific African setting. Not unexpectedly, we are almost paralyzed by the phenomenon of state collapse, which in many ways is the very opposite of state formation (or is it?). While academic intuition tells us that the very characteristics that have affected the pace of state formation are at work, we seem to be unable to isolate the most crucial ones. In Somalia, is it ethnicity; a weak pastoral economic base; the "juridical" nature of the state; weak and myopic, though highly oppressive, leadership (compared with farsighted state-forming leadership)? And so on.

To be fair to the debate on the subject of state formation, one must concede that some of the elements that were isolated as being worthy of study in regard to state building could very well prove to be the most crucial once again in regard to state collapse (the negative phenomenon) and rebuilding (its positive analogue). In the 1960s, social scientists of the modernization school warned that successful state formation would have to confront several crises (Binder 1986). These were (1) the crisis of identity, through which the people learn to identify themselves as citizens of the nation-state rather than as members of a particular ethnic subgroup; (2) the crisis of legitimacy or the development of the sense, on the part of the governed, that the government in power has the right to rule; (3) the crisis of penetration or the development of the state's capacity to enforce all decisions within its territorial jurisdiction; (4) the crisis of participation, or the provision of means and opportunities for the citizens to influence state decisions; and (5) the crisis of distribution, or the evolution of the will and the means to solve at least the most glaring aspects of social, political, and, especially, economic inequalities.

A number of social scientists focused on what was of interest to their own academic disciplines. Thus, sociologist Talcott Parsons (1951) argued that social systems tended to persist because functions common to all tended to reproduce them. Sociologist Neil Smelser (1966) warned of the likely disintegration of social order in the context of rapid economic mobilization that does not keep pace with social differentiation because forces of integration are slower to develop. In a similar vein, political scientist Samuel Huntington (1968) warned that economic development is likely to produce, in the short term, political decay in the context of high social mobilization and low institutionalization. Sociologist Martin Lipset (1959) and political scientist Karl Deutsch (1963) looked at the relationship between economic development and democratic participation, making the now well-known argument that democracy requires a middle class, widespread access to education, and high social mobilization. Political scientists Gabriel Almond, with James Coleman (1960), and with Bingham Powell (1966), made the case for the development of a democratic "civic" culture.

In the African context, Martin Doornbos (1990), Lionel Cliffe (1987), Patrick Chabal (1986), and Goran Hyden (1980, 1983), among others, made the argument that the African state was suffering the crisis of penetration. The counterargument, that the state was indeed "overdeveloped," was made by such scholars as Issa Shivgi (1975), who focused on the exploitative role of the state through the "bureaucratic bourgeoisie." A third group of scholars, including myself (Ng'ethe 1984), refuted the argument of "penetration crisis" from a historical perspective; others, including Nelson Kasfir (1986) and Gavin Williams (1987), refuted the same argument from other points of view, including the international perspective (Doornbos 1977: 183–185).

Analysis of the literature on state formation in Africa shows that a simple question seems to be emerging: Is the African state "developed" or has state formation yet to succeed? In other words: Is the state yet to confront the crises enumerated by the early modernization theorists? Has the enterprise of state formation been successful? Of course, there is not an a priori reason to focus on the modernization theorists alone. It can, for example, be argued convincingly that part of the state crisis in Africa today is the result of external factors (including shrinking the base of resources under the control of the state since the trade and debt crisis was set in motion in the early 1970s). However, it seems to me that in the context in which we are looking at the African state—i.e., the role of the strongman in state reconstruction—we must focus on internal issues; and the modernization theorists did actually enumerate a good many of these issues, though perhaps without adequate explanatory theorizing.

In the Africa of the 1990s, it is clear that there is a "crisis of the state." This crisis goes beyond the early considerations of overdeveloped vs. underdeveloped state, juridical vs. empirical state, and soft vs. hard state. Useful as these classification categories are, the current crisis demands very specific questions and very specific answers, thus posing perhaps the greatest challenge to African social science since the early 1960s. The questions and answers also demand that the specific issues enumerated in the 1960s be disaggregated in order to shed more light.

One issue that poses the greatest challenge is the role of leadership and governance in the evolution and the resolution of the current crisis. Few, if any, scholarly discussions on state formation in Africa have addressed directly the relationship between such evolution/resolution and types of leadership. All that we can expect from past scholarship on state formation is bits and pieces of insights on what has gone wrong: to look for a blueprint on what is to be done is to expect too much. Identity, legitimacy, penetration, participation, distribution, and the overall failure of economic development have something to do with the collapse of the state, and all are somehow conceptually linked to leadership and governance; i.e., the manner in which power is shared and exercised, especially in the types of situations where the leadership and the state have tended to be equated.

Going beyond the theorists, state collapse is now a reality. It is a possibility in more African countries than is perhaps realized. This, in spite of the fact that barely a decade ago one would have argued that, in a majority of cases, state formation was indeed progressing, even if at an agonizingly slow pace. While some of the scholarly works analyzed this slow progress, few anticipated the collapse of the state. Indeed, one could argue that few, if any, were prepared to speculate on the relationship between state formation and state collapse.

☐ *From State Formation to State Collapse*

The characteristics of a collapsed state are well known; what is not so well known is whether a collapsed state represents a failure of state formation, as the earlier theorists would appear to suggest, or whether this is an entirely new phenomenon that can be triggered by a specific combination of factors, even under circumstances where state formation has advanced considerably. What has been the contribution, if any, of governance by strongmen to the collapse of the state in Africa?

■ Strongmen and State Collapse

Looking again at the current state of the states in Africa, it is possible to argue that strongmen have been as much a contribution to the collapse, or the near collapse, of the state as the other factors to which the theorists and the events of the last decade have drawn our attention. Fortunately for Africa, only Rwanda, Somalia, and Liberia have completely collapsed in the current round, but eight other countries—Algeria, Nigeria, Angola, Mozambique, Zaire, Burundi, Chad, and Sierra Leone—are close to collapse (Nellier 1993). Ethiopia, Chad, Ghana, and Uganda have collapsed and risen again. Looking at these fourteen countries together, one can begin to make the case that strongmen, in their various guises, have contributed substantially to the collapse of the state in a number of cases: Somalia under Siyad Barre, Ethiopia under Haile Selassie and then Haile Mariam, Zaire under Mobutu, Uganda under both the first Obote regime and under Idi Amin, Nigeria under Babingida, Chad under Goukouni Weddei, Liberia under Samuel Doe, and perhaps Sierra Leone under Siaka Stevens. Angola and Mozambique are more complicated, in that the ongoing civil wars in these countries seem to have forestalled the emergence of a particular type of leadership and governance. Rwanda and Burundi are cases of ethnic and class conflict that overshadow the role of individual strongmen.

Governance and economic and social factors have combined to lead to the collapse of the state. A few examples illustrate this. In the now classic case of state collapse in Somalia, the inability of the state to command enough resources to pay for its own upkeep seems to have contributed to the state collapse. Somalia under Siyad Barre was one of the most indebted states in Africa, with a debt service ratio of over 180 percent and a nonexistent revenue base. On the other hand, the near collapse of Zaire cannot be, even partly, attributed to the nonexistence of a resource base. It is true that the Zairean state is no longer able to collect taxes and is consequently unable to pay either the military or its civilian servants. However, this is the result of the organizational/institutional failure of the all-powerful leader rather than absence of a resource base. Both cases reflect a strongman style of governance.

Ethiopia under Haile Selassie eventually evolved into a state that lost contact with the countryside and that depended almost solely on the person of the emperor for its legitimacy. Haile Selassie's successor, Mengistu Haile Mariam, was a different type of strongman. He sought to exert control over the countryside through "peasant organizations" that were essentially extensions of the state. The peasant organizations, however, were not a sufficient response to the nationalist question; nor to the characteristic rural poverty in Ethiopia.

Ethnicity and the national question are major factors threatening state collapse in Angola, maybe in Mozambique, and certainly in Rwanda, Burundi, Nigeria, Sudan, and Ethiopia. This has been complicated by religion in a few countries (e.g., Sudan, Algeria, Nigeria). In Uganda, the collapse of Idi Amin's regime was unique: external invasion played a coup-de-grâce role. The state under Amin had already collapsed by the time the Tanzanian forces entered the country and all that was left for the Tanzanian forces to do was remove Amin's army, which alone had continued to give the semblance of a state. It was already, really, a stateless society.

In general, given the so-called relative autonomy of the state and regime from society, the nature of the strongman regime has been a major contributor to the collapse of the state in Africa. The other side of this argument, as implied earlier, is that the state has survived and will, in all probability, continue to institutionalize itself, in those circumstances where the style of governance has allowed state and regime response to societal demands. This positive side of the argument is perhaps easier to anticipate from earlier theorizing on political development and state formation in Africa.

■ Nonstrongmen and State Formation/Survival

A list of the most politically healthy states in Africa at the current moment does not necessarily include Kenya, Tanzania, Algeria, Nigeria, and Cameroon, to name a few where state formation in the past appeared to be progressing fairly well. Tanzania and Kenya, for example, which yesterday would have been described as "overdeveloped states"—indeed, Tanzania was the case study around which this concept was developed—are not currently among those states that are risk free. This complicates the relationship between the *extent* of state formation and the possibility of state collapse (suggesting that state collapse is not a direct consequence of failure of state formation, but rather has its own dynamics). But the overall state of African states equally suggests some sort of a correlation between state survival and nonstrongman leadership.

Namibia, Botswana, Egypt, Ghana, Burkina Faso, and Benin are cases in point. These countries, plus Gabon, Côte d'Ivoire, Morocco, and Tunisia, are arguably the most risk-free states in Africa. Why? Namibia has a terribly fragile economy: its only resource seems to be a constitutional arrangement preventing the emergence of the kind of leadership that has plagued Africa for the last thirty years. Botswana, arguably, is economically healthy on account of its natural resources, particularly diamonds (but

Zaire is also endowed with plenty of natural resources and the state has collapsed). As in Namibia, the stronger argument is that it is political arrangements to ensure legitimate leadership that have ensured Botswana state survival, not the Zaire-like economic resources alone. Egypt, faced with a
fundamentalist challenge, is not showing *any* signs of collapse. Regardless
of individual feelings on the current regime, few would call the Egyptian
regime illegitimate. Burkina Faso and Benin are out of the endangered list
on account of reforms intended to legitimize their leaderships. And similarly, few would argue that the leadership in Morocco or Tunisia is illegitimate.

This line of inquiry, therefore, suggests the hypothesis that, whereas
past successful state formation will not automatically ensure continued
state formation or state survival or prevent state collapse, regime legitimacy, continuous or newly developed, is the best insurance against state collapse, just as strongman leadership could be the best catalyst for state collapse. It remains to consider the lessons from those few cases where
strongmen have ensured state reconstruction.

■ State Reconstruction and Leadership Issues

Although there are only a handful of cases of full state collapse in Africa,
there are even fewer cases of successful reconstruction. Congo (now called
Zaire), Chad and Uganda, Somalia and Liberia are perhaps the only cases
of total, extended state collapse. Congo (Zaire), Uganda, Chad, perhaps
Ethiopia, and from a lesser breakdown Ghana, represent the few cases of
successful reconstruction. Zaire's reconstruction took place in the first few
years after Mobutu took over, followed by a dramatic decline in the 1970s
and thereafter, leading to a virtual state collapse. What can be learned from
these reconstruction processes, and what further questions do they pose?
The collapse of the states created a power and leadership vacuum, but not
the kind of vacuum that just anybody could fill at any old time. To fill the
vacuum required organized force. Museveni, Habré, Rawlings, Meles, and
even Mobutu entered their states' politics as head of some organized force:
the National Resistance Army (NRA), the Armed Forces of the North
(FAT), the Ghanaian Armed Forces, the Tigrean People's Liberation Army
(TPLA). It was their status as leaders of army units that made it possible for
them to emerge as political leaders. The implications are unsettling: that
successors must fight until a victor emerges to consolidate his position as
strongman; that organized force is an essential ingredient of putting together a collapsed state; that, at least, candidacy for legitimacy derives from the
barrel of a gun.

In some cases, one of the problems in state restoration was to create a
national army from victorious fighters and to restore public confidence in

the armed forces. In Uganda, people not surprisingly had come to distrust, if not actually to detest, anybody in uniform because of the terror to which they had been subjected by Idi Amin's forces, which had come to be seen as an occupying army from the northern part of the country (similar perceptions hurt the victors in Chad and Ethiopia, and the victims in Liberia). In reshaping the NRA from a guerilla fighting force to a national army, Museveni did not have much difficulty, since the NRA was a fairly well-disciplined force, obviously aware of the need to refurbish the image of "the men in uniform" and of their role as liberators, in both military and political senses. The NRA therefore was not the traditional neutral army but a highly committed force. The real test for reconstructing leaders is to create an integrated national army, manned by personnel from all parts of the country, who will be willing to support the next government and the next leader. To whom do these institutionalized personal armies owe their loyalty? To the Musevenis, Rawlingses, and Meleses, or to the higher course of liberation and, hopefully, democratization?

A major ingredient in reconstruction is the restoration of security, especially in the countryside. The task requires a twin strategy of military force and political reform. In Uganda, Chad, Ethiopia, Somalia, Angola, and Mozambique, as the crumbling armies and their remnants fled the country, they left in their wake not only a trail of destruction but also a countryside littered with serviceable arms. Any household could acquire a gun if it wished to. In addition, those elements of Amin's, Goukouni's, and Siyad Barre's armies that fled to neighboring countries kept trying to reinvade the country. The new state-builders therefore had to fight these incursions—as well as disarm the countryside through a combination of force and gentle persuasion in order not to alienate the people.

The parallel strategy (the other side of strong leadership) is politically to penetrate the countryside. In Uganda, locally elected and controlled resistance councils had their origins in the NRA's liberated areas during the struggle to overthrow both the Obote and Amin governments. The NRA is always represented in these councils, though it is not clear how much control it actually has over them. In Chad, local acceptance was negotiated, enforced, and then institutionalized in UNIR. Local councils were also coopted and created in Ghana. Securing the countryside has often been the most difficult aspect of state reconstruction, for that is where the inchoate state often meets the most resilient forms of civil society, especially in an agricultural region such as Africa.

■ **Beyond Strongmen**

Strictly speaking, civil society emerges; it is not created. However, in Uganda, Chad, and Ethiopia, as well as Algeria, Angola, Mozambique, and Zaire, civil society has had to be restored, in that civic groups had to be reassured that it was acceptable to express their opinions and state their positions on issues without fear of reprisals from the state. There is some debate as to how much actual leeway the new state has allowed to civic organizations in Chad, Uganda, and Ethiopia. For example, Ugandan newspaper editors have been taken to court for publishing "seditious information" or have lost their jobs for questioning a visiting head of state too forthrightly. Ethnic leaders are arrested after making provocative statements in Ethiopia. But overall, civil society is again vibrant. In Uganda, the print media, church groups, and NGOs are again active, although they are often reminded that they owe their existence to the NRA.

The debate about the "overdeveloped" state is really a debate about the crucial role the civil service has played in Africa in creating state presence, state authority, and state legitimacy. In the 1960s and 1970s, Nyerere's Tanzania and Kenyatta's Kenya (and the first few years of Moi's) were "overdeveloped" in this sense. The crumbling of the civil service, therefore, represents the most ominous sign of the collapse of the state. As noted earlier, one of the most important signals of collapse is the failure of the state to pay salaries to the civil service, and perhaps the final signal—as the Introduction to this book points out—is failure to pay the military. In state restoration, restoring the civil service involves much more than the rehiring and restructuring of government ministries under the control of political ministers. In Uganda, Chad, Ethiopia, and Congo (Zaire), it involved recreating official records, restoring offices, and restoring buildings and the entire administrative infrastructure.

In addition, by the time the leadership issue is settled, the physical infrastructure of the country has so deteriorated that it is difficult to imagine, even for those familiar with the poor infrastructure of most Third World countries. The tarmac roads have gone back to dirt roads, and the dirt roads in the countryside have ceased to be roads. Sewage, telephone, and electricity systems have long ceased to function. In order to restore the infrastructure, Uganda, Chad, Somalia, Zaire, Angola, Mozambique, and Zaire found it necessary to rely heavily on foreign assistance, as the state was in no position to generate its own revenue. This, of course, was also true of other activities: the state could not afford them either. State rebuilding often has to start from near scratch.

The price of foreign assistance is often that the reconstructing state must undertake radical economic reforms. This may begin with currency reform, as happened, for example, in Uganda and Zaire. The old currency must be replaced by a new currency since the old is virtually worthless; and in any case, the new political leadership has to have its own currency. In Uganda, the government liberalized the exchange-rate regime by allowing free purchase and circulation of hard currency within the country. Thus,

Uganda is one of the few countries in Africa where one can purchase hard currency at a kiosk operated by fully licensed foreign exchange dealers. In Ghana, the currency was devalued (as will be necessary in other countries). In Uganda, in addition Museveni restored confidence in the principle of private ownership of property by inviting Asians expelled by Amin to return and reclaim their businesses if they wished. Throughout the process, foreign capital is invited to invest, through new liberal incentives, in order to create "the right investment climate." Ghana and Uganda have become particularly strong showpieces for the World Bank's and IMF's Structural Adjustment Program, which has been posed as a prerequisite for aid and investment from Europe and the United States.

■ Loyalty, Voice, and Exit

The general question that state reconstruction by a strongman seems to raise is: Is a strongman in a position to do things differently from other types of leadership that came into power through other means and therefore exercise his power in a different way? Beyond focusing attention on strongmen, a fruitful line of inquiry is the relationship between state collapse and state reconstruction: Is the latter conditioned by the manner of the former? It would appear that this relationship is as problematic as the relationship between state formation and state collapse. Shedding light on both problems would require extensive comparative analysis. Fortunately for Africa, and unfortunately for purely academic analysis, there are not enough cases for a comparison of significance. I hope there never will be.

The case studies in this book are interesting in that they illustrate some of the theoretical issues that the phenomenon of state collapse and reconstruction raise. What is the relationship between manner of state collapse and manner of entry of the strongman? In Ghana, Chad, Uganda, and Liberia, the appearance of Rawlings, Habré, Museveni, and Taylor marked the coup de grâce to the collapse as well as the first step of reinstatement. The question of the relationship between organized force, leadership, and legitimacy is also crucial. While the four strongmen mentioned above gained prelegitimacy, to use Ferrero's term, by their violent overthrow of tyrants or corrupt weaklings, solid legitimacy comes only with election performance; and presumptive strongmen in Somalia, Angola, and Mozambique face the same test. The importance of the peasantry in power equations (and, in this case, in state reconstruction) normally goes unappreciated.

Ultimately, the biggest test of the success of a strongman in institutionalizing the reinstatement of the state is the problematic of the link between strongman rule and sustainability of the state after the strongman's exit—

and indeed the very nature of this exit (Hirschman 1970). In this test, Habré failed in Chad, being forced in 1992 to exit by the door marked *coup*—the same door by which he came in. In Ghana, Rawlings's success has only been apparent. His election in the democratic conversion of 1993 institutionalized his incumbency but only postponed the exit question. None of the other strongmen who responded to the appeal of a collapsing African state had left office by the end of 1994; and indeed Mobutu's unwillingness to do so, even after his extended term ran out in 1993, was the cause and the mark of impending collapse in Zaire. Fears of a similar problem have reduced support in Liberia and Angola for Taylor and Savimbi: many participants and observers alike predict a brutal settling of accounts if either should come to power, followed by a lifelong incumbency assured by the liquidation of the opposition.

It is significant that in the cases of African state collapse in the late 1980s and early 1990s, Taylor and Savimbi are the only cases of presumptive reinstatement by strongmen, whereas all of the cases of the late 1970s relied on strongmen to restore the state. Even in Somalia, neither Aidid nor Ali Mahdi are likely to rise above their subclan and occupy effective strongman leadership across the country through their Somali National Alliance. Elsewhere in Africa, when states collapse there are no strong candidates who can command armed support and whose charismatic leadership can serve as the vehicle for state restitution. Reconstruction by the democratic path is therefore by far preferable to reliance on a single central autocratic agent.

The South African case is particularly instructive in this respect. In 1992, most analysts classified South Africa among those African states in real danger of collapse. Two years later, following the April 1994 democratic elections in that country and the triumph of the African National Congress (ANC) under Nelson Mandela, the danger of state collapse seems to have considerably receded, though South Africa is by no means risk free yet, as Shezi eloquently analyzes in Chapter 12.

Mandela is not a strongman in the conventional usage of the term and we do not know yet whether he will be a strong leader. He is, however, a legitimate leader through a combination of factors that include history and personal charisma. Through legitimate leadership, Mandela seems poised to nurture the "loyalty" and "voice" options among South Africans while preparing for his own exit, the nature of which still remains an important factor. In the South African case, a particular kind of leadership, in combination with other historical and structural factors, might have been sufficient to forestall state collapse. Also in South Africa, a particular kind of leadership, again in combination with specific structural factors, was instrumental in halting state formation and creating conditions of near state collapse.

■ Conclusion

In this chapter, I have suggested that the phenomenon of state collapse represents the biggest challenge to developmental social science since the 1960s. One of the issues that the social sciences, perhaps, did not fully come to grasp with is the issue of leadership type and its effect on the state.

In Africa, where over the last thirty years the type and manner of exercising leadership has had a strong effect on state, if not society, the leadership question is particularly important in a future research agenda on state survival. This agenda must include a deliberate attempt to clarify the relationship between state formation, collapse, and reconstruction, and the role of leadership in all three aspects of political life, assuming as we must, that "the good life" is only possible within the state; an assumption that is currently by no means universally accepted in Africa.

While in the recent past the strongman type of leadership might have been instrumental, under certain circumstances, in some cases of state reconstruction, theirs is by no means an assured success; not until they have institutionalized "loyalty" and "voice" at the expense of "exit." This will, in turn, depend on the manner of their own "exit."

Given the political, ideological, moral, practical, theoretical, and empirical questions revolving around the "rogue concept" of the strongman, we suggest in conclusion that future energy and resources be invested in trying to understand the role of democratic leadership, or lack of it, in state formation, state collapse, and state reconstruction. For many in Africa, democratic leadership is the preferred investment option.

_____ PART 5

CONCLUSIONS

17

Putting Things Back Together

I. William Zartman

We study how states collapsed in order to learn how to put them back together, for the record of actual reconstructions is thin. The only clear cases are those from 1960 and the late 1970s, and their lessons are as enlightening in the negative as in the positive. The response to colonial state collapse in Congo was the installation of a strongman with foreign backing, which created the problem of Zaire in the 1990s. A similar answer in Chad led to the strongman's replacement by the end of his decade in power, resulting from an overreliance on coercion and distant foreign support that alienated both domestic forces and the traditional foreign patron, France. Ghana and Uganda have shown the importance of a combination: strongman, foreign support, and economic resurrection.

In none of the cases of the late 1970s was direct UN or foreign state intervention a significant factor, and if the reconstructing regimes all tried to gain popular support, only in Ghana was there an opportunity for multi-party democracy to function, more than a decade after the strongman took over power (Boahen 1994). The cases of the 1980s and 1990s only under-score the importance of the question of how to reconstruct.

In the search for answers, it is first necessary to reaffirm that recon-struction of the sovereign state is necessary. While the 1990s have seen a revived debate over the concept of sovereignty, formerly considered absolute and indivisible and now perceived to be weak and porous, that dis-cussion also takes place in an era when more is expected from the state than ever before. Such universal expectations cannot be met by a weakened institution, as Deng (Chapter 13) clearly indicates. State functions cannot be left to even a well-functioning society, any more than society can abdi-cate its activities to the state. Sovereignty needs to be reasserted as a responsibility, not as either a cover for tyranny or a relic of a world order past. The state needs to be restored and its sovereignty needs to be reinstat-ed as the criterion for accountability, short of which its government is not legitimate.

It should also be emphasized that, while statehood needs to be reconsti-tuted in the modern age, it may in some unusual cases be achieved only by changing its dimensions. As the case of Ethiopia has shown (at least for the moment), along with more numerous cases in the former Soviet Union and

its satellites, the restoration of the state to health may require the amputation of an infected member (*infected* in the sense of suffering from a reaction and inflammation against the state's control). But the case for reshaping the restored state has to be made, in each instance, rather than assumed,
and some hard questions must be asked about both the viability of the severed member and the popular basis of support for its continued separate
existence. Independence is still the highest political value available to a
community: it is not to be asserted lightly nor claimed without struggle and
sacrifice.

Indeed, except for the current case of Ethiopia, there is not a case in
this book for which a change in boundaries or secession of a territory is a
necessary condition of state restitution. Moreover, even in those cases
where secession has been posed as a possibility—Somalia, Zaire, South
Africa—the potentially seceding members are likely to be worse off and
the remaining core no better off as a result of the amputation. Just as state
collapse is not just a matter of coups and riots, it is also not a result of foreign conquest or an instance of periodic reconfiguration of political space
(Eisenstadt 1988: 236). Both its cause and remedy relate to sociopolitical
structures within a given sovereign territory and people, not to the shape of
the state itself. It is better to reaffirm the validity of the existing unit and
make it work, using it as a framework for adequate attention to the concerns of its citizens and the responsibilities of sovereignty, rather than
experimenting with smaller units, possibly more homogeneous but less
broadly based and less stable. The logic of secession works against seceding states, threatening an infinite regress of self-determination. In general,
restoration of stateness is dependent on reaffirmation of the precollapse
state.

In addition, the cases, in their positive lessons from the 1980s and negative lessons from the 1990s, strongly underline the notion that the state
can never be reinstituted without a concomitant effort to rebuild civil society and to integrate the workings of the two. Much more analysis needs to
be done to indicate the mechanisms of societal reconstruction, but it is
already clear that a twofold process is under way during state collapse. On
one hand, it has been noted from the outset that state collapse is possible in
part because the last incumbent destroyed much of the support and structure normally found in civil society, to the point where society could not
rebound to fill the vacuum created by the collapse of the incumbent regime.

On the other hand, the cases recall a less recognized phenomenon: that
civil society continues to exist—indeed, even thrive—under state collapse,
its inability to fill the national vacuum being paralleled by its vigor in local
operations. Authority structures around elders, traditional conflict management procedures, active trading networks, and inventive community operations grow up to fill local vacuums, keeping low to avoid the constraining

embrace of the dying state. As a result, there is more raw material from which to reconstruct civil society than there is to rebuild the state. Society's need is above all for political space in which to expand, free of interference; whereas the state has immediate needs for structures within which to function and often requires foreign intervention to provide interim structures and functions until the state can perform them on its own. Thus the reconstruction challenges (for state and society) are different, and state rebuilding needs both to foster and to use societal reconstruction.

The following synthesis attempts to gather together the experience of the few successful cases, the needs of the cases still in collapse, and the lessons of a process of collapse played in reverse to detect crucial moments and ingredients. Needless to say, it does not purport to constitute a blueprint for restitution. The terrain is too different in each case for any one road map to apply, and all the answers are not in yet. Nonetheless, the following discussion can be useful as a basis for immediate practice and further inquiry. It focuses on the three fundamental elements of *power, participation,* and *resources,* and closes with a consideration of foreign roles.

□ Power

Power structures must be reconstituted, from the bottom up. This means that some temporary but effective agent at the top is needed to provide a provisional framework within which a structure of institutions can gradually be erected to allow the state to return to the center of social and political organization in civil society (see Khadiagala's Chapter 3). Only in this way can the loss of confidence that central authority can perform its functions (so characteristic of state collapse) be restored. This was to be the role of Sawyer in Liberia; the UN (under Sahnoun) or the United States (under Oakley) in Somalia; the transitional executive in South Africa; the High Council of State in Algeria; and the High Council of the Republic in Zaire—with highly divergent results. But these efforts require that a difficult choice be made.

Either the rebellion's leaders and local warlords can be brought together, under the theory that the source of the problem must be the source of the solution (foxes will act responsibly in hen coops if given responsibility), and leaders with the mind and means to *break* security must be given the legitimacy to *make* security; or new elites must be helped to emerge from the closet, representing the leaders of a civil society (teachers, labor leaders, elders, religious figures, and civil servants), the best of the ruled being called on to replace the worst of the rulers. If warlords are allowed to form the new state, they assure the return of the system that brought about its own collapse, as Taylor in Liberia, Aidid and Ali Mahdi in Somalia, Savimbi and dos Santos in Angola, and perhaps even Tshisekedi in Zaire indicate. Mechanisms are needed to keep their power under control, to prevent them from bolting or vetoing, and to allow—indeed, force—the entry of new elements. If civil leaders are given power, they need the means to exercise their authority. Mechanisms are needed to give them that power and legitimacy.

At best, both types of leadership need to be brought together in reconstituting the state. It is better to bring in the local powerholders than close them out, lest they make new reconstruction more difficult. At the same time, local civic leadership usually finds room to assert itself, limiting the power of the warlords, if given a chance. Instances as different as Somalia and South Africa provide examples. The experience of several African polities in setting up national conventions of civil leaders to prepare the way for democracy is a striking example (Lancaster 1991; Monga 1994), but the convention needs to be institutionalized as a protoparliament (as in Somaliland and, badly, in Zaire) and retained in the new structures of government as a counterweight to the executive. Such structures form the basis for healthy checks and balances in the system.

☐ *Participation*

Legitimacy must be restored early, through constructive participation and freely expressed support from society. This will necessarily be appointive and cooptive in the early stages, until the structures for institutionalized participation are in place. It is necessary to provide a large, informally representative forum, and if the contenders for power do not do so, an external force to guarantee security and free expression during the legitimization process may be required. A large, pluralistic national convention, composed of many political and professional figures and organizations, needs to establish transitional institutions and prepare a constitution as the normative and legal foundations of the political order, as indicated by Khadiagala (Chapter 3). A national covenant to set up new rules of the game and engage the new players to respect each other should be an early step toward institutionalization and the precondition to any elections, as Ottaway shows in Chapter 15.

A particular problem that combines the needs of power and legitimacy lies in the need—or at least the desire—to build the state around a new type of leadership rather than simply restoring an old order. It does little good to bring peace if it is only to maintain the same type of government that brought about the collapse of the state in the first place. Aidid or Ali Mahdi in Somalia, Taylor in Liberia, Obote in Uganda, Savimbi in Angola, and a series of potential alternatives in Zaire and Algeria all promised to restore the same type of system that caused the problem in the first place, with only a change in the name of the president. To provide a legitimate state reconstruction, a new political system is needed, often requiring new leaders who were not trained under the old system—and therefore are short of experience in governing. That requirement makes reconstruction a larger challenge than even the already daunting job of restoration, and often involves thanking the pretender for completing the removal of the tyrant but excluding him from the succession. Such an effort requires delicate cooperation between external intervenors and civil society.

It is more important that the functions of democracy as a legitimizer, through participation, be fulfilled than that the procedures of a national election or alternance be strictly followed, at least in the early years. Societies need a state before they can hold electoral contests to decide who will run it, and they need some experience in working together before moving on to the next stage of democratic alternance. The vacuum of collapse, with devolving local organization, is not a good spawning ground for national political parties. Local groups need time and experience to develop into national parties.

When elections do come, the dilemma to avoid is between a plebescite for those already in power and a bitter electoral conflict between factions seeking to get there. When electoral competition becomes part of legitimization, it should be to decide the proportions of a national unity government, not to declare a winner-takes-all outcome. National unity governments and powersharing arrangements harness all factions with responsibility and foster the notion that electoral losers still have a stake in the government. They do have drawbacks: unity governments weaken that major attribute of democracy, competitive accountability. But in exchange they condition the expectation—basic to democratic legitimization—that losers in electoral contests remain alive to run again next time. They also open the exercise of government to the pursuit of the conflict *within* (rather than *for*) state offices, perpetuating distrust and killing cooperation. But in exchange they start conflicting parties in the direction of thinking *politics* rather than war.

□ *Resources*

Resources need to be made available for reconstruction. It is hard to overcome the problems of neglect and misallocation that lay at the root of the state's collapse without some resources for the new state to manage. Two state roles in regard to resources must be restored, as Foltz notes in Chapter 2 with regard to Chad: state capacity to extract resources and state ability to allocate resources. The two of course are connected: the inability of states to extract resources from their populations deprived them of resources to distribute; populations got nothing (except interference and repression) from their governments and so gave nothing to them. This kind of vicious circle is hard to reverse. States need some emergency pump-priming to get the machine started, reward compliance and regain confidence, and so restore their extractive capabilities.

Yet, as in the case of power, there is a dilemma inherent in reversing the cycle. The new resources, which can come only from external sources, can only be a stopgap or a pump-primer. Otherwise the new state will fall into the habit of external reliance, weakening its own legitimacy and making itself dependent and vulnerable; or else it will become a reverse tax farmer, living off a percentage of the resources to be distributed and preventing them from reaching society.

□ External Assistance

In all three areas—power, participation, and resources—it is hard to get around the usefulness, if not the outright need, of external assistance. In the cases of the 1960s, 1970s, and 1980s, external intervention in the process of collapse and reconstruction came in many forms: armed UN intervention in Congo in 1960–1961 and U.S. assistance in installing Mobutu in 1965; French and U.S. support in Chad around 1982; the World Bank insistence on structural readjustment in Ghana; Tanzanian troops to topple the tyrant in Uganda in 1979; United States and others' mediation and UN monitoring in Angola and Mozambique; U.S. and UN intervention in Somalia in 1992–1993; ECOMOG in Liberia after 1991; even a brief U.S. mediation in Ethiopia in 1992. Some of these interventions were simply the last push in completing state collapse, but others—particularly in the 1990s—are important to the reconstruction process. In setting up new political structures, a catalyst is necessary, either to turn the warlords from fighting each other to cooperating, or to protect the civilian leaders as they seek to emerge. In providing new economic resources, a new infusion is needed, both to start the machine producing and to win loyalties in the initial stage. Lessons can be drawn from each experience, on what to do and what to avoid, but their general theme points to the need to combine a willingness to stay long enough with the willingness to leave when it is time. External intervention should be available as long as it must; but it should leave as soon as it can.

Foreign intervention may be needed to perform the functions of the state under collapse, but only until local forces can take over the business of putting the state back together. The rare attempts to deal with this subject (Helman and Ratner 1992; Colborne 1993; Ben Yahmed 1993) have revived the notion of a UN trusteeship or its variants. Such solutions err in the arrogant presumption that only the West can govern and in the ignorant fallacy that a 150-member bureaucracy that cannot pay for its emergency interventions is suited to exercising or supervising colonial-like rule.

Unlike the world of a century ago, no state at the end of the twentieth century has an interest in establishing a new colonial rule, and an international condominium is precisely the sort of training in irresponsibility that developing nations do not need.

In the end, it takes conscious efforts of leadership to put a state back together—leadership that can only be indigenous, whatever the usefulness of foreign support. At the same time, leadership alone cannot replace or even accelerate processes that must take place gradually, through repeated efforts, overcoming repeated challenges. The process of reconstructing the state is slow and uncertain, made up of many interacting elements to which leadership must give direction.

Power, participation, and resources are the ingredients behind this leadership process; unfortunately, there is no order of priority among them to prescribe. Elementary security must be restored, most basically through ceasefire; national reconciliation must be begun, through informal negotiations and institutionalizing fora; resources must be secured and mobilized, through foreign stopgap support and restored domestic taxing capacity. All this must be done at once and at the same time, and the steps kept apace of each other as the process moves along. It must also be done with an end in view, as a process that combines order, legitimacy, and authority with policy, production, and extraction, rather than a series of discrete steps taken one step at a time. In addition, it must be done looking backward as well as forward, preparing the introduction of mechanisms that will prevent the new efforts from falling back into the vacuum from which they emerged, victims of the same disabilities that caused the collapse of its predecessors. Finally, it must be done with a keen sense of indigenous orders, customs, and ways of doing things, which are the strongest allies of reconstruction efforts but can also be their undoing. Even with all these guidelines in mind, state restoration is an uphill challenge, not an automatic process. The power of the vacuum can consume even the best efforts to fill it, particularly when the impatience of the tending world insists on quick fixes. It takes time to restitute a state.

Bibliography

Abdulai, David (1992), "Rawlings 'Wins' Ghana's Presidential Elections: Establishing a New Constitutional Order." *Africa Today* 39, No. 4, 1992.

Abir, Mordechai (1968), *The Era of the Princes*. London: Longmans.

Aboagye, Alex R. (1993), "Letter." *New African,* No. 306, March 1993.

Abraham, Philip (1988), "Notes on the Difficulty of Studying the State," in *The Journal of Historical Sociology* 1 (1): 58–89. March.

Adam, Hussein M. (1993), "Somalia: The Military, Military Rule and Militarism." Mimeographed paper, April 1993.

Adams, Bert N. (1981), "Uganda Before, During, and After Amin." *Rural African* 11 (Fall): 15–25.

Addis Ababa Agreement on National Reconciliation in Somalia (1993). Mimeographed document, March 27.

Africa Confidential (1993), "Opening up the World Bank," 34, No. 12: 2, June 11, 1993.

African National Congress (1991). *Strategic Document* [on the ANC's position on power sharing].

——— (1992), *Report on the Deliberations in CODESA I and II.*

——— (1993), *Report on the Multiparty Conference,* April 3, 1993.

Africa Regional Office, Western Africa Department (1993), *Ghana 2000 and Beyond.* Washington, DC: World Bank.

Africa Watch (1991), *Evil Days: 30 Years of War and Famine in Ethiopia*. London: Africa Watch.

Ali, Mohamoud Abdi (1993), "The Grand Peace and National Reconciliation Conference in Borama: Background, Significance and Perspectives." Mimeographed paper, February 14, 1993.

Almond, Gabriel (1988), "The Return of the State." In *The American Political Science Review,* 82:3, September.

——— and Bingham Powell (1966), *Comparative Politics: The Developmental Approach.* Boston: Little Brown.

——— and James Coleman (1960), eds., *The Politics of Developing Areas.* Princeton: Princeton University Press.

"Alphabet Soup: 14 June 1992" (1992), internal document of the Joint International Observer Group (JIOG), June 1992.

Amate, A. O. (1986), *Inside the OAU*. New York: St. Martins.

Amihere, Kabral Blay, and Baffour Ankomah (1993), "Ghana: Easy Victory Brings Trouble." *New African,* No. 305, February 1993.

Anderson, Lisa (1985), *The State and Social Transformation in Tunisia and Libya, 1830–1980*. Princeton: Princeton University Press.

Ankomah, Baffour (1992), "Merry Christmas, Mr. Rawlings," *New African*, No. 302, November 1992.

Anonymous (1989), "Ethnicity and Pseudo-Ethnicity in the Ciskei," in Leroy Vail, ed., *The Creation of Tribalism in Southern Africa*. London: James Currey.

Appiah, Kwame Anthony (1992), *In My Father's House: Africa in the Philosophy of Culture*. Oxford: Oxford University Press.

Arjomand, Said Amir (1992), "Constitutions and the Struggle for Political Order: A Study in the Modernization of Political Traditions." *Archives Europeenes de Sociologie* 33, No. 2.

Askin, Steve, and Carole Collins (1993), "External Collusion with Kleptocracy: Can Zaire Recapture Its Stolen Wealth." *Review of African Political Economy*, No. 57: 72–85.

Azu, Vance (1992), *The Mirror*, Accra, October 31, 1992.

Badie, Bertrand, and Pierre Birnbaum (1983), *The Sociology of the State*. Chicago: University of Chicago Press.

Baroin, Catherine (1985), *Anarchie et cohésion sociale chez les Toubou*. Cambridge, England: Cambridge University Press.

Barongo, Yoramu (1989), "Ethnic Pluralism and Political Centralization: The Basis of Political Conflict," in Kumar Rupesinghe, ed., *Conflict Resolution in Uganda*. London: James Currey.

Battiata, Mary (1989), "Ethiopian Coup Attempt Crushed." *Washington Post*, May 20, 1989.

Bauzon, Kenneth E. (1992), ed., *Developement and Democratization in the Third World*. Bristol, PA: Taylor and Francis.

Bender, Gerald (1978), *Angola Under the Portuguese*. Berkeley: University of California.

Bennoune, Mahfoud (1988), *The Making of Contemporary Algeria: 1830–1987*. Cambridge: Cambridge University Press.

——— (1984), "Industrialization in Algeria: An Overview," in Halim Barakat, ed., *Contemporary North Africa*. Washington, DC: Center For Contemporary Arab Studies.

Ben Yahmed, Bechir (1993), "Images," *Jeune Africa* 1666, No. 1, 10 December.

Berkeley, Bill (1992), "Liberia: Between Repression and Slaughter." *Atlantic Monthly*, December 1992.

Binder, Leonard (1986), "The Natural History of Development Theory." *Comparative Studies in Society and History* 28, No. 1: 3–33.

Boahen, A. Adu (1994), "Governance and Conflict Management in Ghana Since Independence," in I. William Zartman, ed., *Conflict Management in West Africa*. Washington, DC: Brookings Institution.

Boukhobza, Mhammed (1991), *Octobre 88: Evolution ou Rupture?* Algiers: Editions Bouchene.

Boutros-Ghali, Boutros (1992), *An Agenda for Peace: Preventive Diplomacy, Peacemaking and Peacekeeping*. New York: United Nations.

Bradlow, D. (1991), "Debt, Development, and Human Rights: Lessons From South Africa." *Michigan Journal of International Law* 12, Summer.

Braeckman, Colette (1992), *Le Dinosaure: le Zaire de Mobutu*. Brussels: Fayard.

Bratton, Michael, and Nicholas van de Walle (1992), "Toward Governance in Africa: Popular Demands and State Responses," in Goran Hyden and Michael Bratton, eds., *Governance and Politics in Africa*. Boulder: Lynne Rienner.

Brett, E. A. (1991), "Rebuilding Survival Strategies for the Poor: Organizational

Options for Reconstruction in the 1990s," pp. 297–310. In Holger Bernt Hansen and Michael Twaddle, eds., *Changing Uganda: The Dilemmas of Structural Adjustment and Revolutionary Change*. London: James Currey.

———, (1993), "Voluntary Agencies as Development Organizations: Theorizing the Problem of Efficiency and Accountability." *Development and Change* 24, No. 2.

Brittain, Victoria (1986), "The Liberation of Kampala." *New Left Review* 156 (March–April).

Brooks, James (1987), "Ethiopians Officially Joining Ranks of Communist Nations." *New York Times,* February 23.

Buijtenhuis, Robert (1987), *Le Frolinat et les guerres civiles du Tchad (1977–1984)*. Paris: Karthala.

Bull, Hedley (1984), ed., *Intervention in World Politics*. Oxford: Oxford University Press.

Bunker, Stephen (1985), "Peasant Responses to a Dependent State: Uganda, 1983." *Canadian Journal of African Studies* 19: 372–373.

——— (1987), *Peasants Against the State: The Politics of Market Control in Bugisu, Uganda, 1900–1983*. Chicago: University of Chicago.

Callaghy, Thomas (1984), *The State-Society Struggle*. New York: Columbia University Press.

——— (1987), "The State as Lame Leviathan: The Patrimonial Administrative State in Africa," in Zaki Ergas, ed., *The African State in Transition*. New York: St. Martins.

——— (1990), "Lost Between State and Market: The Politics of Economic Adjustment in Ghana, Zambia and Nigeria," in Joan Nelson, ed., *Economic Crisis and Policy Choice: The Politics of Adjustment in the Third World*. Princeton: Princeton University Press.

Carnoy, Martin (1984), *The State and Political Theory*. Princeton: Princeton University.

Chabal, Patrick (1986), *Political Domination in Africa*. New York: Cambridge University Press.

Chapelle, Jean (1980), *Le Peuple tchadien: ses racines, sa vie quotidienne, ses combats*. Paris: Harmattan.

——— (1982), *Nomades noirs du Sahara: les Toubous*. Paris: Harmattan.

Charef, Abed (1990), *Octobre*. Algiers: Laphomic Editions.

Chazan, Naomi (1983), *An Anatomy of Ghanaian Politics*. Boulder: Westview.

——— (1988), "State and Society in Africa: Images and Challenges," in Donald Rothchild and Naomi Chazan, *The Precarious Balance: State and Society in Africa*. Boulder: Westview.

——— (1991), "The PNDC and the Problem of Legitimacy," in Donald Rothchild, ed., *Ghana: The Political Economy of Recovery*. Boulder: Lynne Rienner.

———, Robert Mortimer, John Ravenhill, and Donald Rothchild (1992), *Politics and Society in Contemporary Africa*, 2d ed. Boulder: Lynne Rienner.

Chipman, John (1989), *French Power in Africa*. London: Basil Blackwell.

Clapham, Christopher (1988), *Transformation and Continuity in Revolutionary Ethiopia*. Cambridge, England: Cambridge University Press.

Cliffe, Lionel (1987), *One-Party Democracy*. Dores-Salaam: East Africa Publishing House.

Cohen, Herman J. (1993), *Statement before the Subcommittee on Africa of the Committee on Foreign Affairs of the House of Representatives,* October 26, 1993.

Colborne, Desmond (1993), "Recolonizing Africa: The Right to Intervene?" *South Africa International* 23, No. 4: 162–163 (April).

Colletta, Nat, and Nicole Ball (1993), "War to Peace Transition in Uganda." *Finance and Development* 30, No. 2: 36–39.

Commonwealth Observer Group (1992), Ghana Elections, *Interim Statement,* November 4.

Cooper, Laurie A., Fred M. Hayward, and Anthony W.J. Lee (1992), *Ghana: A Pre-Election Assessment Report, June 1, 1992.* Washington, DC: International Foundation for Electoral Systems.

Crocker, Chester A. (1993), *High Noon in Southern Africa.* New York: Norton.

——— (1992), "The Global Law and Order Deficit: Is the West Ready to Police the World's Bad Neighborhoods?" *Washington Post,* December 20, p. C1.

Cutler, Lloyd (1992), "Foreword," in Morton Halperin and David Scheffer, *Self-determination in the New World Order.* Washington, DC: Carnegie Endowment for International Peace.

Dadi, Abderahman (1987), *Tchad: l'Etat retrouvé.* Paris: Harmattan.

Dagne, Theodros (1992a), "EPRDF's Rise to Political Dominance." *Ethiopian Review,* December 1992.

——— (1992b), "Ethiopia: The Struggle for Unity and Democracy." *Congressional Research Service Report for Congress.* Washington, DC, June 20, 1992.

Daoudi, Zakia (1991), "L'Economie du Maghreb en Difficulté," *Le Monde Diplomatique.* June.

Davidson, Basil (1990), "Precondition For Peace," in *West Africa,* February 1: 175.

Davies, Robert (1991), *Implications for Southern Africa of the Current Impasse in the Peace Process in Mozambique.* Capetown.

Dawisha, Adeed, and I. William Zartman (1988), eds., *Beyond Coercion: The Durability of the Arab State.* London: Croom Helm.

Deng, Francis M. (1993a), "Africa and the New World Dis-Order." *Brookings Review,* Spring 1993.

——— (1993b), *Protecting the Dispossessed: A Challenge for the International Community.* Washington, DC: The Brookings Institution.

de Tocqueville, Alexis (1835), *De la Democracy en Amerique.*

Deutsch, Karl (1963), *The Nerves of Government.* New York: Free Press.

Devoluy, Pierre (1981), "Un Témoignage sur les maquis de Hissene Habré." *Le Monde,* May 13, 1981.

——— (1987), "Stratégie et tactique des forces armées nationales," pp. 33–44 in *Géopolitique Africaine,* Nos. 5–6, April 1987.

Djilas, Milovan (1959), *The Ruling Class: An Analysis of the Communist System.* New York: Praeger.

Doornbos, Martin (1990), "The African State in Academic Debate: Retrospect and Prospect." *Journal of Modern African Studies* 28 (2): 179–198.

———, Lionel Cliffe, and James Coleman (1977), *Government and Rural Development in East Africa.* The Hague. Stanford, CA: Stanford University Press.

Drysdale, John (1992), "Somalia: The Only Way Forward." *Journal of the Anglo-Somali Society.* Winter 1992/93.

Durkheim, Emile (1986), *Politics and the State.* Anthony Giddens, ed., Stanford: Stanford University Press.

——— (1993), *The Division of Labor in Society.* New York: Free Press.

Dyson, Kenneth H. (1980), *The State Tradition in Western Europe: A Study of an Idea and Institution.* Oxford: Martin Robertson.

"Economic Policy" (1990), *Yekatit Quarterly* 13, No. 4, June.

Eisenstadt, S. N. (1988), "Beyond Collapse," in Yoffee and Cowgill 1988.

——— (1969), *Political Systems of Empires,* New York: Free Press.

——— (1967), *Decline of Empires.* Englewood Cliffs, NJ: Prentice Hall.

El-Kenz, Ali (1989), ed., *L'Algérie et la Modernité.* Dakar, Senegal: CODESRIA.

Ekwe-Ekwe, Herbert (1990), *Conflict and Intervention in Africa.* London: Macmillan.

EPLF (1987), "Eritrean People's Liberation Front Statement on the Regional Autonomy of the Derg's Shengo." Washington, DC: EPLF. September.

Ergas, Zaki (1987), ed., *The African State in Transition.* New York: Saint Martins.

"Ethnicity and Pseudo-Ethnicity in the Ciskei" (1989), in Leroy Vail, ed., *The Creation of Tribalism in Southern Africa.* London: James Currey.

Evaluation of the June 21, 1992 Elections in Ethiopia (1992). Washington, DC: National Democratic Institute.

Evans, Peter D.R., and Theda Skocpol (1987), eds., *Bringing the State Back In.* Cambridge: Cambridge University Press.

Fanon, Frantz (1968), *The Wretched of the Earth.* New York: Grove.

Fatton, Robert (1992), *Predatory Rule: State and Civil Society in Africa.* Boulder: Lynne Rienner.

Ferrero, Gigliermo (1942), *Principles of Power.* Salem, NH: Ayer.

Foltz, Anne-Marie, and William J. Foltz (1991), "The Politics of Health Reform in Chad," in Dwight H. Perkins and Michael Roemer, eds., *Reforming Economic Systems in Developing Countries.* Cambridge, MA: Harvard University Press.

Foltz, William J. (1987), "Chad's Third Republic: Strengths, Problems, and Prospects." *CSIS Africa Notes,* No. 77, October 30.

——— (1988), "Libya's Military Power," in René Lemarchand, ed., *The Green and the Black: Qadhafi's Policies in Africa.* Bloomington: Indiana University Press.

——— and Henry Bienen (1985), *Arms and the African.* New Haven: Yale University Press.

Forrest, Joshua (1988), "The Quest for 'Hardness' in Africa." *Comparative Politics* 20, No. 4: 432–442. July.

Freid, Morton H. (1968), "State: The Institution," in David L. Sills (ed.).

Galaydh, Ali Khalif (1990), "Notes on the State of the Somali State," *Horn of Africa* 13, Nos. 1 and 2, January–March and April–June.

Gambari, Ibrahim A. (1991), *Political and Comparative Dimensions of Regional Integration: The Case of ECOWAS.* Atlantic Highlands, NJ: Humanities Press.

Gbabendu, A., et al. (1991), *Volonte de Changement au Zaire,* I and II. Paris: Harmattan.

Geffray, C. (1990), *A Causa Das Armas en Mocabique: Antropologia de Uma Guerra Civil.* Paris.

George, Kevin O. (1993), *The Civil War in Liberia,* unpublished manuscript.

Gertzel, Cherry (1990), "Uganda's Continuing Search for Peace." *Current History,* 205–208 (May).

Ghana, Republic of (1977), *Five-Year Development Plan 1975/76–1979/80.* Part II. Accra: Ghana Publishing Corp.

Ghana Elections, Commonwealth Observer Group (1992), interim statement, November 4, 1992.

Gingyera-Pinychwa, A.G.G. (1991), "Toward Constitutional Renovation: Some Political Considerations," in Holger Bernt Hansen and Michael Twaddle, eds., *Changing Uganda: The Dilemmas of Structural Adjustment and Revolutionary Change.* London: James Currey.

Goldstone Commission (1992). *Goldstone Report on the causes of violence in Bruntville*. Johannesburg: Government of South Africa.

Goulbourne, Harry (1987), "The State, Development, and the Need for Participatory Democracy in Africa," in Peter Anyang' Nyong'o, *Popular Struggles for Democracy in Africa*. London: Zed.

Gramsci, Antonio (1967), *The Modern Prince*. New York: International Publishers.

Green, Reginald (1981), "Magendo in the Political Economy of Uganda. Pathology, Parallel System, or Dominat Sub-Mode of Production?" Discussion Paper No. 165, Institute of Development Studies, University of Sussex.

Greenfeld, Liah (1992), *Nationalism: Five Roads to Modernity*. Cambridge, MA: Harvard University Press.

Grundy, Kenneth (1986), *The Militarization of South African Politics*. Bloomington: Indiana University Press.

Gurr, Ted Robert, Keith Jaggers, and Will H. Moore (1990), "The Transformation of the Western State: The Growth of Democracy, Autocracy, and State Power Since 1800." *Studies in Comparative International Development*. 25, No. 1.

——— and Barbara Harf (1994), eds., "Early Warning of Communal Conflicts," *Journal of Ethno-Political Development* 4, No. 1 (Special Issue), July.

Gyan-Apenteng, K. (1992), "Winners and Losers." *West Africa,* November 16–22, 1992.

Haireche, Abdelkader (1993), *Conflict Management and Cooperation in North Africa*. Ph.D. Dissertation, New York University.

Halliday, Fred, and Maxine Molyneux (1981), *The Ethiopian Revolution*. London: Verso.

Hanlon, Joseph (1984), *Revolution Under Fire*. London: Zed.

——— (1986), *Beggar Your Neighbours: Apartheid Power in Southern Africa*. London: James Currey.

——— (1991), *Mozambique: Who Calls the Shots*. Bloomington: Indiana University Press.

Harbeson, John (1988), *The Ethiopian Transformation*. Boulder: Westview.

Hegel, G. W. (1952), *Philosophy of Right*. Oxford: Oxford University Press.

Helleiner, G. K. (1981), "Economic Collapse and Rehabilitation in Uganda." *Rural Africana* 11 (Fall): 27–35.

Helman, Gerald, and Steven Ratner (1992), "Saving Failed States," *Foreign Policy* 89 (Winter): 3–20.

Henze, Paul B. (1992), "Ethiopia in Transition." *Ethiopian Review,* July.

Herbst, Jeffrey (1990), "Economic Reform in Africa: The Lessons of Ghana," *UFS Field Staff Reports,* Africa/Middle East 1989–1990, No. 15. Indianapolis: Universities Field Staff International.

——— (1993), *The Politics of Reform in Ghana, 1982–1991*. Berkeley: University of California Press.

Hirschman, Albert O. (1970), *Exit, Voice and Loyalty*. Cambridge: Harvard University.

Holcomb, Bonnie K., and Sisai Ibssa (1990), *The Invention of Ethiopia: The Making of a Dependent Colonial State in Northeast Africa*. Trenton, NJ: Red Sea.

Hull, Galen (1979), "The French Connection in Africa: Zaire and South Africa." *Journal of Southern Africa Studies* 5, No. 2.

Human Rights Commission (1993), "Report on Political Violence." Discussion Paper on the South African Economy: International Monetary Fund. January. Johannesburg.

Huntington, Samuel (1965), "Political Development and Political Decay" *World Politics* 17, No. 3: 27–35.

———— (1968), *Political Order in Changing Societies*. New Haven: Yale University Press.

Hyden, Goran (1980), *Beyond Ujamaa in Tanzania*. London: Heineman.

———— (1983), *No Shortcuts to Progress*. London: Heineman.

———— (1983), "Problems and Prospects of State Coherence," in Donald Rothchild and Victor Olorunsola, eds., *States Versus Ethnic Claims: African Policy Dilemmas*. Boulder: Westview.

———— (1992), "Governance and the Study of Politics," in Goran Hyden and Michael Bratton, eds., *Governance and Politics in Africa*. Boulder: Lynne Rienner.

Ibingira, Grace (1980), *Africa's Upheavals since Independence*. Boulder: Westview.

Inter-Action Council (1993), *Bring Africa Back into the Mainstream of the International System*. New York: Inter-Action Council.

International Monetary Fund (1981 and 1985), *Government Finance Statistics Yearbook* 1981–1985. Washington, DC: IMF.

———— (1984), *International Financial Statistics Yearbook* 37. Washington, DC: IMF.

Jackson, Robert, and Carl Rosberg (1982), *Personal Rule in Black Africa*. Berkeley: University of California Press.

———— (1986a), "The Marginality of the African State," in Gwendolyn M. Carter and Patrick O'Meara, eds., *African Independence: The First Twenty-Five Years*. Bloomington: Indiana University Press.

———— (1986b), "Why Africa's Weak States Persist: The Empirical and the Juridical in Statehood," in Atul Kohli, ed., *The State and Development in the Third World*. Princeton: Princeton University Press.

Jamal, Vali (1988), "Coping under Crisis in Uganda." *International Labor Review* 127, No. 6: 679–701.

———— (1991), "The Agrarian Context of the Ugandan Crisis," in Holger Bernt Hansen, and Michael Twaddle, eds., *Changing Uganda: The Dilemmas of Structural Adjustment and Revolutionary Change*. London: James Currey.

Jaycox, Edward V.K. (1993), "Structural Adjustment Spurs African Development," *AfricaNews* 38, Nos. 2–3, March 8–21, 1993.

Jeffries, Richard (1983).

———— (1991), "Leadership Commitment and Political Opposition to Structural Adjustment in Ghana," in Donald Rothchild, ed., *Ghana: The Political Economy of Recovery*. Boulder: Lynne Rienner.

———— (1993), "The State, Structural Adjustment, and Good Government in Africa." *Journal of Commonwealth and Comparative Politics* 31, No. 1: 20–35.

Jessop, Bob (1989), *State Theory: Putting the Capitalist State in Its Place*. Cambridge: Polity Press.

Johnson, Phyllis, and David Martin (1989), *Apartheid Terrorism: The Destabilization Report*. London: James Currey.

Kasfir, Nelson (1983), "State, Magendo and Class Formation in Uganda." *Journal of Commonwealth and Comparative Politics* 21, No. 3: 85–103.

———— (1986), "Explaining Ethnic Political Participation," in Atul Kohli, ed., *The State and Development in the Third World*. Princeton: Princeton University Press.

———— (1991), "The Ugandan Elections of 1989: Power, Populism, and

Democratization," in Holger Bernt Hansen and Michael Twaddle, eds., *Changing Uganda: The Dilemmas of Structural Adjustment and Revolutionary Change*. London: James Currey.

—— (1993), "Popular Sovereignty and Popular Participation: Mixed Constitutional Democracy in the Third World." *Third World Quarterly* 13, No. 4: 597–606.

Kaufman, Herbert (1988), "The Collapse of Ancient Sates and Civilizatons as an Organizational Problem," in Norman Yoffee and George L. Cowgill, eds., *The Collapse of Ancient States and Civilizations*. Tucson: University of Arizona Press.

Kayizzi-Mugerwa, Steve, and Arne Bigsten (1992), "On Structural Adjustment in Uganda." *Canadian Journal of Development* 13, No. 1: 57–75.

Kean, John (1988), "Despotism and Democracy: The Origins of the Distinction Between Civil Society and the State," in John Kean, ed., *Civil Society and the State: New European Perspectives*. New York: Verso.

Keller, Edmond J. (1993), "Government and Politics," in *Ethiopia: A Country Profile*. Washington, DC: Library of Congress.

—— (1988), *Revolutionary Ethiopia: From Empire to People's Republic*. Bloomington: Indiana University Press.

Khadiagala, Gilbert (1993), "Uganda's Domestic and Regional Security Since the 1970s." *Journal of Modern African Studies* 31, No. 2, (June): 231–255.

Kiapi, Abraham (1989), "The Constitution as a Mediator in Internal Conflict," in Kumar Rupesinghe, ed., *Conflict Resolution in Uganda*. London: James Currey.

Kitchen, Helen (1987), *Anglo, Mozambique and the West*. Washington, DC: Center for Strategic and International Studies.

Kizito, Edmond (1993), "Uganda's Economy Grows but Poverty Still Bites." *International Press Service Feature*. March 5.

Kouassi, Edmond Kwam (1993), "The Impact of Reduced European Security Roles on African Relations" (with John White), in I. W. Zartman, ed., *Europe and Africa: The New Phase*. Boulder: Lynne Rienner.

Kraft, Scott (1988), "Ethiopia Forgets Its Famine to Concentrate on Civil War." *Los Angeles Times,* May 30, 1988.

Krasner, Stephen (1984), "Aproaches to the State: Alternative Conceptions and Historical Dynamics," *Comparative Politics* 16, No. 2.

Kraus, Jon (1991), "The Political Economy of Stabilization and Structural Adjustment in Ghana," in Donald Rothchild, ed., *Ghana: The Political Economy of Recovery*. Boulder: Lynne Rienner.

Laitin, David, and Said Samatar (1987), *Somalia: Nation in Search of a State*. Boulder: Westview.

Lancaster, Carol (1991), "Democracy in Africa." *Foreign Policy* 85, Winter 1991/92.

Landell-Mills, Pierre (1992), "Governance, Civil Society and Empowerment in Sub-Saharan Africa." World Bank Africa Technical Department, May 1992.

—— (1993), *Sovereign National Conventions in Africa*. Washington, DC: World Bank.

Lanne, Bernard (1979), "Les Populations du sud du Tchad." *Revue Française d'Etudes Politiques Africaines,* Nos. 163–164, July–August 1979.

—— (1984), "Le Sud, l'état et la révolution." *Politique Africaine* 16, December 1984.

Lawyers Committee for Human Rights (1986), *Liberia: A Promise Betrayed*. Washington, DC: Lawyers Committee for Human Rights.

Layachi, Azzedine, and Abdelkader Haireche (1992), "National Development and Political Protest: The Islamists in the Maghreb Countries," in *Arab Studies Quarterly* 14, Nos. 2 and 3: 69–92, Spring/Summer.

Lemarchand, René (1988), "The Case of Chad," in René Lemarchand, ed., *The Green and the Black: Qadhafi's Policies in Africa*. Bloomington: Indiana University Press.

——— (1992), "Uncivil State and Civil Societies: How Illusion Became Reality." *The Journal of Modern African Studies* 30, No. 2, p. 180.

Lemoine, (1991), "L'Algerie." *Le Monde Diplomatique*. July.

Leslie, Winsome (1993), "Collapse in the Congo, 1960–65," paper presented to the 1993 Africa Country Day Program, Nitze School of Advanced International Studies, Johns Hopkins University, Washington, D.C.

Lewis, I. M. (1969), *A Pastoral Democracy*. Oxford, England: Oxford University Press.

——— (1988), *A Modern History of Somalia*. Boulder, Colo.: Westview Press.

——— (1990), "The Ogaden and the Fragility of Somali Segmentary Nationalism," *Hour of Africa*, 13.

Liebenow, J. Gus (1987), *Liberia: The Quest for Democracy*. Bloomington: Indiana University.

Lijphart, Arend (1985), *Power-sharing in South Africa*. Berkeley: Institute of International Studies.

Lipset, Seymour Martin (1959), *Political Man*. New York: Doubleday Anchor.

Lopez-Pinter, Rafael (1992), "Comprehensive Mission Report from Consultant in Electoral Administration in Liberia." July.

Lowenkopf, Martin (1974), *Liberia: The Conservative Road to Development*. Stanford, CA: Hoover Institution.

Lund, Michael (1994), *Preventive Diplomacy*. Washington, DC: United States Institute of Peace.

Lycett, Andrew (1993), "Meles Zenawi Takes Control." *New African*, February 1993.

Lyons, Terrence (1991), "The Transition in Ethiopia." *CSIS Africa Notes*, 127, August.

Magnant, Jean-Pierre (1986), *La Terre Sara, Terre Tchadienne*. Paris: Harmattan.

Mamdani, Mahmood (1976), *Politics and Class Formation in Uganda*. New York: Monthly Review.

——— (1990a), "Uganda: Contradictions of the IMF Program and Perspective." *Development and Change* 21: 427–467.

——— (1990b), "The Social Bases of Constitutionalism in Africa." *Journal of Modern African Studies* 28, No. 3.

Mann, Michael (1984), "The Autonomous Power of the State: Its Origins, Mechanisms, and Results." *Archives Europeenes de Sociologies* 25, No. 2: 185–213.

Mare, G. (1992), "History and Dimension of the Violence in Natal: Inkatha's Role in Negotiating Peace." *Social Justice* 18, Nos. 1–2.

Marennin, Otwin (1987), "The Managerial State in Africa: A Conflict Coalition Perspective," in Zaki Ergas, ed., *The African State in Transition*. New York: St. Martins.

Marks, Shula (1989), "Patriotism, Patriarchy and Purity: Natal and the Politics of Zulu Ethnic Consciousness," in Leroy Vail, ed., *The Creation of Tribalism in Southern Africa*. London: James Currey.

Martin, Matthew (1991), "Negotiating Adjustment and External Finance: Ghana and the International Community, 1982–1989," in Donald Rothchild, ed., *Ghana: The Political Economy of Recovery*. Boulder: Lynne Rienner.

Martone, Gerald R. (1993), "Friends of Liberia: Project Opportunity Statement," May 21–June 6, 1993.

Marx, Karl (1968), "Manifesto of the Communist Party," in Karl Marx and Frederick Engels, *Selected Works*. New York: International.

—— (1970), *The German Ideology*. New York: International.

Mazrui, Ali (1980), "Between Development and Decay: Anarchy, Tyranny, and Progress under Idi Amin." *Third World Quarterly* 11, No. 1: 44–53.

—— (1988), "Is Africa Decaying? The View from Uganda," in Holger Bernt Hansen and Michael Twaddle, eds., *Uganda Now: Between Decay and Development*. London: James Currey.

McDougal, G. (1992), "Testimony Prepared for the Subcommittee of the U.S. House of Representatives." July 23.

McNamara, Francis (1989), *France in Black Africa*. Washington, DC: National Defense University Press.

MERIP Report (1990), "Europe's Other Frontier: North Africa Faces the 1990s" 163, March–April.

Merton, Robert (1951), *Social Theory and Social Structure*. New York: Free Press.

Messoudi, M. T. (1993), "ONDH: Une dizaine de Cas de Torture." *El Watan*, February 6.

Migdal, Joel (1988), *Strong Societies and Weak States: State Society Relations in the Third World*. Princeton: Princeton University Press.

Mitchell, Timothy (1991), "The Limits of the State: Beyond Statist Appoaches and Their Critics." *American Political Science Review* 85, No. 1: 77–96.

Monga, Celestin (1994), "After the National Convention," in Daniel Simpson, ed., *Democratization and Its Outcomes*. Boulder: Lynne Rienner.

Mudoola, Dan (1989), "Communal Conflicts in the Military and Political Consequences," in Kumar Rupesinghe, ed., *Conflict Resolution in Uganda*. London: James Currey.

—— (1991), "Institution-Building: The Case of the NRM and the Military, 1986–89," in Holger Bernt Hansen and Michael Twaddle, eds., *Changing Uganda: The Dilemmas of Structural Adjustment and Revolutionary Change*. London: James Currey.

Mugyenyi, Joshua B. (1991), "IMF Conditionality and Structural Adjustment under the National Resistance Movement," in Holger Bernt Hansen and Michael Twaddle, eds., *Changing Uganda: The Dilemmas of Structural Adjustment and Revolutionary Change*. London: James Currey.

Museveni, Yoweri K. (1992), *What Is Africa's Problem?* Kampala: NRM Publications.

Mutibwa, Phares (1992), *Uganda Since Independence: The Story of Unfulfilled Hopes*. Trenton, NJ: Africa World Press.

Myrdal, Gunnar (1971), *Asian Drama*. New York: Vintage.

National Democratic Institute for International Affairs/African American Institute (1992), *An Evaluation of the June 21, 1992 Elections in Ethiopia*. Washington, DC: National Democratic Institute for International Affairs.

National Democratic Lawyers (1992), *An Overview of Political Violence*. Washington, DC.

Nellier, John (1993), "States in Danger," mimeo.

New Economic Policy (1990), *Yekatit Quarterly* 13, No. 4, June.

New Patriotic Party (1993), *The Stolen Verdict: Ghana, November 1992 Presidential Election*. Accra: NPP.

Ng'ethe, Njuguna (1984) ???

Niblock, Tim (1991), "The Background to the Change of Government in 1985," in Peter Woodward, ed., *The Sudan After Nimeiri*. London: Routledge.

Nietzsche, Friedrich (1966 edition), *Beyond Good and Evil*. New York: Vintage.

Nolutshungu, Samuel (1992), "Africa in a World of Democracies: Interpretation and Retrieval." *Journal of Commonwealth and Comparative Politics* 30, No. 3: 316–334.

Nordlinger, Eric (1981), *On the Autonomy of the Democratic State*. Cambridge: Harvard University Press.

—— (1987), "Taking the State Seriously," in Myron Weiner and Samuel P. Huntington, *Understanding Political Development*. Boston: Little Brown.

Nzongola-Ntalaja, George (1985), "The National Question and the Crisis of Instability in Africa." *Alternatives* 5, No. 4: 533–563.

—— (1987), "The National Question and the Crisis of Instability in Africa," in Emmanuel Hansen (ed.), *Africa: Perspectives on Peace and Development*. London: Zed.

—— (1993), Taped interview, May 12.

—— (1993), *Statement before the Subcommittee on Africa of the Committee on Foreign Affairs, U.S. House of Representatives*, October 26.

Oakley, Robert and John Hirsch (1995), *Somalia and Operation Restore Hope: Reflections on Peacekeeping and Peacemaking*. Washington, DC: United States Institute of Peace.

Ochieng, E. O. (1991), "Economic Adjustment Programs in Uganda, 1985–1988," in Holger Bernt Hansen and Michael Twaddle, eds., *Changing Uganda: The Dilemmas of Structural Adjustment and Revolutionary Change*. London: James Currey.

O'Donnell, Guillermo (1988), "Tensions in the Bureaucratic State and the Question of Democracy," in Roy Macridis and Bernard Brown, eds., *Comparative Politics: Notes and Readings*, 6th ed. Chicago: Dorsey Press.

"Ogaden and the Fragility of Somali Segmentary Nationalism" (1990), *Horn of Africa* 13.

Ohlson, Thomas and Stephen John Stedman (1994), *The New is Not Yet Born: Conflict Resolution in South Africa*. Washington, DC: Brookings.

Omara-Otunnu, Amii (1987), *Politics and the Military in Uganda, 1980–1985*. London: St. Martins.

—— (1992), "The Struggle for Democracy in Uganda." *Journal of Modern African Studies* 30, No. 3: 443–464.

Onuf, Nicholas G. (1991), "Sovereignty: Outline of a Conceptual History." *Alternatives* 16, No. 4: 425–446.

"Opening up the World Bank" (1993), *Africa Confidential* 34, No. 12, June 11.

Oppenheim, L. (1985), *International Law, Vol. 1*. London: Longmans.

Ottaway, Marina (1987), "Post-Numeiri Sudan: One Year On." *Third World Quarterly* 9, No. 3, July.

——, ed. (1990), *Political Economy of Ethiopia*. New York: Praeger.

—— (1992), "Nationalism Unbound: The Horn of Africa Revisited," *SAIS Review* 12, No. 2, Summer–Fall.

—— (1993), "Should Elections Be the Criterion of Democratization in Africa?" *CSIS Africa Notes*, No. 145, February.

Ouma, Stephen (1991), "Corruption in Public Policy and Its Impact on

Development: The Case of Uganda since 1979." *Public Adminisration and Development* 11: 473–490.

Owen, Roger (1992), *State, Power and Politics in the Making of Modern Middle East*. New York: Routledge.

Parekh, Bikhu (1990), "When Will the State Wither Away?" *Alternatives* 15, No. 3: 247–262.

Parsons, Talcott (1951), *The Social Ssytem*. New York: Free Press.

Pelezynski, Zbigniew A. (1988), "Solidarity and the 'Rebirth of Civil Society' in Poland," in John Kean, ed., *Civil Society and the State: New European Perspectives*. New York: Verso.

Perlez, Jane (1989), "Ethiopia Starts to Come Unglued After String of Military Setbacks." *New York Times,* March 22, 1989.

Pittman, Dean (1984), "The OAU and Chad," in Yassin El-Ayouty and I. William Zartman, eds., *The OAU after Twenty Years*. New York: Praeger.

Poggi, Gianfranco (1978), *The Development of the Modern State: A Sociological Introduction*. San Francisco: Stanford University.

——— (1982), "The Modern State and the Idea of Progress," in Gabriel Almond, et al., eds., *Progress and Its Discontents*. Berkeley: University of California Press.

Report by Mengistu Haile Mariam: Resolutions Adopted by the Plenum (1990), *Documents of the 11th Plenum of the CC WPE,* Addis Ababa, March.

Report of the Secretary-General on the Question of Liberia (1993), March 8.

Republic of Ghana (1977), *Five-Year Development Plan 1975/76–1979/80* 2. Accra: Ghana Publishing.

Revolution Africaine (1989), "Associations a Caractere Politique." No. 1324, July.

Reyna, Stephen P. (1990), *Wars Without End: The Political Economy of a Precolonial African State*. Hanover, NH: University Press of New England.

Roberts, Hugh (1980), *Political Development in Algeria: The Regime of Greater Kabylia*. Oxford University Press.

——— (1983), "The Algerian Bureaucracy," in Talal Asad and Roger Owen, eds., *Sociology of Developing Societies: The Middle East*. London: MacMillan.

——— (1984), "The Politics of Algerian Socialism," in R. I. Lawless and Alan M. Findley, eds., *North Africa: Contemporary Politics and Economic Development*. London: Croom Helm.

Ronen, Dov (1986), ed., *Democracy and Pluralism in Africa*. Boulder: Lynne Rienner.

Rothchild, Donald (1981), "An African Test Case for Political Democracy: President Limann's Economic Alternatives," in Colin Legum, ed., *Africa Contemporary Record, 1979–80*. New York: Africana.

———, and E. Gyimah-Boadi (1981), "Ghana's Return to Civilian Rule." *Africa Today* 28, No. 1.

———, and John Harbeson (1981), "Rehabilitation in Uganda." *Current History* 80, No. 463: 115–119, 134–138.

———, and Victor Olorunsola (1983), *State Versus Ethnic Claims: African Policy Dilemmas*. Boulder: Westview.

——— (1985), "The Rawlings Revolution in Ghana: Pragmatism with Populist Rhetoric." *CSIS Africa Notes* 42 (May 2, 1985).

——— (1987), "Hegemony and State Softness," in Zaki Ergas, ed., *The African State in Transition*. New York: St. Martins.

——— and Naomi Chazan (1988), eds., *The Precarious Balance: State and Society in Africa*. Boulder: Westview.

————, and E. Gyimah-Boadi (1989), "Populism in Ghana and Burkina Faso." *Current History* 88, No. 538: 221–224, 241–244.

———— (1991), "Ghana and Structural Adjustment: An Overview," in Rothchild, ed., *Ghana: The Political Economy of Recovery*. Boulder: Lynne Rienner.

————, and Letitia Lawson (1994), "The Interactions Between State and Civil Society in Africa: From Deadlock to New Routines," in John W. Harbeson, Donald Rothchild, and Naomi Chazan, eds., *Civil Society and the State in Africa*. Boulder: Lynne Rienner.

Ruiz, Hiram A. (1992), *Uprooted Liberians: Casualties of a Brutal War*. U.S. Committee for Refugees.

Sabine, George H. (1962), *A History of Political Theory*. New York: Holt, Rhinehart and Winston.

Sahnoun, Mohammed 1994, *Somalia: Missed Opportunities*. Washington, DC: US Institute of Peace.

Salih, Kamal Osman (1991), "The Sudan 1985–89: The Fading Democracy," in Peter Woodward, ed., *The Sudan After Nimeiri*. London: Routledge.

Samatar, Ahmed (1988), *Socialist Somalia: Rhetoric and Reality*. London: Zed.

Sami, Zubaida (1989), *Islam, The People and The State*. New York: Routledge.

Sandbrook, Richard (1985), *The Politics of Africa's Economic Stagnation*. Cambridge: Cambridge University Press.

Sarwar Lateef, Sarwar K. (1991), "Structural Adustment in Uganda: The Intitial Experience," in Holger Bernt Hansen and Michael Twaddle, eds., *Changing Uganda: The Dilemmas of Structural Adjustment and Revolutionary Change*. London: James Currey.

Saul, John (1979), *The State and Revolution in Eastern Africa*. New York: Monthly Review Press.

Sawyer, Amos (1992), *The Emergence of Autocracy in Liberia*. San Francisco: Institute for Contemporary Studies.

Schatzberg, Michael (1991), *Mobutu or Chaos: The United States and Zaire, 1960–1990*. Lauham, MD: University Press of America.

Schneidman, Witney (1991), *Conflict Resolution in Mozambique: A Status Report*. Washington, DC.

Schutz, Barry (1992), "A Multi-Level Perspective of Conflict Mitigation: The Role of Region in a Restructured Global System," in Barry Schutz, Robert O. Slater, Steven Dorr, *Global Transformation and the Third World*. Boulder: Lynne Rienner.

———— and Robert O. Slater (1992), *Revolution and Political Change in the Third World*. Boulder: Lynne Rienner.

Shivgi, Issa (1975), *Class Struggles in Tanzania*. Dares Salaam: East Africa Publishing House.

Smelser, Neal (1966), *Social Structure and Mobility in Economic Development*. Chicago: Aldine Publishing Co.

Smith, Steven B. (1983), "Hegel's View on War, the State and International Relations," in *The American Political Science Review* 77, No. 3: 625–632.

Snider, Lewis (1987), "Identifying Elements of State Power: Where Do We Begin?" *Comparative Political Studies* 20, No. 3: 314–356.

Soulas de Russel, Dominique (1981), *Tschad—Objekt nationaler und internationaler Machtkampfe*. Hamburg: Institut fur Afrika-Kunde.

Southall, Aidan (1980), "Social Disorganization in Uganda: Before, During, and After Amin." *Journal of Modern African Studies* 18, No. 4: 627–656.

Spartacus, Colonel (1985), *Opération Manta: Tchad 1983–1984*. Paris: Plon.

Steinbruner, John (1992) "Civil Violence as an International Security Problem." (A memorandum addressed to the Foreign Policy Studies Program staff dated November 23). Washington, DC: Brookings Institution.

Tainter, J. A. (1988), *The Collapse of Complex Societies*. New York: Cambridge University Press.

Temmar, Hamid (1983), *Stratégy de Développement Indépendent, le Cas de l'Algérie: un Bilan*. Algiers: OPU.

Thompson, Virginia, and Richard Adloff (1981), *Conflict in Chad*. Berkeley: Institute of International Studies.

Tindigarukayo, Jimmy (1988), "Uganda, 1979–85: Leadership in Transition." *Journal of Modern African Studies* 26, No. 3: 607–622.

———— (1990), "On the Way to Recovery? Museveni's Uganda in 1988." *Canadian Journal of Development Studies* 11, No. 2: 347–357.

Turner, John (1990), "Zaire's Future: On the Threshold of the Third Republic." *International Freedom Review* 4, No. 1.

Uhomoibhi, M. I., et al. (1991), *History of Nigeria: Nigeria in the Nineteenth Century*. London: Longmans.

United Nations (1993), Document E/CN.4.35

United Nations Security Council Note of the President (1993), S/25344 of 26 February.

Vandewalle, Dirk (1993), "The Second Stage of State-Building in North Africa," in I. William Zartman, *State and Society in North Africa*. New York: Praeger.

Vines, Alex (1991), *Renamo: Terrorism in Mozambique*. London: Bloomington: University of Indiana Press.

———— (1993), "Change and the Military in Mozambique," paper presented to the US Defense Intelligence College Conference in Alconbury, UK, 6 May.

Vogt, Margaret (1993), *The Nigerian Crisis and ECOMOG*. Lagos: Gabuno.

Waddington Report on the Boipatong Massacre, June 17, 1992.

Weber, Max (1958), *Essays in Sociology*, H. H. Gerth and C. Wright Mills, eds. New York: Galaxy.

Wilson, Ernest (1984), "Contested Terrain: A Comparative and Theoretical Reassessment of State-Owned Enterprise in Africa." *Journal of Commonwealth and Comparative Politics* 22, No. 1: 4–27.

Woods, Dwayne (1992), "Civil Society in Europe and Africa: Limiting State Power Through a Public Sphere." *African Studies Review* 35, No. 2: 77–100.

Woodward, Bob (1987), *Veil: The Secret Wars of the CIA 1981–1987*. New York: Simon & Schuster.

Workers' Party of Ethiopia, 11th Plenum of the Central Committee (1990), *New Economic Policy*. Addis Ababa: WPE.

World Bank (1991), *Public Choices for Private Initiatives: Prioritizing Public Expenditures for Sustainable and Equitable Growth in Uganda*. Washington, DC: World Bank.

———— (1993a), Africa Regional Office, Western Africa Department, *Ghana 2000 and Beyond*, p. 10. Washington, DC: World Bank.

———— (1993b), *World Development Report*. Washington, DC: IBRD.

Wrigley, Christopher (1988), "Four Steps Toward Disaster," in Holger Bernt Hansen and Michael Twaddle, eds., *Uganda Now: Between Decay and Development*. London: James Currey.

Yeats, W. B. (1983 edition), *The Poems—A New Edition*. New York: Macmillan.

Yefsah, Abdelkader (1990), *La Question du Pouvoir en Algérie*. Algiers: ENAP.

Yoffee, Norman, and George L. Cowgill, eds., (1988), *The Collapse of Ancient States and Civilizations*. Tucson: University of Arizona Press.

Young, Crawford (1982), "Patterns of Social Conflict: State, Class and Ethnicity in Africa." *Daedalus* 59, No. 2: 71–98.

——— (1984), "Zaire: Is There a State?" *Canadian Journal of African Studies* 18, No. 1: 80–82.

———, and Babacar Kante (1992), "Governance in Senegal," in Goran Hyden and Michael Bratton, eds., *Governance and Politics in Africa*. Boulder: Lynne Rienner.

Zaire: Cabinet du President (1993), *Chronologie du processus de democratisation au Zaire*. Kinshasa, Zaire, February.

Zartman, I. William (1989, 2nd edition), *Ripe for Resolution*. New York: Oxford University Press.

——— (1995), "Negotiating in South Africa," in I. William Zartman, ed., *Elusive Peace: Negotiating an End to Civil Wars*. Washington, DC: Brookings Institution.

———, and Victor Kremenyuk (1994), eds., *Cooperative Security: Reducing Third World Wars*. Syracuse: Syracuse University.

——— (1993), ed., *Europe and Africa: The New Phase*. Boulder: Lynne Rienner.

———, and Samuel Amoo (1992), "Mediation by Regional Organizations: The OAU in Chad," in Jacob Bercovitch and Jeffrey Rubin, eds., *Mediation in International Relations*. New York: St. Martins.

——— (1986), "Conflict in Chad," in Arthur Day and Michael Doyle, eds., *Escalation and Intervention*. Boulder: Westview.

Zolberg, Aristide (1992), "The Spector of Anarchy in Africa: African States Verging on Dissolution." *Dissent*, 303–311.

About the Contributors

Hussein M. Adam, born in Tanzania of Somali parents, is associate professor in political science at College of the Holy Cross in Worcester, Massachusetts. He was educated at Princeton, Makerere University in Uganda, and Harvard. He has edited two volumes on Somalia, as well as a monograph on language policies and several articles on African and development studies. His current research is on militarism and the Somali state crisis. He has headed the African and African American Studies Department at Brandeis University (1970–1974), and the Social Sciences Division of the Somali National University (1975–1987).

Francis Deng is senior fellow of the African studies branch of the Foreign Studies Program at the Brookings Institution. He has been a guest scholar at the Woodrow Wilson International Center for Scholars, one of the first Rockefeller Brothers Fund Distinguished Fellows, and a Jennings Randolph Distinguished Fellow of the United States Institute of Peace. He has authored or edited over a dozen books in the fields of law, anthropology, history, politics, and folklore. He has also written two novels. Among his titles are *Conflict Resolution in Africa* (with I. William Zartman) and *Cry of the Owl,* his second novel. Dr. Deng holds a law degree from Khartoum University and a doctorate from Yale Law School.

Leonid Fituni is director of the Center for Strategic Global Studies of the Russian Academy of Sciences and was formerly section director of the academy's Africa Institute. He is the author of a dozen books in Russian, English, and Portuguese on African economic and political issues, the most recent of which is *Africa 30 Years After Independence: Development Crises and Structural Reform.*

William J. Foltz is the H. J. Heinz Professor of African Studies and Political Science and acting director of the Yale Center for International and Area Studies at Yale University. He has written extensively on the politics and international relations of African states and on ethnic and religious conflict. He recently chaired the Bujumbura Conference, "The Role of the Military in Democratization in Africa."

Ibrahim A. Gambari is permanent representative of Nigeria's mission to the United Nations. He was foreign minister of Nigeria from January 1984 to August 1985. Dr. Gambari has been professor of international relations at Ahmadu Bello University, Zaria, Nigeria, since 1983, and was a visiting professor of African studies at the Johns Hopkins Nitze School of Advanced International Studies. In addition to authoring a number of articles, he is author of the book *Theory and Reality in Foreign Policy Making: Nigeria After the Second Republic.*

Edmond J. Keller is professor of political science and director of the James S. Coleman African Studies Center at UCLA. He is the author of *Education, Manpower and Development: The Impact of Educational Policy in Kenya* and *Revolutionary Ethiopia: From Empire to People's Republic.* He also coedited *Afro-Marxist Regimes* and *South African in Southern Africa,* and has written numerous articles on African and African American politics.

Gilbert M. Khadiagala is assistant professor of comparative politics and African studies at Kent State University, Ohio. He studied in Kenya, Canada, and the United States, earning his doctorate at the Johns Hopkins Nitze School of Advanced International Studies. Dr. Khadiagala has published articles on African politics and Southern African security. He is currently at work on a book, *Allies in Adversity: The Frontline States in Southern African Security.*

Azzedine Layachi is assistant professor at St. John's University, in Jamaica, New York. He studied politics and international relations at New York University. His chapter, "The OAU and the Western Sahara Conflict," will appear in the forthcoming *The Organization of African Unity After 30 Years,* edited by Yassin el-Ayouti. Other recent works include *The United States and North Africa: A Cognitive Approach to Foreign Policy* and "National Development and Political Protest: Islamists in the Maghreb Countries," in *Arab Studies Quarterly* 14 (2/3), spring 1992.

Martin Lowenkopf retired in 1989 from his position as director of the Office of Research and Analysis in the U.S. State Department's Bureau of Research and Analysis. In recent years he has written in *CSIS Africa Notes:* "What Can We Hope For/Expect in a Clinton Africa Policy?" (December 1992); "Some Lessons from the Past and Some Thoughts for the Future on

U.S. Policy in Africa" (January 1992); and "If the Cold War Is Over in Africa, Will the United States Still Care?" (May 1989). His doctorate is from the University of London.

Njuguna Ng'ethe, a Fulbright visiting scholar and professor in the Department of Political Science, University of Iowa, is a research professor and director of the Institute for Development Studies, University of Nairobi, Kenya. His recent research has focused on civil society and state formation in Africa, with emphasis on the role of grassroots resources in state formation, including the informal sector, community movements, and rural-urban centers.

Marina Ottaway is a professor at Georgetown University and an adjunct professor at the Johns Hopkins Nitze School of Advanced International Studies (SAIS). She has written extensively on the Horn of Africa and Southern Africa. Her latest book, *South Africa: The Struggle for a New Order,* was published by the Brookings Institution in 1993. Dr. Ottaway is editor of a SAIS study on Africa, *The Political Economy of Ethiopia* (1990).

Donald Rothchild is professor of political science at the University of California, Davis, and a visiting scholar at the Brookings Institution. He has taught in the Africa program at SAIS, Johns Hopkins University, and from 1975 to 1977 (and in 1985) he was a visiting professor of political science at the University of Ghana, Legon. He was a member of the Carter Center Ghana Election Mission in November 1992. Dr. Rothchild has published widely. He is coauthor of *Politics and Society in Contemporary Africa;* editor of the SAIS African Studies Library volume, *Ghana: The Political Economy of Recovery;* and, with Naomi Chazan and John Harbeson, coeditor of *Civil Society and the State in Africa.*

Barry Schutz is currently in the Office of the Secretary of Defense and was on the faculty of the Defense Intelligence College. As both an analyst and a government-linked academic, he has worked for the Rand Corporation and the Science Applications International Corporation. He has been a senior research fellow at the Research Institute on International Change and recently completed a Fulbright at the Higher Institute of International Relations in Maputo, Mozambique. Dr. Schutz has recently coedited *Global Transformation and the Third World* and *Revolution and Political Change in the Third World.* Dr. Schutz's doctorate in political science is from the University of California at Los Angeles.

Sipho Shezi was a predoctoral student at SAIS and a former lecturer in political studies at the University of Natal, Pietermaritzburg. He has a long involvement in antiapartheid activities and recently spearheaded a peace initiative in Natal as a member of the African National Congress. Mr. Shezi has an M.A. from Sussex and a postgraduate diploma in international relations from Lancaster, in addition to his first degree from the University of Natal.

Herbert Weiss, a member of the Political Science Department at Brooklyn College and Research Fellow at the Institute of African Studies, Columbia University, served as special assistant to the special representative of the UN Secretary-General in South Africa in 1993–1994. His study of the Congolese independence struggle, *Political Protest in the Congo,* is republished in a French translation. He also studied the postindependence revolutionary movements of the 1960s and cochaired the international conference on the Congo Rebellions/Revolution in Paris in 1984, the proceedings of which were published by Harmattan in two volumes, *Rebellion-Revolution au Zaire, 1963–1965.* In 1991, Dr. Weiss served on an AID mission in Zaire that sought to identify measures that could be taken to help the democratization process.

I. William Zartman is Jacob Blaustein Professor of International Organization and Conflict Resolution and director of African Studies at SAIS, Johns Hopkins. Dr. Zartman is the author of a number of works on Africa, including *Africa in the 1980's* and *Ripe for Resolution: Conflict and Intervention in Africa* (1989). He has also developed the field of negotiation analysis, editing and coauthoring *The 50% Solution, The Negotiation Process* (1978), *Positive Sum: Improving North-South Negotiations* (1987), and *International Mediation in Theory and Practice* (1985), and has written *The Practical Negotiator* (1982), and contributed to *Dynamics of Third Party Intervention, Managing U.S.-Soviet Rivalry,* and *New Issues in International Crisis Management.*

Index

About the Book

The collapse of states—a phenomenon that goes far beyond rebellion or the change of regimes to involve the literal implosion of structures of authority and legitimacy—has until now received little scholarly attention, despite the fact that a number of states have actually ceased to exist as entities in the aftermath of the collapse of the dominant international system.

The authors of this book address the problem by comparatively examining eleven African cases. In each case, they consider what caused the state to collapse, what the symptoms and early warning signs were, and how the situation was or can be dealt with. They also assess more generally the potential strengths and weaknesses of various responses (e.g. democratization, "strongmen," UN action, foreign intervention) to impending state collapse.

I. William Zartman is Jacob Blaustein Professor of International Organization and Conflict Resolution and director of African studies at the Johns Hopkins University School of Advanced International Studies. His numerous publications on Africa include *Government and Politics in North Africa, International Relations in the New Africa,* and *Africa in the 1980s.*